A Note to the Reader

The New American Library, in its continual endeavor to publish the best reading for every taste and mood, is particularly proud to bring before a large new audience this instructive, penetrating, and timely analysis of Lenin, the man whose thoughts and actions best personify the whole sweep—implacable and tragic—of Russia today. The thoughtful reader will discover three levels in Mr. Shub's book: the turbulent life of Lenin himself; a short, pertinent history of Russia before and after the Revolution of 1917; and the ideological growth of those ideas and policies that have culminated in what the Western world now refers to as Communism. To make possible its production and wide distribution in Mentor format, this wealth of critical information has been carefully abridged by Donald Porter Geddes, one of today's outstanding editors, whose condensation of the Mentor edition of *The Age of Jackson* retained its superb mood, content and importance. No whole sections in *Lenin* have been removed; thinning has been entirely by word, phrase and paragraph.

The Publishers

THE COMPLETE HARDCOVER EDITION OF *Lenin* WAS PUBLISHED BY DOUBLEDAY AND COMPANY

Other MENTOR Books of Special Interest

RUSSIA AND AMERICA: Dangers and Prospects
                    by *Henry L. Roberts*

In this penetrating analysis, the author discusses global tension created by atomic and thermonuclear discoveries and our relations with Russia.
                                    (#MD182—50¢)

AMERICAN DIPLOMACY: 1900-1950
                    by *George F. Kennan*

A trenchant appraisal of United States' foreign relations during the past fifty years by a distinguished diplomat.   (#MP360—60¢)

THE DYNAMICS OF SOVIET SOCIETY
                    by *W. W. Rostow and others*

An authoritative volume which presents a synthesis of the whole political, economic and social structure of Soviet Russia today.   (#MD121—50¢)

THE NATURE OF THE NON-WESTERN WORLD
                    by *Vera Micheles Dean*

A noted expert on foreign affairs throws new light on the conflict between East and West as she probes the background of more than one-half of the world.
                                    (#MD190—50¢)

LENIN

A Biography by

DAVID SHUB

Abridgment by Donald Porter Geddes

A MENTOR BOOK
Published by THE NEW AMERICAN LIBRARY

*Published as a MENTOR BOOK
By Arrangement with Doubleday and Company, Inc.*

FIRST PRINTING, DECEMBER, 1950
SECOND PRINTING, JULY, 1951
THIRD PRINTING, JULY, 1952
FOURTH PRINTING, MAY, 1953
FIFTH PRINTING, MAY, 1954
SIXTH PRINTING, MAY, 1955
SEVENTH PRINTING, MARCH, 1957
EIGHTH PRINTING, OCTOBER, 1958
NINTH PRINTING, SEPTEMBER, 1959
TENTH PRINTING, AUGUST, 1960
ELEVENTH PRINTING, NOVEMBER, 1961

This edition of *Lenin* has been abridged
with the author's approval to make
possible its production in this form.

*MENTOR BOOKS are published by
The New American Library of World Literature, Inc.
501 Madison Avenue, New York 22, New York*

PRINTED IN THE UNITED STATES OF AMERICA

EDITOR'S NOTE

David Shub was born and educated in Russia. Over a period of more than forty years he has had intimate contact with the leaders of every faction in the Russian revolutionary movement, both as a revolutionary and as a close student of Russian affairs.

Mr. Shub became a member of the Russian Social Democratic Party in 1903, at a time when Lenin was one of its leaders. From 1904 to 1905 he lived in the western European centers of Russian revolutionary activity (London, Paris, Geneva), where he often met Lenin and the other leaders of the Social Democratic Party—Bolshevik and Menshevik—including Plekhanov, Axelrod, Zasulich, Bogdanov, Lunacharsky, Bonch-Bruyevich, Martov, Potresov, and Dan.

In September, 1905, Mr. Shub returned to Russia and participated in the Russian Revolution of 1905-6. Late in 1906 he was arrested for revolutionary activity and sentenced to exile in Siberia, whence he escaped a year later.

He arrived in the United States in 1908. Since then he has maintained close contact with the leading figures of the Russian Revolutionary movement and has written extensively on Russian affairs. He was personally acquainted with many of the Bolshevik leaders, including Lenin, Trotsky, and Bukharin, as well as outstanding liberals and Socialists, such as Kerensky, Miliukov, Chernov, Catherine Breshkovsky (the Grandmother of the Russian Revolution), and others.

Mr. Shub's lead article on Stalin in the magazine section of the New York *Times* (March 22, 1930) was probably the first authoritative profile of the Soviet leader to appear in the American press. The *Times* referred to the author as "a veteran of the Russian revolutionary movement and an authority on Russian affairs." For many years he has edited and contributed to liberal, labor, and socialist publications in several languages.

An understanding of Lenin, the founder of world communism, provides the key to the Russian enigma of today. The publisher is glad to be able to meet the need for a full and authoritative biography of this historic figure.

In this book the human Lenin appears, as revealed by his relations with his family, his friends, and his enemies, and with the leading figures in Russia's revolutionary struggle. It traces Lenin's life on the basis of original source material both of pre-revolutionary and post-revolutionary periods. Mr. Shub's personal knowledge and contact with Lenin and the other leaders give his story an authenticity that could never be achieved by research. For the first time we are shown the environment which influenced Lenin's career from his childhood and youth to his end in the Kremlin.

With copious extracts from Lenin's writings and speeches, many for the first time available in English, Mr. Shub's book provides the reader with an intimate understanding of the principles and mainsprings of action which guide not only the rulers of the Soviet Union but also Communists all over the globe.

Weaving around the life of Lenin a complete history of Bolshevism, the author traces the Russian Revolutionary movement from 1825, describes the revolutions of 1905 and 1917, the role played in both by Lenin, and the trend of revolutionary thought in Russia which culminated in Leninism. The story is presented in a manner which enables even the uninitiated reader to gain an understanding of those events which have so profoundly influenced the course of world history.

The words and deeds of Lenin today guide the destinies of one sixth of the world. "Lenin is our teacher," said Joseph Stalin to Harold Stassen on April 9, 1947, "and we Soviet people are Lenin's disciples."

1948   HUGH GIBSON

CONTENTS

PROLOGUE: BITTER HERITAGE

VLADIMIR ULIANOV CAME RUNNING HOME FROM SCHOOL, breathless and frightened.

"What is it?" his mother demanded.

"Alexander! He's been arrested."

Maria Alexandrovna clutched the table. "Alexander arrested! What for?"

"He's charged with plotting to assassinate the Czar."

"How do you know?"

"Kashkadamova told me. She asked me to step out of the classroom—showed me a letter she had just received from her father's friend in St. Petersburg."

Maria Alexandrovna decided to take the next train to the capital.

She hoped, however, that she would not have to travel alone. The Ulianovs were a highly respected family in Simbirsk. Ilya Nikolaievich, her husband who had died a year before, had been an "active state counselor," had taught mathematics and physics in Penza and Nizhnii Novgorod, and, a few months before Vladimir's birth, had been named school inspector for the entire province. But Maria Alexandrovna was disappointed. Friends and neighbors would have nothing to do with the mother of a political prisoner. She left for the capital alone.

On the long, dismal journey she thought of her son about to be tried for high treason. Alexander, twenty-one years old, was the eldest of her six children and young Vladimir's idol. Outwardly he was soft, but where principles were concerned she knew him to be adamant. Slow and cautious, he had wanted to be sure before joining the revolutionary movement. Only a year before he had said:

"It is absurd, even immoral, for a man who has no understanding of medicine to cure the sick. How much more absurd and immoral it is to seek to heal social ills without understanding their cause."

At that time Alexander's chief interest had been zoology. He had written a prize paper on the subject and even Vladimir had been deceived by his brother's preoccupation with natural science. He had explained to friends:

"Alexander will never be a revolutionist. Last summer he spent his time preparing a dissertation on Annelides. A revolutionist cannot possibly devote so much time to the study of Annelides."

9

But a few months later, the scientist was making bombs. As a member of the revolutionary party, the People's Will, he became a leader of a group of St. Petersburg student terrorists. In secret meetings at his apartment plans were laid to kill Alexander III on March 1, 1887, the sixth anniversary of the assassination of his father, Alexander II.

Ulianov also prepared a manifesto, to be published immediately after the Czar's death. It began: "The spirit of the Russian land lives and the truth is not extinguished in the hearts of her sons. On ———, 1887, Czar Alexander III was executed."

The date was advanced several days when the terrorists learned that the Czar was planning to leave for his summer palace. Assassins were planted in the square before St. Isaac's Cathedral. But the Czar did not appear and at twilight the conspirators returned to their underground headquarters. Ulianov then heard that on February 28 the Czar was to drive along the Nevsky Prospect. Once more the terrorists waited, but no Czar's carriage appeared. The secret police, suspecting an assassination plot, had warned the monarch to remain in the Winter Palace.

Hours later the terrorists met in a tavern. One of them, Andreiushkin, had been shadowed for days by detectives. They followed him to the tavern, where he and his comrades were seized.

Ulianov and his lieutenant, Lukashevich, after waiting impatiently all day, proceeded to their headquarters. The police were there to meet them. In Ulianov's possession they found a code book with a number of incriminating names and addresses.

Within the next few days hundreds of suspects were picked up, the police having obtained the key to the code by torturing one of the terrorists. They singled out fifteen men, including Alexander Ulianov, for trial. The charge: conspiracy to assassinate the Czar.

Maria Alexandrovna reached St. Petersburg seven days after her son's arrest. For weeks she tried to see him. In despair, she wrote a letter to the Czar, in the margin of which Alexander III made this note:

"I think it would be advisable to allow her to visit her son, so that she might see for herself the kind of person this precious son of hers is."

Alexander embraced his mother, wept, asked her to forgive him. But his first allegiance, he insisted, was to the revolutionary movement. He had no alternative but to fight for his country's liberation.

"But your way of achieving this liberation is so terrible."

"There is no other way," Alexander replied.

At the preliminary hearing Ulianov refused to talk. But

when he realized that many of his comrades faced execution, he decided to shoulder the main responsibility himself.

Alexander was his own advocate. It was a curious defense. In order to save his comrades Alexander confessed to acts he had never committed.

In his concluding address, Ulianov cried: "My purpose was to aid in the liberation of the unhappy Russian people. Under a system which permits no freedom of expression and crushes every attempt to work for their welfare and enlightenment by legal means, the only instrument that remains is terror. Therefore, any individual sensitive to injustice must resort to terror. Terror is our answer to the violence of the state. It is the only way to force a despotic regime to grant political freedom to the people."

Speaking for himself, and for his comrades beside him, he declared "there is no death more honorable than death for the common good."

Alexander Ulianov was sentenced to die on the gallows. Frantically his mother pleaded with him to ask for imperial clemency. Alexander refused, although some of his co-defendants petitioned the Czar and their death sentences were commuted.

In the early morning of May 8, 1887, Alexander and four of his comrades were hanged in the courtyard of the Schlusselburg fortress.

When the St. Petersburg newspaper carrying the news of Alexander's execution reached Vladimir in Simbirsk, he threw the paper to the floor and cried:

"I'll make them pay for this! I swear it!"

"You'll make who pay?" asked a neighbor, Maria Savenko.

"Never mind, I know," Vladimir replied.

The world knows Vladimir Ulianov as Lenin.

1   SEEDS OF REVOLUTION

THE MARTYRED IDEALIST WHO DREAMED OF FREEDOM THROUGH assassination, and his brother Vladimir, who took a more pragmatic road to reach another goal, drew their inspiration from the same source. They were both bred in a revolutionary tradition uniquely Russian, whose spirit contained incredible contradictions of nobility and baseness, virtue and criminality, love and hate.

When Alexander died on the gallows, the ingredients that were to shape the destiny of his brother had already been prepared.

The Russian revolutionary movement dates back to the

Napoleonic era, when Russian officers returned infected with
the ideas of the French Revolution. The first conscious revolutionists were, for the most part, army officers. The earliest
overt act against autocratic power was the attempt by a group
of these officers, known as the Decembrists, to deny the throne
to Grand Duke Nicholas, on the death of Czar Alexander I,
and to install his brother Constantine as a constitutional monarch.

On December 26, 1825, the day Nicholas was to ascend the
throne, a regiment of the Guards refused to swear allegiance
to Nicholas, proclaimed Constantine the lawful Emperor, and
demanded a constitution for Russia. The emissaries sent by
Nicholas to negotiate with the rebel leaders were fired upon;
in the meantime the populace began to join the insurgents.
Before the revolt could gain momentum, Nicholas ordered a
battery to open fire on the rebels. The Decembrists were put
to flight, leaving many dead and wounded on the streets. Five
of their leaders were hanged, thirty-one were sentenced to long
terms of hard labor, others were exiled to Siberia.

While western Europe had for centuries been the scene of
struggle between kings and cities against feudal lords, and
then of the third estate against the absolute power of the king,
in Russia those centuries saw only the ever-greater subjuga-
tion of the people.

The peasants harbored smoldering hatred against their oppressors. As a result Russia in the early nineteenth century
was sharply divided into two camps: the Czarist government,
its powerful bureaucracy and nobility on the one hand and the
multi-million-headed servile peasantry on the other.

The French Revolution of 1830 gave fresh impetus to revolutionary ideas. Clandestine circles were organized to discuss political, literary, and social problems. The pioneers were
members of the nobility, professors, writers, and students.
Their most vivid figure was Alexander Herzen. Herzen and
his friends wanted the end of serfdom and autocratic rule.
Few among these men welcomed the rise of the bourgeoisie.
The majority were hostile toward the merchant class and capitalism. Russian democratic thought was steeped in Socialism.

The early rebels adopted Fourier, Saint-Simon, and other
French Socialists as their teachers. The educated landowners
supported the Czar.

"The people have a desire for potatoes," wrote Byelinski in
1847, "but none whatsoever for a constitution; the latter is
wanted by the educated urban classes who are powerless to do
anything."

The European revolutions of 1848 were greeted by these intellectuals with great hope, but the subsequent collapse caused
even stronger reaction against the bourgeoisie. A German

scholar wrote that since Russia had no working class and since the peasant commune really secured land to each peasant, revolution was impossible in Russia. Herzen drew the opposite conclusion. Precisely because of the weakness of Russian capitalism and the existence of the peasant communes Socialism could be introduced more easily in Russia than anywhere else. And he continued: "What can be accomplished only by a series of cataclysms in the West can develop in Russia out of existing conditions."

The growing popularity of heterodox political thought led to a tightening of censorship and increased persecution of intellectuals. Turgenev was arrested in 1852 for displeasing the censor. The members of a literary circle, whose main crime consisted of nightly discussion of Fourier's theories, were condemned to death in a body. Among them was Dostoevsky. The prisoners were forced to go through final preparations for execution before their sentences were commuted to long terms of hard labor in Siberia.

When Nicholas I died in 1855 there was no immediate change. But after Russia's defeat in the Crimean War, Alexander II, yielding to persistent agitation, appointed a committee to draw up a decree for the abolition of serfdom. Encouraged by the apparent turn toward liberalism, the press began a bold discussion of all political questions.

The Czar's Act of Liberation abolishing serfdom in 1861 proved a disappointment. The peasants, who expected to receive land free and clear, were saddled with such heavy mortgages and taxes that they could not hope to redeem their land within a reasonable period. But the peasants could not conceive that the Czar had given them freedom under such disadvantages. Blaming the landowners, their dissatisfaction expressed itself in arson and riots. In reprisal, the government sent punitive expeditions against the villages.

Meanwhile, the liberal publications adopted a more revolutionary tone. Illegal pamphlets were distributed. One of these accused the government of provoking a new Pugachev rebellion by its agrarian policy. The "educated classes" were called on to take power. If they failed to do so the "patriots" would be forced to summon the people to revolt. Another demanded the convocation of a Constituent Assembly to give Russia a democratic regime. A third concluded that if the government did not remove the causes of popular discontent, Russia would see an insurrection by the summer of 1863.

During the same year a proclamation "To the Young Generation" argued that the 1848 defeat of Socialism in western Europe proved nothing as far as Russia was concerned. For, in contrast to the West, Russia had peasant communes "and enough land to last 10,000 years. We are a retarded people, and therein lies our salvation. . . . We believe that we are destined to bring a new principle into history . . . and not to ape Europe's outlived ideas."

In the winter of 1862 proclamations urging revolution appeared. One called for armed uprising and ruthless extermination of the enemies of freedom. The author was Zaichnevsky.

"Soon the day will come," this proclamation declared, "when we shall unfurl the great banner of the future, the red banner, and . . . march upon the Winter Palace. . . . It is quite possible that the affair will end with the extirpation of the Imperial family alone. . . . But it is also possible that the entire Imperial Party will rise . . . to defend its Emperor. In that case . . . we shall utter the cry, 'Use the ax,' and then crush the Imperial Party . . . as mercilessly as it is now dealing with us.

". . . Remember that when that time comes, whoever is not with us is against us! We are convinced that the revolutionary party . . . must maintain its present centralized organization so that it may build the foundation for a new . . . order in the shortest possible time. This organization must usurp . . . power through a dictatorship. . . . Elections to the National Assembly must be directed by the government which shall immediately make certain that its members include none of those who are in favor of the present order, should any such persons still be found alive."

Herzen condemned proclamations of this violent character on the ground that their effect was to tighten the bonds between the autocracy and the propertied classes and force the regime to take further repressive measures. As a matter of fact, wholesale arrests and new political restrictions usually followed such leaflets.

Playing upon the Emperor's fear, his advisers induced him to sign one reactionary measure after another. The new Minister of Education changed the high school curriculum. A spy system was introduced among the students.

Again students took the lead in demonstrations. Punishment was swift and summary. Many were expelled and banished to Siberia.

A new leader became known—a nobleman and former artillery officer named Michael Bakunin. Bakunin regarded the repudiation of religion as the first step toward progress. He preached the abolition of hereditary property, advocated the transfer of land to agricultural communes and factories to labor associations. He urged equality for women, the abolition of marriage and the family, and free education for all children. The abolition of the state was the keynote. His credo was that the entire structure of society must be demolished before a new and better one could be built.

Bakunin's most remarkable disciple, Sergei Nechaiev, the son of a priest, passionately embraced the cause of revolution. In 1869 he organized a society in Moscow for the purpose of preparing a mass insurrection. He shrank from nothing to attract followers, resorting to deceit, terrorism, and murder.

Implicated in the student riots of 1869, Nechaiev fled to Switzerland, where he issued an appeal to Russian students to join his organization. Here he was befriended by Bakunin, whom he impressed with his strong character and fanaticism. Together with Bakunin, Nechaiev published a periodical— *The People's Justice*—which advocated the most desperate acts, not only against the Czar, but also against liberal writers and journalists. In their *Catechism* Nechaiev and Bakunin wrote:

"The Revolutionist is a doomed man. He has no private interests, no affairs, sentiments, ties, property nor even a name of his own. . . . Heart and soul, not merely by word but by deed, he has severed every link with the social order and . . . the . . . civilized world. . . . He is its merciless enemy and continues to inhabit it with only one purpose—to destroy it. . . . Everything which promotes the success of the revolution is moral, everything which hinders it is immoral. . . . The nature of the true revolutionist excludes all romanticism, all tenderness, all ecstasy, all love."

Bakunin issued a paper certifying Nechaiev as leader of the Russian branch of the "Revolutionary Union of the World." With this document, Nechaiev returned to Russia and began to recruit members.

He persuaded his comrades to assassinate a student named Ivanov, by telling them that Ivanov was a spy.

The murder of Ivanov led to the unearthing of Nechaiev's secret organization and the arrest of some three hundred persons. Nechaiev fled to Switzerland and continued to issue proclamations, but his methods, described by Dostoevsky in *The Possessed*, finally cost him his following, including Bakunin.

"Nechaiev is one of the most . . . energetic men I have ever met," Bakunin wrote. "Whenever it is necesary to render some service to what he calls the 'cause,' he . . . is as ruthless with himself as he is with others. He is a fanatic . . . but . . . a very dangerous one, association with whom may be fatal to all concerned. His methods are abhorrent. He has come to the conclusion that . . . to create a workable . . . organization one must use as a basis the philosophy of Machiavelli and adopt the motto of the Jesuits: 'Violence for the Body; lies for the Soul.'

"With the exception of . . . the chosen leaders, all the members should serve as blind tools in the hands of those leaders. . . . It is permissible to deceive these members . . .

rob them, and even murder them if necessary. They are merely cannon fodder for conspiracies. For the good of the cause, he must be allowed to gain full mastery over your person, even against your will. When all of us came together and exposed him, he had the audacity to say: 'Well, that is our method. We consider all those who disapprove of this method and refuse to apply it our enemies and we think it our duty to deceive and discredit all who refuse to go with us the whole way.' "

Nechaiev was extradited for the murder of Ivanov and sentenced to twenty years at hard labor. In 1883 he died in the fortress of St. Peter and St. Paul.

Another guiding spirit among the colony in Switzerland, Peter Lavrov, a former officer and St. Petersburg professor, favored the gradual education of the masses.

"The reconstruction of Russian society," wrote Lavrov, "must be achieved not only for the sake of . . . but also through the people. But the masses are not ready. . . . Therefore the triumph of our ideas . . . requires preparation and clear understanding of what is possible at the given moment."

According to Lavrov, the role of the intellectuals was to imbue the people with the knowledge that would help them to attain "the moral ideal of Socialism."

To Bakunin, the only sure path to revolution was by unleashing the elemental fury latent in the Russian people. Both Lavrov and Bakunin called on the youth to "go to the people."

With similar ideas was Peter Tkachev, who came to Switzerland in 1874, after several years in Czarist prisons. Tkachev believed in the dictatorship of a revolutionary minority. He advocated the forcible seizure of power. Tkachev drew the following picture of the peasant paradise after the social revolution:

"The peasant would live a life of ease and joy. His purse would be filled . . . with gold coin. His cattle and fowl would be uncounted. . . . And he would eat and drink all his belly could hold, and would work only when he had a mind to, and no one would dare to force his will on him. . . ."

Lavrov refused to print this article, on the ground that "no desire to hasten the revolution can justify such attempts to inflame the people to passions of greed and sloth."

"A revolutionist," Tkachev wrote in 1875, "always has the right . . . to call the people to an insurrection. He should regard the people as always ready for a revolution. Every people that is oppressed by an arbitrary government (and such is the condition under which all peoples live) is always able and willing to make a revolution. . . .

"A real revolution can be brought about only in one way: through the seizure of power. . . . In other words, the immediate and most important task . . . must be solely the overthrow of the government and the transformation of the . . .

conservative state into a revolutionary state. The capture of a government . . . in itself does not yet constitute a revolution. . . . The revolution is brought about by the revolutionary government, which . . . eradicates all the conservative . . . elements . . . eliminating all those institutions which hinder the establishment of equality and brotherhood . . . and . . . introduces such institutions as favor the development of these principles. . . ."

Lavrov completely rejected the dictatorship of the minority: "History has shown us . . . that the possession of great power corrupts the best people, and that even the ablest leaders, who meant to benefit the people by decree, failed. Every dictatorship must surround itself by compulsory means of defense which must serve as obedient tools in its hands. Every dictatorship is called upon to suppress not only its reactionary opponents but also those who disagree with its methods and actions. Whenever a dictatorship succeeded in establishing itself it had to spend more time and effort in retaining its power and defending it against its rivals than upon the realization of its program with the aid of that power."

He was only echoing the beliefs of Herzen, who years before had written: "Social progress is possible only under complete republican freedom, under full democratic equality. A republic that would not lead to Socialism seems an absurdity . . . a transitional stage regarding itself as the goal. On the other hand, Socialism which might try to dispense with political freedom would rapidly degenerate into an autocratic Communism."

To check the influence of the émigré revolutionists, the government ordered all students abroad to return to Russia by January 1874. Most students complied with the decree as a welcome opportunity for going out among the Russian people to preach the theories of Socialism.

In 1876 the revolutionists, under Bakunin's influence, formed a society called "Land and Freedom." Its program called for a social revolution from the "bottom," by fomenting uprisings and passive resistance among the peasants, as well as strikes among the workers. "Fighting units" were formed to lead the coming insurrection.

A split occurred in the Land and Freedom group in 1879, when an executive committee was set up to organize terrorist acts. A small faction, headed by George Plekhanov, rejected the policy of terrorism and became known as the "Black Repartition." The larger group called itself the People's Will.

Both groups believed that the peasant was by nature strongly inclined to Socialism. Contrary to the Marxist notion that only the industrial working class could bring Socialism, they believed that in Russia the peasant could play the same role. But the People's Will believed that Socialism could not be realized for some time; the immediate goal was the expropriation of the estates in favor of the peasantry and the establishment of civil liberty. The party stipulated that a Provisional Government would be set up until an elected Constituent Assembly gave the Russian people a system of their own choosing; the only road to democratic freedom in an autocratic state was through political assassination, the party asserted.

On Sunday, March 13, 1881, Czar Alexander II was assassinated.

If the terrorists thought that their act would strike fear into the heart of the new Emperor, Alexander III, their hopes were soon shattered. In a manifesto dated May 13, 1881, Alexander III proclaimed: "In the midst of our great grief the voice of God commands us to stand bravely at the helm of the state, to trust Divine Providence, with faith in the power and truth of Absolutism."

Five participants in the assassination were executed, most of the party leaders were sentenced to long prison terms and Siberian exile. A score, including Vera Figner, the "Madonna of the Schlusselburg," were immured for decades in the dungeons of the famous fortress, where some died and others went insane.

But the People's Will, despite its belief in terrorist acts against the Czar and his reactionary Ministers, had little in common with Bakunin, Nechaiev, or Tkachev.

"None of us," wrote Vera Figner in 1918, "was a Jacobin. We never thought of forcing upon the majority of the people the will of the minority, and we never planned a government which would bring about revolutionary, socialistic, economic, and political changes by decree. . . . Should the people's representatives favor some measure that is directly opposed to the demands of the revolutionary party, this party would under no circumstances resort to acts of violence and terrorism to enforce its program, but would limit itself to peaceful propaganda. . . ."

And from their fortress dungeons the members of the Executive Committee sent a message to the Russian people in June 1882, called "From the Dead to the Living," which stressed their repudiation of violence and bloodshed.

"Brethren and sisters," said the message, "out of our graves we send you what may be our last greeting, our testament. On the day of our triumph do not soil the glory of the revolution by any acts of cruelty or brutality against the vanquished foe. May our unhappy lot not only be the price of Russian freedom, but also serve to bring a more beautiful, more humane society. We salute our country, we salute all mankind."

After the decimation of the People's Will leadership, a few revolutionists succeeded in escaping abroad. Among them were George Plekhanov, Paul Axelrod, Vera Zasulich, and Leo

Deutch of the Black Repartition. In 1883 they organized the "Group for the Emancipation of Labor," in order to propagate Marxism in Russia. This organization published books and pamphlets rejecting the notion that Russia was destined to follow a unique path to Socialism either through a peasant uprising or a *coup d'état* by a revolutionary minority.

The members maintained that the struggle for Socialism could be successful only when the revolutionary parties were supported by an organized and class-conscious working class. To attain the final objective of a socialist society, political freedom was the necessary stepping-stone.

The leader of the Marxists was Plekhanov. Under his guidance the first Social Democratic circles were formed.

But all over Russia there still existed young revolutionists' organizations which tried to revive the People's Will. One of these was the terrorist group headed by Alexander Ulianov.

The program of the St. Petersburg Terrorists as drawn up by Ulianov contained the following revealing passage: "Convinced that terror results wholly from the absence of a minimum of freedom, we can state with complete confidence that terrorist activities will cease, if the Government grants this 'minimum of Freedom.' "

When Alexander Ulianov became convinced that the Czar would not grant them the "minimum" he turned to the terrorist action which led him to the gallows. His younger brother, Vladimir, did not take the path of terror. He embraced Marxism instead. But although he turned to the teaching of Marx, his whole being was profoundly influenced by the conflicting cross-currents of the Revolutionary movement. At the time of his brother's death—and before he had read a word of Marx—Lenin was already drawing from both the humanitarian teachings of Herzen and Lavrov, and the demoniac visions of Bakunin, Tkachev, and Nechaiev.

The current of thinking that ran from Herzen and Lavrov through the People's Will to Alexander Ulianov produced greater idealism and self-sacrifice than any other movement in history. The theories of universal destruction propagated by men like Nechaiev were still to be tested.

The apostles of enlightenment looked toward the liberation of man. Even when they resorted to individual terrorism, they sought moral justification for their acts, never masking their true aims, and always preferring to sacrifice their own lives rather than send others to their death.

Nechaiev and his followers, on the other hand, advocated the use of deception, calumny, and murder for the attainment of their objectives. They regarded the Russian people mainly as a means toward their apocalyptic end, envisaging either ideal anarchy or the dictatorship of a minority ruling by means of unlimited force and terror.

The early revolutionary parties contained adherents of both schools. But by the time Lenin's brother was executed the humanitarian current dominated the Russian revolutionary movement. And Herzen's precept of 1867—"Socialism which would dispense with political freedom would soon degenerate into autocratic Communism"—was accepted as a truism. The doctrines of Nechaiev seemed to be buried forever. No one, except perhaps Dostoevsky, foresaw that they would be revived to play a decisive role in the history of Russia and the world.

2 YOUTH

VLADIMIR ILICH ULIANOV WAS BORN IN SIMBIRSK, ON THE Volga, on April 22, 1870. His mother, Maria Alexandrovna, was the daughter of a physician named Alexander Blank, who left his St. Petersburg hospital to settle on a small estate in the village of Kokushkino, province of Kazan.

She married Ilya Ulianov in the summer of 1863, and went to live with him in Penza. Ilya was "a strong man of firm character who was very stern in his relations with his subordinates." He was conservative in his politics and a devout member of the Russian Orthodox Church. In 1866 Maria bore him the first of their six children, Alexander, or Sasha as the family called him. In September 1869, when Ilya was appointed provincial school inspector, they rented the house in Simbirsk where Vladimir was born the following spring.

Vladimir—little Volodya—was a boisterous child with lively gray eyes and a top-heavy body. He learned to walk at about the same time as his younger sister Olga. Olga was his playmate, Alexander his hero.

Vladimir mastered his lessons with almost disconcerting thoroughness. His brother Dmitri recalls the meticulous care that Vladimir put into his compositions.

". . . On a quarter . . . sheet of paper he would make an outline. . . . He would then take another sheet, fold it in half, and make a rough draft on the left side of the paper, in accordance with his outline. The right side or margin remained clear. Here he would enter additions, explanations, corrections, as well as source indications. . . ."

In this early capacity for systematic work an essential facet of the coming man reveals itself for the first time.

From all that the reminiscences of his family and early friends reveal, his childhood and adolescence were almost idyllic.

Although the Ulianovs were not wealthy, their style of life compared favorably with that of the minor nobility, in whose ranks Ilya Nikolaievich was enrolled by virtue of his official

position. His death, when Vladimir was sixteen, was th_
blow, followed within a year by the tragic death of Alexan
But Maria Alexandrovna was a strong woman and the family
always remained intimately bound to one another.

A month after Alexander's death, Vladimir was graduated
from the Simbirsk gymnasium with a gold medal as the
school's best student.

But his admission to Kazan University seemed unlikely because he was the brother of an executed terrorist. It is an
ironic commentary that the man who made this possible was
the father of Alexander Kerensky, whose Provisional Government he was to overthrow in 1917.

Feodor Kerensky was not only the director of the Simbirsk
gymnasium; he had also been named guardian of the Ulianov
family by Ilya Nikolaievich's will.

"Neither in nor out of school," wrote Feodor Kerensky,
"has a single instance been observed when Ulianov . . .
caused dissatisfaction to his teachers or the school authorities.

"His mental and moral instruction," he continued, "has always been thoroughly looked after. . . . Religion and discipline were the basis of this upbringing, whose fruits are apparent in Ulianov's exemplary conduct."

What Vladimir thought of this document at the time is not
known, but many years later, in reply to a Bolshevik Party
questionnaire asking when he ceased to believe in God, Lenin
wrote: "At the age of sixteen."

When Vladimir entered Kazan University, in the fall of
1887, he found himself drawn almost at once into student
disorders. Professors were being expelled for mildly liberal
opinions and students who were suspected of engaging in any
political activity were being sent into exile. These measures
only stiffened student resistance. On December 4, 1887, the
assembled student body presented the dean with a program
of their demands.

Vladimir, who was observed standing in the front row with
clenched fists, was arrested that very night with forty other
students and expelled.

At his mother's request, he was permitted to live under
police surveillance at the Kokushkino estate. Here the family
spent the winter in virtual isolation. But Vladimir was not
particularly unhappy. The house was filled with books, and
for recreation there were skiing and hunting.

In the fall Vladimir was permitted to reside in Kazan once
more, but his application for return to the university was denied. The family rented a two-story house with a balcony and
pleasant garden. A spare kitchen became his study. It was in
this kitchen, at the age of eighteen, that he began reading
Karl Marx.

The following year the family moved to Samara, where

...nized a small Marxist group. In the meantime
...s making repeated efforts to have him readmitted
...ity. The matter was referred to the warden of
...chool district, who turned in an unfavorable

...xandrovna then took her son's case to the Ministry of Education in St. Petersburg, and through her persistence he was finally allowed to take his law examinations at the St. Petersburg University.

During the summer before going to the capital, Vladimir studied intensively.

He passed his law examinations with honors in 1891 and was admitted to the bar. But his moment of success was marred when Olga, his childhood playmate, who was studying in the capital at the same time, contracted typhoid fever and died.

Probably for his mother's sake he returned to Samara and went through the motions of starting a law practice. Actually the clandestine Marxist club he had started was soon consuming most of his time. His first real disciples were his sisters, Anna and Maria, and his brother Dmitri.

The two younger Ulianovs, Dmitri and Maria, were of much the same cast as their late brother Alexander—deep-set eyes, high foreheads, pale, handsome. Vladimir, with his small thick nose and broad high cheekbones, had a rather plain face, except for the piercing intelligence of his eyes. At twenty-one he was rapidly losing his hair.

Early in 1892 a famine hit the province of Samara, and when the peasants flocked to the city in search of bread, a committee of citizens was organized to aid the destitute. But Vladimir took an unexpected stand.

"The famine," he asserted, "is the direct consequence of a particular social order. So long as that order exists, famines are inevitable. They can be abolished only by the abolition of that order of society. Being in this sense inevitable, famine today performs a progressive function. . . .

"It is easy to understand the desire of so-called 'society' to come to the assistance of the starving, to ameliorate their lot. . . . The famine threatens to create serious disturbances and possibly the destruction of the entire bourgeois order. Hence the efforts of the well-to-do to mitigate the effect of the famine are quite natural. . . . *Psychologically this talk of feeding the starving is nothing but an expression of the saccharine sweet sentimentality so characteristic of our intelligentsia.*"

The authentic voice of Lenin had spoken for the first time.

In the autumn of 1893 Vladimir Ulianov left for St. Petersburg and joined an underground Social Democratic circle called the "Elders." He arrived during the period of Russia's great industrial awakening, with peasants flocking into the cities to become factory hands. The Social Democrats were concentrating their propaganda on small groups of workers, whom they secretly instructed in the Communist Manifesto. But this was propaganda on a fairly high plane, with the result that these groups remained isolated from the mass of the people.

Workers who "graduated" from the propaganda seminars were ordered to stay out of trouble; they practically never took part in strikes and other labor disturbances.

Ulianov at once suggested proceeding from select propaganda to mass agitation. His scheme was opposed by the more conservative members, but by 1895 those who remained with him agreed to start a campaign of mass agitation among the workers.

Ulianov became the leader of the Elders. He was the author of its first proclamation addressed to the workers of a St. Petersburg factory.

To the autocracy, writings of the Marxist school were at first not unwelcome. "A small clique," said Police Director Zvolianski. "Nothing will come of them for at least fifty years." The revolutionary organization the regime still dreaded was the terrorist People's Will. Marxists, the authorities calculated, could do more to counteract the influence of the People's Will than the Czar's secret police. Furthermore, their writings were so ponderous and scientific that the revolutionary implications seemed too remote to be dangerous. At this time two such works were published with the censor's approval. One was Plekhanov's; the other was Peter Struve's.

At a meeting in a St. Petersburg suburb on Christmas Day 1894 Ulianov read a paper on these two works. Praising Plekhanov's work almost reverently, he severely criticized Struve's departure from orthodox Marxism. It was at this meeting that an early Social Democratic associate, Alexander Potresov, first spoke with Ulianov.

"I remember to this day," Potresov wrote many years later, "the vigor and acuteness of Ulianov's criticism. . . . My opinion was that he undoubtedly represented a great force. . . . His face was worn; his entire head bald, except for some thin hair at the temples, and he had a scanty reddish beard. His squinting eyes peered slyly from under his brows." At twenty-four he was already known as the "old man."

Overwork was a contributing cause to a severe attack of pneumonia in the early part of 1895. In April Ulianov went abroad for medical treatment. This at last gave him an opportunity for first-hand contacts with Plekhanov and Axelrod, the founding fathers of Russian Marxism, as well as with foreign Socialist leaders. In Paris he met Paul Lafargue, Marx's son-in-law.

When Plekhanov and Ulianov met near Geneva early in 1895, Plekhanov was the teacher, Ulianov the disciple.

Plekhanov was a man of deep humanist roots. His was the temperament of the philosopher. Yet, not satisfied with the power of the written word alone, he became a political leader. When unable to cope with the ruthlessness of the man of action, he retreated to the written word.

"A noble desire," wrote Lunacharsky, "to defend culture and its further progress from Czarist and bourgeois barbarism led him to assume the role of a political fighter. Lenin, on the contrary, was above all a political fighter. . . . Lenin cast aside every vestige of nationalism. From basic divergence, evident in their work, their manner, their physiognomy, came the difference in tactics and political destiny."

When the conversation turned to literature or art, Plekhanov found the young man unimaginative and uninspired. But no sooner did Ulianov return to politics than "he became a changed man, thoroughly aroused and revealing a mind of great brilliance and power. Every remark showed deep reflection. One felt that his opinions were backed by life experience, and while his life experience was quite simple and not extensive, it was sufficient to make him an expert in revolutionary work."

Plekhanov felt he had found the leader needed by the party. Here was the man with the fire and force to turn strikes into a revolutionary struggle against absolutism. Ulianov seemed to remind him of Alexander Mikhailov, the great leader of the People's Will. Like Mikhailov, Ulianov was a master of organizational detail. Yet Potresov had "a vague feeling that the two men who apparently believed in the same goal spoke different languages."

From Geneva, Ulianov went to Zurich to see Axelrod with Plekhanov's introduction. Axelrod knew little of the young man and talk did not flow freely. Ulianov handed him a recently published volume of Marxist articles.

Axelrod became engrossed in one article, which revealed an original and forceful mind. But he was disturbed by the author's animosity toward liberals. The article was signed "K. Tulin."

"Who is Tulin?" Axelrod asked.

"That is my pseudonym."

A warm debate followed. "We believe," said Axelrod, "that . . . the immediate interests of the Russian workers are identical with those of the other progressive forces in society. In Russia, the workers and Liberals are faced with the same task, the overthrow of absolutism."

Ulianov smiled. "Plekhanov said the same thing. . . . He expressed his opinion figuratively. 'You,' he said, 'turn your back upon the Liberals. We turn our faces toward them.'"

They devoted the better part of a week to arguing the question. Finally Ulianov declared that he was convinced. These first talks impressed Axelrod as deeply as they had Plekhanov. The movement had had no one who combined a grasp of Marxist theory with practical organizing ability.

"Now we have that man," said Axelrod. "He is Ulianov. . . ."

In September 1895 Ulianov returned to Russia.

In St. Petersburg, Ulianov became acquainted with Jules Martov, who in the years to come was to be one of his main political antagonists. Martov studied at the University of St. Petersburg, where he had become a revolutionist and a Marxist. He was later expelled for participating in revolutionary demonstrations. Exiled for a number of years from the capital, he played an important part in the rise of the labor movement in Vilna. The two young men used to meet in the public library under the watchful eyes of the secret police. "At that time," says Martov, "Vladimir Ulianov was in that stage of development when a man of high caliber seeks to learn rather than teach others. . . ."

During that winter and fall Lenin was closely watched by the secret police. Anticipating trouble, he warned his sister Anna to restrain his mother from coming to St. Petersburg in the event of his arrest. Prison would only bring back somber memories of Alexander.

* * *

The game of hide-and-seek continued for several months, and still the secret police groped blindly. It seemed impossible to get a clear picture of what the man was doing or who his co-conspirators were. The Okhrana tried another tack: surely there was one Judas in the organization. In due time he was found; a few rubles gave him eloquence. On December 20, 1895, Ulianov and Martov were arrested; the proofs for the first issue of the clandestine newspaper they were to publish were seized.

3 PRISON AND SIBERIA

REGULATIONS OF THE ST. PETERSBURG PRISON WERE NOT harsh. Visits were allowed twice a week, once in the prisoner's cell, the other time in the general anteroom. The first, in a guard's presence, lasted a half hour; the second, a full hour with one file of guards standing behind the visitors and another behind the prisoners. But there was so much noise that anything could be discussed. Relatives were allowed to bring books and food several times a week. The reading matter was only carelessly checked. Thus prisoners could maintain contact with political affairs outside.

Despite Ulianov's protests, Maria Alexandrovna visited him regularly. She came with Anna as often as regulations allowed, bringing bundles of books. Ulianov had taught Anna to write in a dot-dash code, minute enough to pass unnoticed. By this and other means Ulianov carried on an active correspondence with his party comrades outside.

After his arrest, the various Social Democratic groups banded together in the "League for the Liberation of Labor." This was a ruse aimed at persuading the government that those in prison were not the actual Social Democratic leaders. It didn't work. A month later many members of the league, including Potresov, were arrested. But new men took their places and revolutionary propaganda continued.

While in prison Ulianov became recognized as the real head of the League, directing many of its activities.

In 1896 he wrote a pamphlet on strikes which became effective propaganda, in connection with the walkout of 35,000 textile workers. He also began his first major work, *The Development of Capitalism in Russia*. To prepare the documentation for this book he read everything he could find on economics and finance.

Apart from losing some weight, he emerged from the St. Petersburg prison, after fourteen months, in excellent health. The time had not been wasted.

Upon being released, Ulianov was banished for three years to the village of Shushenskoe in eastern Siberia. He arrived there in May 1897. From the government he received an allowance of seven rubles and forty kopecks a month, enough to pay for room, board, and laundry.

Ulianov did not find existence in Siberia intolerable. His life was tranquil, his health good. Hunting, fishing, and swimming were enjoyable pastimes; forced isolation an excellent setting for study and writing. In the evening, when tired, he played the guitar of his peasant neighbor. Except for the initial absence of newspapers, he scarcely missed civilization. His relative contentment with life was mirrored in his letters home.

Food was simple—plenty of milk and a steady diet of mutton. A ram would be slaughtered and there would be meat for the week. When the stock was depleted another week's supply was laid in. The meat was chopped in a large cattle trough, made into hamburgers, and served twice a day.

Most of the simple townsfolk became very fond of him. Zavertkin, a peasant, relates that he was having tea one day with Ulianov when he noticed men in uniform prowling around the windows. No sooner had he seen this when three men burst into the house—the local assistant district attorney, the captain, and sergeant of gendarmes. Without a word of greeting or removing his hat, one of the men arrogantly demanded, "Where is Ulianov's study?"

Ulianov pointed to the table littered with books and papers and to the few shelves filled with books. The search began, followed by a cross-examination. But in a few minutes the roles were reversed; caps were removed, and Ulianov was the commanding officer.

In May 1898 Nadezhda Krupskaya arrived in Shushenskoe. She had met Ulianov in St. Petersburg where she taught in an evening school for workers. They had become friends and had continued corresponding while Ulianov was in prison. When Krupskaya herself was exiled to Ufa, she requested to be transferred to Shushenskoe. "For this purpose," she writes, "I described him as my 'fiancé.'"

In Krupskaya, Ulianov found the ideal comrade and secretary who subordinated herself completely to his work. Their marriage was to last for life.

It was a curious honeymoon. Mornings were spent translating Sidney and Beatrice Webb's *Theory and Practice of Trade Unionism*. For two hours each afternoon they copied the text of the *Development of Capitalism in Russia*. Published in St. Petersburg in 1899, under the pseudonym of Vladimir Ilin, this work established Ulianov's reputation among Russian radicals as an important Marxist theoretician.

On Sundays, Ulianov ran a legal information bureau, which soon gave him the reputation of being a great lawyer, particularly after he helped a gold miner win a case against his employers.

Lenin's home became the general headquarters for exiled politicals. Correspondence was extensive. Books, newspapers, and magazines, Russian and foreign, were exchanged. Although meetings were forbidden, conferences were arranged on one pretext or another.

Mail arrived twice a week, bringing letters, papers, and books from European Russia. Lenin's sister Anna wrote them frequently, as did several St. Petersburg friends. There was mail from Martov in Turukhansk, Potresov in Orlov, and fellow exiles closer to Shushenskoe. They corresponded about events in Russia, made plans for the future.

"Vladimir Ilich was the central figure in the community of exiled Social Democrats," according to Z. Krzhizhanovskaya, an old friend. "His busy, cheerful mode of living, full of inner meaning, acted as a stimulus, set the pace for all of us, kept us from lapsing into indolence."

Under his influence, "there was neither the boredom of idleness, nor the feeling of dejection, nor intrigue. Everybody was busy, preparing himself for the future, instructing the workers, following Russian events. Everybody felt alive, alert, happy." Not even the bitter Siberian cold kept visitors away.

During his final year of exile Ulianov developed the ambitious plan which he later elaborated in *What Is to Be Done* and *Letter to a Comrade*. He proposed the establishment of an official Social Democratic newspaper outside of Russia. From abroad it would direct Marxist political action throughout Russia by means of an underground network of smugglers and party agents. He talked over the project night after night with Krzhizhanovsky, corresponded with Martov and Potresov, discussed the prospects for going abroad as soon as his term of exile was over.

Ulianov received disturbing news from Potresov several months before leaving Siberia. The magazine published by the "legal Marxists" in St. Petersburg was running articles by Peter Struve and Professor Tugan-Baranovsky which challenged some of the revolutionary tenets of Marxism. Ulianov was also greatly perturbed to hear that Eduard Bernstein, a leading German Social Democrat, had written a book which called for the revision of Marxist theory and practice. Ulianov promptly declared war on these heretics.

With Potresov and Martov also completing their terms of exile, the three men planned their future campaigns together. For the moment it was agreed that Ulianov and Potresov would proceed to Pskov—pending their departure for western Europe.

The largest problem ahead was organization. "It is absolutely essential," wrote Ulianov, "that we improve our revolutionary organization and discipline, and perfect our conspiratorial methods. We must frankly admit that in this respect we lag behind the old Russian revolutionary parties, and we must put forth every effort to overtake and surpass them."

The period of exile was ending, but not before Ulianov had completed *The Aims of Russian Social Democrats* which was to appear in Switzerland under the signature of N. Lenin —his first use of that name. He chose "Lenin" after the River Lena, which flowed through the region of his exile.

In March 1900 the long and arduous journey back to European Russia began.

They stopped in Ufa, where Lenin entrusted his wife to the care of local comrades. Then he continued on alone to Pskov. His appeal to the Director of State Police to permit Krupskaya to join him in Pskov was rejected, but he was allowed to spend a week with his mother in Moscow. Not until the end of the year could he visit his wife in Ufa.

The Social Democratic movement had gathered considerable momentum during Lenin's absence. Influenced by strikes in St. Petersburg and other cities, a new faction, known as the

Economists, maintained that workers would achieve better results by fighting for their economic interests than by revolutionary action. The Social Democrats, they argued, should champion higher wages, shorter hours, and better factory conditions. Some Economists went so far as to assert that providing political leadership was the business of liberal intellectuals; that the workers needed no party of their own; that their sole political function was to support the middle class in its struggle against absolutism.

In 1897 the secret Jewish Social Democratic cells of Russian Poland and Lithuania held a clandestine conference in Vilna and organized the General Jewish Workers' Alliance. This organization, which became known as the Bund, was Russia's first Social Democratic mass organization. Its members were mainly factory workers and artisans.

In March 1898 the first all-Russian Congress of Social Democratic organizations met in Minsk, with six delegates from the Russian organization and three from the Bund. The Congress proclaimed the birth of the Russian Social Democratic Labor Party, elected a three-man Central Committee, and published a general manifesto of Social Democratic aims. Composed by Struve and edited by the Central Committee, the manifesto claimed for the new party the revolutionary mantle of the People's Will.

The Minsk Congress whipped together the separate units which had worked independently of one another. A second party congress was scheduled to meet within six months, but a few weeks later the Minsk delegates were all arrested, imprisoned, and later exiled.

In the same year—1898—the Economists founded *The Worker's Cause,* which urged the Social Democratic organizations to subordinate their Marxist propaganda to a campaign for the right to strike and for freedom of speech, press, and assembly. Lenin, who had combated this group from Siberia, was now preparing to launch a full-scale offensive against it.

In May 1900 Lenin, Martov, Potresov, and other Marxists met secretly in Pskov to draw up final plans for publishing their paper abroad. Its first task would be to fight the Economists and others who deviated from the Marxist line. The paper was to be called *Iskra*—the Spark. Lenin and Potresov were to go abroad to enlist Plekhanov's support.

Shortly thereafter Lenin crossed the frontier into Germany. Soon Potresov joined him, after conferring with Plekhanov and Axelrod in Switzerland. Secret printing facilities would be supplied by the German Social Democratic Party. Potresov enlisted the aid of Clara Zetkin and Adolf Braun, who arranged that the paper be printed in Leipzig while the editorial board was to reside in Munich.

A final conference was held in Geneva. A statement announcing the forthcoming appearance of the new revolutionary organ declared that its first function would be to rally all the Party forces around it. The secret distributing agents of *Iskra* would also be the connecting links of the Party network. Uncompromising war would be waged against all "opportunist" and wavering elements until a powerful revolutionary party was forged.

The *Spark* was ready to be ignited.

4 THE BIRTH OF BOLSHEVISM

THE FIRST ISSUE OF THE "ISKRA" ROLLED OFF THE PRESS IN Leipzig on December 21, 1900. It was printed in small type on onion-skin paper, designed for convenient smuggling and distribution by underground agents.

The issues were shipped to Berlin and stored in the cellars of the *Vorwaerts,* official organ of the German Social Democratic Party. In this subterranean storeroom a handful of trusted German Social Democrats carefully folded copies in small parcels and concealed them in packing cases. These were routed to towns close to the frontier, where they were picked up by professional smugglers who ran the contraband across the border to waiting *Iskra* agents.

The men who worked for this underground chain had to run the gamut of the Prussian police, who assisted undercover Okhrana agents in Germany. Often large batches of papers were confiscated, and *Iskra* smugglers were arrested and exiled to Siberia.

From its birth *Iskra* was more than a revolutionary newspaper. It became one of the fountainheads of the Russian Social Democratic movement. From *Iskra* editorial headquarters instructions radiated to hundreds of party cells throughout Russia. The party doctrines formulated in the pages of *Iskra* became the fighting program for groups of party members everywhere. *Iskra* spread its gospel and stamped out heresies.

"If we have a strongly organized party," Lenin wrote in the first issue, "a single strike may grow into a political demonstration, into a political victory over the regime. If we have a strongly organized party, a rebellion in a single locality may spread into a victorious revolution."

To build that "strongly organized party" was Lenin's main objective. He allowed Martov, Potresov, and Zasulich to do much of the editing, while he followed closely the workings of the *Iskra* machinery inside Russia. There the fight against the Economists and other revisionist groups was carried by *Iskra* supporters into the underground Social Democratic

committees and workers' organizations. *Iskra* also conducted
a strong campaign against the use of individual terrorism as
a political weapon. It was not easy to convince men bred in
the tradition of the People's Will to abandon political assassination.

To combat all forms of heresy *Iskra* agents in Russia started
an intensive campaign of propaganda and agitation among
workers and students. Lenin drew this distinction between
propaganda and agitation:

"A propagandist . . . must give many ideas concentrated
all together, so many that all of them will not be understood
by the average person, and in their totality they will be understood by relatively few.

"The agitator, on the other hand, will pick out one more or
less familiar and concrete aspect of the entire problem. . . .
His efforts will be concentrated on this fact, to impart to the
masses a single idea. . . . He will strive to evoke among the
masses discontent and revolt against this great injustice and
will leave the full explanation for this contradiction to the
propagandists."

Iskra agents distributed leaflets and newspapers at every
opportunity. Often the Social Democratic committees took the
lead in organizing strikes. More intensive propaganda was
conducted in small clandestine groups called "circles."

But systematic work was impossible. It was difficult to find
safe quarters, arrests were frequent, propagandizing was a
dangerous business. Moreover, educated propagandists were
hard to find; when one was arrested his circle usually disin-
tegrated because there was no one to take his place. Although
the curriculum of the propaganda circles called for between
six and ten lectures, the course was seldom completed. In
many cases the lecture consisted of reading *Iskra* to the members. Each issue gave the propagandists material for discussion, for winning new adherents. Workers to whom the propagandists read several copies often became sufficiently interested to read the paper to their comrades. Thus *Iskra* passed
from hand to hand, until the newsprint was so worn it could
barely be read.

Agitation was carried on by various means. In some cases
one trained man read the latest issue of a legal newspaper to
his fellow workers, injecting his comments. At the same time
he tried to pick out those among his listeners who showed
promise. These he took in hand, and furnished with "legal"
books on current problems. If the worker showed interest, he
was given clandestine literature. After a probationary period
he became a member of the Party.

Copies of *Iskra* leaflets were distributed not only in the factories but in army barracks, and through the mail. In large
cities they were widely scattered through the streets. In small

towns and villages they were pasted on walls. In workers' districts pamphlets were showered down in factory courtyards, or near water pumps.

But the most spectacular form of paper warfare was waged in the theaters of Moscow, St. Petersburg, Kharkov, Kiev, and Odessa. Here groups of men took their seats in the gallery and dropped their literature out over the audience below.

The systematic dissemination of clandestine revolutionary literature was by no means an *Iskra* monopoly. The unique feature of the *Iskra* machine was that its agents were becoming the nucleus of a tight band of professional revolutionists. And it was Lenin himself who referred to these men as "agents" in order to stress their special revolutionary function.

* * *

Unregistered, under the name of Meyer, Lenin took up his abode in Munich in a little room offered him by a German saloonkeeper, a Social Democrat.

Engrossed though he was in his revolutionary work, he did not forget his family in Russia. He wrote on February 20, 1901:

DARLING MOTHER:

The carnival ended here some days ago. It was the first time I had ever seen the last day of the carnival abroad . . . a procession of masked paraders on the streets; wholesale tomfoolery; clouds of confetti thrown into the faces of passersby; little paper kites. Here they know how to make merry on the streets! . . . Nadya's exile will soon be over. I will send a request for a passport for her one of these days. I should like to ask Maniasha to send me with her a little box of "my" pen points. Can you imagine, I have not been able to get them here in any place. Silly people, the Czechs and the Germans. English pen points are not to be gotten here. Only "their own" products. But they are good for nothing. . . .

"Nadya" was Krupskaya, whose term of restricted residence in Russia was almost over.

On her arrival in western Europe she was forced to travel from city to city looking for Lenin. For two days she did not know whether she was Modraczek, Ritmeyer, Lenina, Ulianova, Krupskaya, or what. First she came to Prague, and began to search for Modraczek, the alias under which she believed Lenin lived. She had wired ahead about her coming, but there was no one to meet her.

"I waited and waited," she relates. "In perplexity I . . . proceeded to Modraczek's address. We came to a narrow street in the workers' quarters and stopped in front of a huge house with mattresses hanging out of the windows for airing. I climbed to the fourth floor. A blonde Czech woman opened the door. I asked for Herr Modraczek. Whereupon a workman appeared and said: 'I am Modraczek.' Bewildered, I muttered: 'No, my husband!' Modraczek at last divined the meaning of it all. 'Ah, you are probably the wife of Herr Ritmeyer. He lives in Munich. . . ,' "

And so she set out for Munich. This time she took the streetcar to the part of the city where she hoped to locate Ritmeyer. She found the house but the address turned out to be that of a beer hall. She stepped up to the bar, behind which stood a small corpulent German, and asked him about Herr Ritmeyer, feeling that there was something wrong again. The barkeeper answered: "Yes, that is me. What is it?" Utterly confused, she murmured, "No, it's my husband I am looking for."

"Was there no end to this Labyrinth?" she writes. At last the wife of Ritmeyer entered, and surmised who Krupskaya was. "Ah, that must be the wife of Herr Meyer. He has been expecting his wife from Siberia. I'll take you to him." She followed the woman into the yard of the big house.

She found Lenin seated at a table with his sister Anna and Martov.

Lenin and his wife moved into a crowded three-room apartment, two rooms of which were occupied by a worker, his wife and their six children. Their single room served as their sleeping quarters, parlor, kitchen, and study.

A month later they settled in a new apartment in the Schwabing district of Munich.

In a letter to Lenin's mother Krupskaya wrote on August 2, 1901: "Volodya [Lenin] is working diligently these days. I am very pleased with him. When he becomes completely engrossed in a certain work, he is in excellent spirits. This is his nature. His health is very good. Not the slightest trace of his cold lingers. Nor does he suffer from insomnia. He invigorates himself daily with a cold-water rubdown. In addition we go bathing almost every day."

But the following spring they were on the move again. The printing plant in Leipzig had been abandoned in favor of Munich. Now the owner of the Munich plant refused to continue turning out *Iskra*. It was too great a risk. Plekhanov and Axelrod favored transferring operations to Switzerland but the majority voted for London.

Lenin and Krupskaya arrived in England in April 1902, in the midst of a dense fog.

Very promptly Lenin and Krupskaya discovered that their knowledge of English bore only a remote resemblance to the native product. With his usual zest Lenin set to work learning the language. He hired two English teachers whom he taught Russian in exchange for English lessons. With these efforts his English soon became fairly proficient if not fluent.

The library of the British Museum was a treasure house for his research, even as it had been for Karl Marx before him.

While in London, Lenin met Trotsky for the first time. Friends in Samarna had already written about an enthusiastic *Iskra* man who had recently escaped from Siberia. "The young eagle" was the way they had described him. And by his prolific writings he had also earned the nickname of the "Pen."

Trotsky himself arrived with a loud knock at the front door. "I knew from the sound that it must be someone calling on us and hurried downstairs," says Krupskaya. "The caller was Trotsky, and I led him into our room. Vladimir Ilich had just awakened and was still in bed.

". . . . The enthusiastic references to the man as a 'young eagle' made Vladimir Ilich study the caller very closely. . . ." Evidently he passed muster, for thereafter "they walked and discussed things together a great deal." Moreover, when Trotsky received word to return to Russia, Lenin asked him to remain abroad, to familiarize himself with party matters and assist in the work of *Iskra*. And he fought for Trotsky in the teeth of opposition by other members of the editorial board.

Plekhanov regarded Trotsky with immediate suspicion. He saw him as an ally of the younger element, Lenin, Martov, and Potresov. When Lenin sent Trotsky's articles to Plekhanov, the latter's comment was: "The pen of our 'Pen' does not please me."

"Style is a matter of practice," Lenin replied. "The man is capable of learning and will prove very useful." In March 1903 he considered Trotsky's apprenticeship completed and proposed his election to the editorial board.

Iskra had called into existence a group of "professional revolutionists" whose duty it was, in Lenin's words, to "devote . . . their whole life to working for the Revolution."

By the end of 1902 the majority of the Social Democratic Party committees in Russia had already been fused into the *Iskra* network. The general quickening of the social tempo of the country helped speed this process. The earlier industrial strikes were followed by student walkouts, street demonstrations, and peasant riots. In 1903 disorders among students and peasants intensified.

Meanwhile Lenin published his book *What Is to Be Done* in which he forcefully presented his views regarding the relations between the Party intellectuals and workers, between the revolutionary elite and the politically inarticulate mass. This work was to become a revolutionary bible to his adherents. Here the doctrine of the "professional revolutionists" was explicitly stated for the first time.

"The history of every country teaches us," he wrote, "that by its own ability the working class can attain only a trade-unionist self-consciousness, that is to say, an appreciation of the need to fight the bosses, to wrest from the government this or that legislative enactment for the benefit of the workers. The Socialist doctrine, on the other hand, is the outgrowth of those philosophical, historical, and economic theories which had been developed by the representatives of the well to do, the intellectuals.

"By their social origin, Marx and Engels, the founders of modern scientific Socialism, were themselves members of the bourgeois intelligentsia. Similarly, in Russia, the theoretical principles of the Social Democracy originated independently of the unconscious strivings of the laboring classes. They were a natural and inevitable result of the development of the ideas of the revolutionary Socialist intellectuals." Only revolutionary intellectuals, "professional revolutionists," could rescue the working class from bourgeois influence and convert it to Socialism.

During this period he was consistently advocating and gradually building up a party apparatus of the "professional revolutionists."

This departure from the prevailing Marxist line slowly prepared the ground for the split that was to come in 1903. Potresov and Martov felt that Lenin was returning to the sectarianism which had characterized him at the time of their first meeting. Lenin, on the other hand, was becoming increasingly skeptical of the revolutionary single-mindedness of his colleagues. Frictions in the editorial office of *Iskra* were mounting. Among other things, Plekhanov could not tolerate Lenin's manner of writing.

Plekhanov measured his sentences for their prose effect. Lenin wrote only to influence the actions of men. In a debate the same was true. Before a highly sophisticated audience he was no match for Plekhanov's erudition. But the words that left the party intellectuals cold stirred the masses, whom he swayed through invective and the constant reiteration of simple slogans. In other words, Lenin was a natural political leader, which his antagonists—even in the early intra-party struggle—were not.

When Struve deserted the Marxist ranks for the Liberal camp, Lenin wrote an article in *Iskra* calling him a renegade and traitor. Takhtarev, who was then Lenin's close friend, asked him how he could permit himself to use such language, since any worker who read the article might feel it was his duty to kill Struve as a "traitor."

"He deserves to die," was Lenin's calm reply. That was in 1903, and Takhtarev did not take Lenin seriously, neither did his Social Democratic colleagues. His strong, often abusive, language was merely taken for rhetoric.

Serious differences of opinion between *Iskra* editors had

begun in 1902, when the Party program satisfied neither
Lenin, Martov, nor Axelrod.

Lenin demanded that the program state clearly that the
Party was fighting for the dictatorship of the proletariat.

Plekhanov retorted that the lower middle class was destined
to play a large part in the revolution. Martov and Potresov
stood by Lenin somewhat half-heartedly. After much haggling,
Martov, Zasulich, and Theodore Dan composed a new compromise draft which attempted to reconcile the differences between Plekhanov and Lenin. The new text, although finally
accepted, did not satisfy Lenin.

Other differences followed, and the breach between the
London office of *Iskra* and the Plekhanov-Axelrod headquarters in Switzerland widened. Finally, in April 1903, *Iskra*
was transferred to Geneva, where controversial articles were
henceforth to be submitted to the vote of the six members of
the board, Lenin, Plekhanov, Martov, Potresov, Zasulich, and
Axelrod. Often this led to a 3-3 deadlock, with Lenin, Martov,
and Potresov lining up against the three older Social Democrats.

Leaving England behind him in April 1903, Lenin settled
in a small house in Secheron, a working-class district on the
outskirts of Geneva. The struggles inside *Iskra* were now
growing more frequent and more explosive. Potresov, who
often sided with Lenin, reported that "it was impossible to
work with him."

Lenin, he concluded, divided the world sharply between
those who were with him and those who were against him.
There was no middle ground.

Despite the gathering storm clouds, the other editors of
Iskra did not grasp the far-reaching implications of their daily
tussles with Lenin. They regarded these quarrels as a family
affair and did not suspect that Lenin wanted to build up a
rival organization responsible to him alone. Yet that is precisely what Lenin was beginning to do. This organization,
conceived by Lenin and fostered by the myopic consent of the
other Social Democratic leaders, was in fact the embryo of
the Communist Party machine. For even in this period Lenin
was surrounding himself with men whose obedience to him
was absolute and unquestioning.

Lenin, the splendid organizer, was an even more thorough
disciplinarian. "In Lenin's organization, discipline reached the
point of almost military obedience." It was, according to
Potresov, "an organization uniting the superior command and
the 'agents' of the Party executives. . . . It was an organization
of the revolutionary minority; at the proper moment this
minority was to seize the reins of power. . . ."

It was an organization groomed to give practical effect to

Lenin's theory that in the struggle for power the masses were to be pliant instruments in the hands of a determined general staff of "professional revolutionists."

Because Lenin's ideas were so explicitly bound with his theory of the "professional revolutionist," a showdown was inevitable. The stage was set in November 1902 when, at the initiative of *Iskra,* a committee was organized inside Russia to call a Party Congress—the first in which Lenin was to participate.

In the early summer of 1903 delegates from all parts of Russia began to congregate in Geneva.

Among the first delegates to arrive was Shotman, a St. Petersburg worker. Shotman had an unusual opportunity for intimate contact with the émigré leaders, eager to receive first-hand news from Russia.

Shotman writes of his first contact with Lenin: "I do not remember what was discussed at the meeting. . . . But I remember very vividly that immediately after his first address I was won over to his side, so simple, clear, and convincing was his manner of speaking.

"When Plekhanov spoke, I enjoyed the beauty of his speech, the remarkable incisiveness of his words. But when Lenin arose in opposition, I was always on Lenin's side. Why? I cannot explain it to myself. But so it was, and not only with me, but my comrades, also workers."

Despite the simmering differences between Plekhanov and Lenin, the preliminary caucuses pointed to substantial agreement among the delegates. It seemed as if the congress sessions would be harmonious and brief. It was in this spirit that the delegates left Geneva for Brussels for the opening on July 30, 1903.

For security reasons, the sessions moved from one site to another, mainly to local trade-union halls in the working-class districts of Brussels. After four or five sessions devoted to heated debates on the party program, the police warned four delegates to leave the city within twenty-four hours. With police spies watching the movements of all the delegates, the Congress voted for transfer to London.

Sessions were resumed on the morning following the arrival of the delegation in the British capital. Of the forty-three delegates present only three or four were workers; the rest were "professional revolutionists." These delegates, holding a total of fifty-one votes, represented three main trends: *Iskra,* the Jewish Socialist Bund, and the Economists. Their differences were substantial. The Bund preferred a loose federation. Nor did the Economists wish to bow to the will of the *Iskra* high command.

Lenin understood that the success of his blueprint for tight party organization depended on the degree of discipline he could enforce from the start. He began, therefore, by pushing through a motion which set up a presidium consisting entirely of *Iskra* men, with Plekhanov as chairman and himself and Pavlovich-Krasikov as vice-chairmen. He won on this motion, despite the protests of Martov. This was the opening skirmish in the Lenin-Martov battle.

Later, Lenin admitted that the purpose of his move had been to wield the "iron fist" against all Social Democratic groups that resisted *Iskra's* control over the Party.

Lenin lost to Martov, however, on the wording of the rules defining Party membership. Lenin wanted to limit membership to those who not only subscribed to the party program but participated actively in one of its organizations. Martov, on the other hand, was willing to admit all who accepted the program and gave the Party "regular personal cooperation under the guidance of one of its organizations."

To many this difference seemed merely verbal. Actually the minor variation in language contained the fissionable element that was to smash the Social Democratic Party into its ultimately irreconcilable Bolshevik and Menshevik factions. According to an official interpretation of 1937, the treasonable error of Martov and his supporters in 1903 was that they wanted a party "which after the autocracy was overthrown would conduct its struggle entirely within the framework of bourgeois democracy."

The Mensheviks of 1903 would have been offended by the charge that they intended to conduct their fight "entirely within the framework of bourgeois democracy." They professed much the same general doctrines as Lenin, but in every critical situation from 1903 to 1917 their actions did not tally with their words. Whatever their theories, they were unprepared and unwilling to sacrifice "bourgeois" democracy in order to achieve Socialism. This inconsistency between Menshevik words and Menshevik deeds was to be the hallmark of their political weakness.

Although Martov carried the Congress by a small margin on the paragraph defining party membership, Lenin won on almost every other important issue. And he owed his victories largely to Plekhanov.

The members of Lenin's 1903 majority became known as Bolsheviks (after *bolshinstvo,* for majority), Martov's group were dubbed Mensheviks (after *menshinstvo,* meaning minority).

Plekhanov sided with Lenin on the issue of tight party organization. The Congress voted for the dissolution of all independent Party organizations and their fusion into a single party apparatus. After this vote the Bund and a number of other groups walked out. This left *Iskra* in complete command. But the elimination of the dissident factions brought no harmony. The fight between Martov and Lenin continued, with Plekhanov lining up on Lenin's side.

Lenin won on his motion for cutting the *Iskra* editorial board to three—himself, Plekhanov, and Martov. This meant the elimination of Axelrod, Potresov, and Zasulich—all of whom were Martov supporters. Lenin was confident that in this three-man board he could wield control.

His confidence was reinforced by Plekhanov's fateful speech. On Lenin's insistence Plekhanov had already written in the program draft that the concept of proletarian dictatorship includes "the suppression of all social movements which directly or indirectly threaten the interests of the proletariat."

Plekhanov, in his last years, deeply regretted his London oration. A few weeks after the Congress, when Plekhanov had already begun to backtrack on his support of Lenin, Martov tried to explain away Plekhanov's speech.

"Plekhanov's words," he said, "evoked indignation on the part of some delegates which might easily have been avoided had Comrade Plekhanov added that it was impossible to imagine a situation so tragic that the proletariat, in order to fortify its victory, should resort to such methods."

It was a brave attempt to undo the words which justified the suppression of freedom but Plekhanov thanked him ironically for this afterthought. In later years, when he was reminded that Leninism could be considered a legitimate offspring of that speech, Plekhanov tried to explain that he had spoken of dispersing a democratically elected parliament as only "theoretically possible," not as desirable or necessary. It was a lame excuse. The record is clear that at the Congress Plekhanov stood with Lenin. His change of heart and switch to Martov's side came later.

At one point during the Congress Plekhanov was so impressed with Lenin that he exclaimed to Axelrod: "Of such stuff are Robespierres made!" Plekhanov meant this as a high compliment. And when Akimov tried to drive a wedge between Plekhanov and Lenin, Plekhanov retorted:

"Napoleon had a passion for getting his marshals divorced from their wives. Comrade Akimov is like Napoleon in this respect. He wants to divorce me from Lenin at all cost. But I am not out to divorce Lenin, and I hope he doesn't intend to divorce me."

But the divorce was to come. The Congress, which began in harmony, ended in an uproar. On the morning following the last session Martov and his followers left for Paris, Lenin and his cohorts for Geneva. The two groups were not on speaking terms. Martov had refused to serve on the three-man *Iskra* board on the ground that he could not accept the vote of non-confidence in Axelrod, Potresov, and Zasulich.

A short time thereafter another conference was held in

Geneva which, if anything, widened the split. Plekhanov still stood by Lenin, although Martov tried to convince him that Lenin was seeking control of *Iskra*. In Geneva Trotsky joined Martov in the fight against Lenin. Finally Plekhanov tried to restore harmony by reconstituting the board on its old basis, with the return of Axelrod, Potresov, Martov, and Zasulich. Lenin refused. When Plekhanov insisted that there was no other way to restore unity, Lenin handed in his resignation.

"I am absolutely convinced," said Lenin, "that you will come to the conclusion that it is impossible to work with the Mensheviks. I resign from the editorship of *Iskra*. You can . . . be responsible for the future developments."

The "divorce" had come, after all. For Lenin, the decision to resign rather than continue to share authority with his old Social Democratic comrades was one of the most difficult of his career. He knew that for the moment he would be isolated and without an effective weapon in the propaganda war for the triumph of his ideas.

Lenin's stand brought a barrage of criticism from his former comrades. "Autocrat," "bureaucrat," "formalist," "centralist," "copperhead," "obstinate," and "narrow-minded" were some of the epithets fired at him, as he himself ironically enumerated in his 1904 pamphlet *One Step Forward, Two Steps Back*.

The most vigorous attack came from Trotsky, who described Lenin as a "despot and terrorist who sought to turn the Central Committee of the Party into a Committee of Public Safety— in order to be able to play the role of Robespierre."

Replying to Lenin's *One Step Forward, Two Steps Back,* Trotsky wrote that if Lenin ever took power "the entire international movement of the proletariat would be accused by a revolutionary tribunal of 'moderatism' and the leonine head of Marx would be the first to fall under the guillotine."

When Lenin spoke of the dictatorship of the proletariat, wrote Trotsky, he meant "a dictatorship over the proletariat."

No longer was this a family squabble. The early differences had finally cleared the air to reveal a profound rift between Lenin and the Mensheviks.

Back in his home in Secheron, Lenin was on the verge of a nervous breakdown as a result of the many months of tense jockeying for power.

By summer his nerves were almost completely shattered. Krupskaya decided to take him "as far as possible from people, to forget for a time all work and worry." They spent a month tramping through the Swiss countryside, from Geneva to Lausanne to Interlaken to Lucerne, with knapsacks on their backs. "Volodya and I have made a pact not to discuss business affairs," she wrote to Lenin's mother on July 2, 1904. "We sleep ten hours a day, swim, and walk. Volodya doesn't even read the papers properly."

Lenin returned to Geneva refreshed and greatly heartened by the decision of A. A. Bogdanov, a Marxist writer on economics and philosophy, to join the Bolshevik nucleus in Switzerland. Bogdanov's conversion was the stimulant Lenin badly needed. They spent the month of August drawing up new plans.

With Bogdanov's contacts he mobilized a group of young Marxist writers for a new fighting newspaper to compete with *Iskra,* which was now firmly in Menshevik hands.

In the autumn Lenin called together a group of twenty-two Bolsheviks in Geneva to outline his final scheme. Among those present were Lepeshinsky, Olminsky, Lunacharsky and Vorovsky.

Lenin announced that the new paper would be "the real organ of the working-class movement in Russia . . ."

The first issue appeared in December 1904. It was called *Vperiod (Forward);* later the name was changed to *Proletari (Proletarian).* Serving under Lenin's supreme editorial command were Bogdanov, Lunacharsky, Olminsky, and Vorovsky.

With the appearance of *Vperiod* Lenin's spirits soared once again. The atmosphere in the editorial office was very different from that of the old *Iskra.* Instead of bitter fighting, good spirits and complete harmony prevailed. Lenin's eyes beamed when the first copy was ready. Around him sat men on whom he could count.

But there were more substantial reasons for Lenin's new optimism. In February 1904 the Czarist government had blundered into war with Japan. Spring and summer had brought an unbroken series of military defeats and with them rumblings of revolt. In January 1905 the Japanese took Port Arthur.

"It is not the Russian people, but the autocracy that has suffered shameful defeat," Lenin wrote. "The Russian people gained by the defeat of the autocracy. The capitulation of Port Arthur is the prologue to the capitulation of Czarism."

The seeds which generations of rebels had sown were about to yield their first real harvest: Russia was on the verge of revolution.

Lenin, on the eve of the great upheaval of 1905, was thirty-four. Behind him he had a decade of revolutionary experience —a familiar pattern of conspiracy, imprisonment, Siberian exile, and the shuttling existence of a political émigré. Four years of hectic life abroad had not made him a western European. He learned the languages of this alien world but his outlook remained profoundly Russian.

The tough core of his political lines had firmly set; despite his Marxist and European schooling, his philosophy was conditioned by powerful ingredients of Russian revolutionary absolutism and by a sense of his own unique mission. Arbitrary and dictatorial in the eyes of his former mentors and Social

Democratic comrades, he regarded them with increasing disdain for their "bourgeois" aversion to a monolithic party of revolutionary conspirators; for their constant preoccupation with the moral aspects of revolution.

If the man had inner doubts, he did not permit himself to express them. In his writings he was becoming more and more dogmatic, more intolerant of differences of opinion. And while he was to reverse himself on many basic issues of the revolution, he always managed to present these as merely "tactical" shifts, while lambasting his opponents as "opportunists" and "traitors" for much less.

Within his own circle he already commanded veneration and blind loyalty. Of the great political leaders in modern history none had less personal vanity, less desire to flaunt his own person rather than his ideas. But despite his personal reticence and keen sense of humor he was well aware of the enormous political value of the adulation he inspired. In 1905 it never occurred to his followers to call him the "Leader," yet the respectful patronymic "Ilich" set him apart from his contemporaries.

Whether Lenin saw himself as a future dictator is hard to say. He never stated it in so many words until power was in his hands. Then he put his cards on the table with remarkable frankness.

"Classes are led by parties," said Lenin in 1920, "and parties are led by individuals who are called leaders. . . . This is the ABC. The will of a class is sometimes fulfilled by a dictator. . . . Soviet socialist democracy is not in the least incompatible with individual rule and dictatorship. . . . What is necessary is individual rule, the recognition of the dictatorial powers of one man. . . . All phrases about equal rights are nonsense."

But although Lenin did not use such language in his Geneva days, the man's general approach to the coming revolution was already clear enough.

Valentinov, for example, was surprised at Lenin's interest in the details of street fighting which he had seen in Kiev in July 1903. Seeing Valentinov's perplexity with his preoccupation in the "jaw-breaking" aspect of the Kiev disorders, Lenin replied passionately:

"But you must understand, the moment has come when it is necessary to fight not only in the figurative, political meaning of the word, but in its simplest, most direct physical sense. The time when demonstrators unfurled the Red Flag, shouted 'down with absolutism!' and then scattered in all directions, is past. It is necessary to begin its *physical* destruction by mass attack, to deal physical blows against the apparatus of absolutism and its defenders. . . . What is necessary now is not argumentation in the manner of our namby-pamby intellectuals but learning to give proletarian punches on the jaw. We must know how and want to fight."

In *Materialism and Empiro-Criticism* Lenin declared: "Marx's theory is the objective truth. Following the path of this theory, we will approach the objective truth more and more closely, while if we follow any other path we cannot arrive at anything except confusion and falsehood. From the philosophy of Marxism, cast of one piece of steel, it is impossible to expunge a single basic premise, a single essential part, without deviating from objective truth, without falling into the arms of bourgeois-reactionary falsehood. . . ."

Armed with this passionate faith in the proletarian fist and in the "objective truth" of Marxism, Lenin was ready to return to the Russian battle front.

5   THE FIRST REVOLUTION

WHILE CONFLICT RAGED IN SOCIAL DEMOCRATIC RANKS, A NEW party had come on the scene and had stirred fresh currents in the Russian people. This was the Socialist Revolutionary Party. The leaders were Catherine Breshkovsky, who had served six prison terms and spent more than twenty years in Siberia; Mikhail Gotz, son of a Moscow millionaire and a famous Siberian exile; Gregory Gershuni, whose Terrorist Brigade carried out the assassination of leading reactionary Ministers and Governors; Victor Chernov, and a number of old revolutionists of the People's Will. Terrorism was the most spectacular phase of Socialist Revolutionary action, but hardly the most important.

The Socialist Revolutionaries did not take much stock in the Marxist theory. Their general approach to social problems was to proceed from the bottom up. Hence their emphasis on the *people,* on the *mir,* and on a cooperation between consumer and producer in the form of cooperatives. The coming revolution had to be national in character, expressing the aspirations of workers, peasants, and intellectuals. The proletariat was no sacred cow; student, teacher, peasant, scientist, and writer were equally important in a democratic society. Placing a high value on the labor of the mind, they fought for complete intellectual liberty. To the new party liberty was as much an end as a means. To build Socialism without intellectual freedom meant quartering all humanity in barracks. Their ultimate goal was the reorganization of production and the entire social order according to Socialist principles, albeit they believed that Russia was not yet ready for the complete realization of this aim. Nevertheless, in accordance with the traditions of the Russian peasantry and its con-

viction that the land belongs to no individual, the Socialist
Revolutionary program demanded the immediate socialization
of the land.

The Marxist group could not accept the Socialist Revolutionary contention that the peasant communes could serve as
a departing point for Socialism in the rural districts. The older
party maintained that the peasants were indeed a potential
revolutionary force, but not a socialist one. The Social Democrats, in fact, regarded the village mir as a reactionary institution "in the bosom of which the class struggle was already
developing."

The Socialist Revolutionaries' use of individual terror also
came in for denunciation. The Marxist group condemned
these tactics, seeing only "a means of struggle used by the
petty bourgeois bound to put the masses to sleep by making
them believe that the arm of a hero can bring liberation."

Generally the Socialist Revolutionaries were more romantic
and sentimental than their Social Democratic contemporaries.

While the Socialist Revolutionaries aligned themselves with
the older party in demands for a Constituent Assembly and a
democratic republic, they placed as great an emphasis on
"recognition of the inalienable rights of man and citizen,"
wide autonomy for urban and rural communities and regions,
the broadest possible application of federalist principles to
the separate nationalities, and recognition of the rights of self-
determination of nationalities.

Socialist theory did not completely monopolize Russian
political thinking. Liberalism also began to organize for
political action. When Nicholas II ascended the throne in
1894, the zemstvo of the Tver province appealed to the new
monarch with "the hope that the voice of the people and the
expression of its desires will be heard on the heights of the
throne and will be heeded." To this moderate appeal the Czar
replied that the zemstvo was indulging in idle dreams.

Pobedonostsev, procurator of the Holy Synod, was entrusted with blanket authority to promote such policies as he
thought best. Pobedonostsev cracked down on the zemstvos
and embarked on the systematic persecution of religious and
racial minorities. The Czar, relying on his adviser's judgment,
ignored the approaching storm clouds.

"The Emperor lacks real education or experience in affairs
of state and most particularly any strength of character," said
A. A. Polovtzev, the Secretary of State and member of the
Imperial Council. "Anyone can convince him to change his
mind. The Emperor's Uncle Sergei has the greatest influence
on him, but Sergei is, in every sense of the word, a worthless
individual. . . ."

Pobedonostsev himself was not much kinder in his judgment
of the Czar. "He has a naturally bright mind, he is shrewd,

quickly grasps the meaning of what he hears, but only understands the significance of some isolated fact, without connection with the rest, without appreciating the interrelation of all other pertinent facts, events, trends, occurrences. He sticks to his insignificant petty point of view. This is the result of his military-school education, as well probably as the influence of the many chambermaids who surround his mother."

With the court hopelessly absorbed in petty intrigues, the Liberals began to press for constitutional changes. In 1903, under the leadership of Professor Paul Miliukov, Princes Paul and Peter Dolgorukov, Ivan Petrunkevich, Feodor Kokoshkin, Feodor Rodichev, and Vladimir Nabokov, a Union of Liberation was founded. In Stuttgart this new group published a newspaper under the editorship of Peter Struve, the former Marxist. In the summer of 1905 the Union of Liberation was instrumental in the founding of the Constitutional Democratic (Cadet) Party headed by Miliukov.

In the midst of Russian military defeat Von Plehve, the reactionary Minister of Interior, was assassinated by a member of the Terrorist Brigade of the Socialist Revolutionary Party; street demonstrations broke out, opposition from every side grew bolder. For the first time the Czar retreated, summoning Prince Sviatopolk-Mirsky, a liberal, to Von Plehve's post. Censorship was relaxed and reforms were pledged. In November 1904 a great congress of the zemstvos met in St. Petersburg and demanded freedom of speech and press, inviolability of person, equality for national minorities, and the convocation of a representative assembly.

In the meantime, the Ministry of Interior and the political police, in the effort to wean the workers away from radicalism, had organized a Union of Russian Workers, whose program called for the defense of the economic rights of labor and loyalty to the Czar. Father Gapon, a priest, was placed at the head of the union. But the logic of events pushed this organization far beyond the objectives intended by its police sponsors.

On Sunday, January 22, 1905, the union organized a procession to the Winter Palace to present a petition to the Czar. The marchers, numbering many thousands of unarmed workers, accompanied by their wives and children, carried ikons and placards. They were not received by the Czar or his Ministers. Instead, they were brought to a halt by troops ordered to keep the demonstration out of the Winter Palace square. The soldiers opened fire on the multitude as it approached the Troitski Bridge, and continued firing indiscriminately. More than seventy were killed and many hundreds wounded. This massacre destroyed the last particle of public faith in the regime. "Bloody Sunday" produced universal indignation and a wave of protest strikes.

Less than a month after the massacre, the Terrorist Brigade of the Socialist Revolutionary Party assassinated the detested Grand Duke Sergei, then Governor General of Moscow.

"Learn to look the coming revolution straight in the eye," Kaliaiev, the assassin, told the judges who sentenced him to death. "Our generation will end this autocracy forever. . . ."

In May 1905 a Union of Unions was organized under the chairmanship of Profesor Miliukov. This brought together all the liberal and radical groups in a renewed demand for parliamentary government and the institution of universal suffrage.

On August 19, 1905, the Czar signed a manifesto summoning a popular assembly, the Imperial Duma, with advisory powers, but without legislative authority. This half measure, like so many concessions the Czar granted under duress, satisfied no one, serving only to whet the appetite of the people for political freedom.

Strikes, demonstrations, riots gained momentum and scope. In mid-September the Typographical Union of Moscow went out on strike. They were joined by the bakers, then the telegraph and postal operators. The strike grew into nationwide proportions without direction from any party. In this strike for liberty the leaders were legion, the people themselves without central direction.

On October 22, 1905, Count Witte, a former Minister of Finance, warned the Czar that Russia was on the verge of a bloody revolution.

Late in October the All-Russian Railway Workers' Union called a general strike. On October 25 railroad transportation came to a halt throughout the Empire. The strike had at last paralyzed the government.

At the same time a strange new "government" appeared in St. Petersburg, the Soviet Workers' Deputies. Elections to the new body began in the factories on the twenty-sixth of October. A young lawyer named Khrustalev-Nosar was elected chairman, with Trotsky and the Socialist Revolutionary Nikolai Avksentiev as vice-chairman of the first Soviet.

The initiative for this proletarian parliament came from the Menshevik wing of the St. Petersburg Social Democratic Party. The general strike needed a non-partisan directorate to give it political direction and this body was the answer. On October 26 the first meeting of the Soviet took place in the Technological Institute. It was attended by only forty delegates, representing 20,000 workers; not all the St. Petersburg factories had had time to elect their delegates.

The Soviet's first appeal called on the entire working class to join the strike. "In the next few days," said the appeal, "decisive events will take place in Russia, which will determine for many years the fate of the working class in Russia. We must be fully prepared to cope with these events united through our common Soviet."

The Soviet acted openly. Overnight it became known and popular everywhere as an institution of power in the hands of the masses.

Khrustalev assumed the role of the tribune of the people, but his political leadership was jostled on the third day by Trotsky. The latter's talents as an orator immediately pushed him to the forefront.

Although the Soviet was conceived merely as a central strike committee, its leaders soon realized that it could become an effective organ for political agitation. Within a few days it became an instrument of revolutionary power.

On the twenty-eighth the Soviet ordered the shutdown of all shops; grocery stores were permitted to be open only in the morning. The same day it warned factory owners and shopkeepers that they would face the "people's vengeance" if they tried to conduct their business. Two days later life in St. Petersburg was at a complete standstill.

Although not a shot had been fired this was revolution, and the Czar's advisers knew it. From Berlin, Kaiser Wilhelm advised his cousin to grant a constitution. Wilhelm also offered to provide the Czar with a haven. His offer caused great excitement at the court. Those opposed to constitutional concessions were in favor of the Czar's departure. Witte, on the other hand, argued that this step meant the end of the dynasty.

Realizing that further delay would be fatal, Nicholas dismissed Pobedonostsev, appointed Count Witte Premier of Russia, and on October 30, issued a brand-new manifesto. This document granted freedom of speech, conscience, and assembly, the right of labor to organize, and a more liberal suffrage law for elections to the Duma. Nicholas also promised, for the first time, that no laws would be decreed without the Duma's sanction. When Trepov, the governor of St. Petersburg, heard the news, he exclaimed:

"Thank God the manifesto has been signed. Freedom has been granted; the people will choose their own representatives. A new life is beginning."

When the first issue of the Soviet newspaper *Izvestia* appeared, Trotsky had this to say of the Czar's promises: "We are given a Witte, but Trepov remains; we are given a constitution, but absolutism remains. All is given and nothing is given."

The Soviet voted to continue the strike. On the thirty-first there was a tremendous demonstration, with flags and revolutionary songs, led by three members of the Soviet. But no soldiers or sailors took part; the military was still faithful to the government.

On November 3 the strike ended. But *Izvestia* continued the fight with words: "The proletariat knows what it wants and what it doesn't want. It doesn't want the police hooligan Trepov, nor the 'liberal' mediator Witte—neither the jaws of a wolf nor the tail of a fox. It doesn't want Cossack whips wrapped up in a constitution."

The Prime Minister played politics with both the Right and the Left. He conferred with Khrustalev and threatened him with Trepov, and threatened Trepov with Khrustalev. While the government hesitated, the Soviet came out with the slogan "Disarm the autocracy and arm the Revolution." The Soviet demanded an eight-hour workday and a raise in wages for all the workers of St. Petersburg. This move drove the capitalists and the middle class into the arms of the regime. The peasants remained passive.

On November 8 a mutiny broke out among the sailors of Kronstadt fortress, but it was quickly suppressed and the leaders faced possible execution. The Petrograd workers again called a strike. The demand of the strike was the abolition of courts-martial and the death penalty. At the same time the Soviet decided to start agitation in the Army. The strike was more successful than authorities had expected. Count Witte had to appeal to the workers in a language never before used by a Minister of the Czar.

"Brother workers, go back to your jobs. Stop your rebellion. Pity your wives and children," begged the Premier. "Listen to the advice of a man who is favorably disposed to you and desires only your welfare."

The Soviet Executive Committee promptly replied: "The Soviet of Workers' Deputies . . . expresses its extreme amazement that the Czarist Minister unceremoniously allows himself to call the Petrograd workers 'brothers.' The proletarians are no relatives of Count Witte."

It was at this time, November 1905, that Lenin returned to Russia. What had he been doing since Bloody Sunday?

Believing that an insurrection was imminent, Lenin set out to wrest control of the Party from the Mensheviks. In April he summoned his followers for what he designated as the Third Congress of the All-Russian Social Democratic Party. Convening in London from April 25 to May 10, 1905, this Congress was attended only by Bolsheviks, including Litvinov, Kamenev, Rykov, Krassin, and Lunacharsky.

Lenin had little difficulty getting his program adopted. The delegates accepted him as their leader, and gave him carte blanche. The immediate task was to organize an armed uprising, the Congress declared. The Mensheviks were virtually excommunicated, a fact which had no practical significance, inasmuch as they did not recognize the authority of the Third Congress. As far as they were concerned, the London gathering was the first Congress of the Bolshevik Party.

In the summer of 1905 a young Bolshevik from Kazan came to Lenin asking for instructions. What were the rank and file of Russia to do?

"What is to be done? One thing—an armed uprising—an immediate armed uprising."

The comrade hinted that Bolsheviks doubted whether an uprising at this time could bring victory. Lenin stood still for a moment.

"Victory?" he rasped. "What do we care about victory?"

The young man gaped in astonishment. Lenin seemed to be declaiming to a large gathering.

"We do not live by illusions. Tell that to the comrades in my name. We are sober realists. Let no one believe that we shall necessarily win. We are still very weak, but this is by no means a question of victory alone. We want the uprising to shake the foundation of the autocracy and set the broad masses into motion. Our task then will be to attract those masses to our cause. That is the main point! *The uprising is what matters.* Talk that 'we can't win' and therefore don't need the uprising is the talk of cowards with whom we must have no relations."

The Bolshevik left with the slogan "armed uprising" ringing in his ears.

All the Bolshevik activities were directed by Lenin, under the slogans of armed rebellion, the formation of a revolutionary army, and the establishment of a Provisional Revolutionary Government. Lenin took energetic measures for the purchase and smuggling of arms into Russia. He established contact with the mutineers on the *SS Potemkin,* pointing to the lessons that could be drawn from that sailors' revolt. "The revolutionary army," he said, "is needed because great historical questions can be solved only by force, and in the modern struggle organized force means military organization."

In a letter to the Military Organization of the St. Petersburg Committtee of the Social Democratic Party he gave instructions on the struggle:

It requires furious *energy* and *more energy.* I am appalled, truly appalled, to see that more than half a year has been spent in talk about bombs—and not a single bomb has yet been made. . . . Go to the youth. Organize at once and everywhere fighting brigades among students, and particularly among workers. Let them arm themselves immediately with whatever weapons they can obtain—a knife, a revolver, a kerosene-soaked rag for setting fires.

Do not demand obligatory entry into the Social Democratic Party. For Christ's sake, throw out all your schemes, consign all functions, rights, and privileges to the devil. . . . Let the squads begin to train for immediate operations. Some can undertake to assassinate a spy or blow up a police station, others can attack a bank to expropriate funds for an insurrection. Let every squad learn, if only by beating up police. The dozens of sacrifices will be repaid with interest by producing hundreds of experienced fighters who will lead hundreds of thousands tomorrow.

The general strike came as a complete surprise to Lenin. It did not fit the slogans of his newspaper nor the resolutions of the Third Congress. But it loomed so large across the face of Russia that he was forced to recognize its importance and he was compelled to reckon with the newly established Soviet Workers' Deputies. At first the novel revolutionary institution alarmed him more than it did the Czar. When the Mensheviks and the Socialist Revolutionaries organized the Soviet, Lenin regarded this undisciplined organism as a dangerous rival to the Party, a spontaneous proletarian assembly which a small group of "professional revolutionists" would not be able to control.

When Lenin returned to Russia in November, the Soviet was an established force in the revolution. *Novoye Vremya,* a reactionary newspaper, wrote that there are "two governments in Russia, Premier Witte's and Khrustalev's, and that it is a question which will succeed in arresting the other."

This was a somewhat exaggerated picture of the Soviet's importance in 1905, but it showed clearly that its enemies sensed its potential power. Somewhat later the question posed by *Novoye Vremya* was settled by the arrest of Khrustalev, and the leadership of the Soviet went to a committee of three headed by Leon Trotsky.

Quick to realize that his initial opposition to the Soviet had been a mistake, Lenin now became an advocate of expanding its role to that of the nucleus for a Provisional Government.

The temporary era of civil liberty brought into the open the first Bolshevik daily newspaper in St. Petersburg, *Novaya Zhizn,* and Lenin for the first time had a legal forum. But he was not content with this weapon; his mind was set on an armed uprising and he divided his time between the newspaper's offices and underground conferences to map insurrectionary plans.

For a time he found it safer to live apart from his wife on a false passport under the name of William Frey. One evening while "Frey" was dining with one of his chief lieutenants in a Tartar restaurant in St. Petersburg, he saw an attractive young woman sitting alone at an adjoining table. His companion, quick to note that Lenin was interested, approached the woman, whom he knew, and said:

"If you aren't waiting for anyone, why not join us? You'll meet a very interesting man"—indicating Lenin's table. "He is very well known, but don't ask for particulars."

Elizabeth K, who was a rather wealthy young woman, was

sufficiently curious to welcome an introduction to "William Frey."

"Are you British?" she asked.

"Not quite," he replied sardonically.

They spent more than an hour in pleasant banter before parting. A few days later she dropped into the *Novaya Zhizn* office to visit one of the contributors. Mysterious Mr. Frey was there greeting her with his habitual mocking smile.

"How do you do? I am very happy to see you again. Don't you patronize the Tartar restaurant any longer?"

Elizabeth quite properly understood this to be an invitation. When she told it to the Bolshevik who had introduced them, he laughed.

"My good friend 'Frey' is, of course, interested in the feminine question, but primarily from a collective, social, and political viewpoint. I should never have supposed that he was capable of dealing with the question on a personal plane. Allow me to add this: After our dinner that evening he asked me whether I could vouch for you. He is inclined to be suspicious and to avoid new acquaintances, so as not to run into informers. I was forced to tell him who you were, and that your apartment was excellently suited for secret gatherings."

Two days later the three dined once more in the Tartar restaurant. Madame K consented to Frey using her apartment twice a week for meetings with comrades which could not safely be held elsewhere. On the appointed day she would send her maid away and personally admit visitors who answered to the password. She was never present in the room where the sessions took place, scrupulously retiring beyond the reach of the voices.

Several evenings Lenin came alone. He would help Elizabeth prepare the samovar and carry it into the dining room. A warm friendship developed between them. Sometimes she played the piano for him. But she was puzzled by his interest in a particular passage in Beethoven's "Appassionata Sonata," which he asked her to repeat time and again. Invariably as she reached that passage Lenin became animated. One evening he asked her to indicate the spot in the score where the passage occurred. It developed that the reason for his interest was that it reminded him of the revolutionary hymn of the Jewish Socialist Bund. Madame K, who was far more at home in the musical and literary world of St. Petersburg than among Marxists, laughed scornfully.

The high tide of revolution had now passed and reactionaries had begun a strong counter-offensive. Behind Premier Witte's back, Minister of Interior Durnovo obtained the Czar's approval for his plans to restore the autocratic powers of the throne.

"It's their heads or ours," said Nicholas. ". . . I authorize you to take all measures that you consider necessary."

Uprisings of soldiers and sailors, badly planned and ill-directed, were taking place in various parts of the country. A strike of postal and telegraph workers again tied up communications. The industrialists saw the specter of social revolution and demanded that the government take drastic action.

The Soviet issued a manifesto calling for a boycott of tax payments, the overthrow of the regime, and the convocation of a Constituent Assembly. On December 16, 1905, the day after this appeal was published, the entire Executive Committee of the Soviet was arrested and all newspapers which had carried the text were suppressed.

The Bolsheviks meanwhile continued their own preparations, purchasing contraband arms and organizing units of twenty-five armed men as fighting brigades. Lenin fixed his main hopes on Moscow. In St. Petersburg no other political faction favored insurrection. But Moscow seemed ripe for revolt.

When a new general strike was called for the twentieth of December, St. Petersburg did not respond, but in Moscow the strike changed swiftly into an insurrection. Party fighting brigades, supported by a section of the populace, threw up barricades. The walls of Moscow were plastered with leaflets containing tactical instructions on the conduct of the insurrection: fight in groups of three and four—attack suddenly and disappear just as fast.

St. Petersburg seemed in no hurry to send reinforcements to government forces commanded by Dubassov, the Governor-General. The troops stationed there were insufficient. After permitting the insurrectionary stew to boil for a week, the government finally sent the crack Semionovsky Guards and artillery from St. Petersburg. On the twenty-ninth Dubassov began mopping up the barricades. The last stronghold fell on the morning of the thirty-first.

Lenin was in Finland from the twenty-fourth until the suppression of the insurrection. The collapse brought strong intra-Bolshevik opposition to Lenin into the open for the first time. He was accused of "Nechaievism," of "adventurist tactics," of a deliberate policy of bloodletting. For his part, however, he regarded the abortive revolt as an important lesson to the masses and to the Party leadership. It was a dress rehearsal for 1917.

As the Czar regained self-confidence, his Ministers violated the guarantees of civil liberty. Radical newspapers were suppressed and Socialist leaders arrested.

In this period, when absolutism was reasserting itself but the spell of the October general strike and the Manifesto was still not entirely destroyed, the decisive question was the role which the Duma would play. For although the regime had clamped down on the extremists it had not yet regained sufficient strength to rescind the Manifesto. The Liberals continued to hope that the Duma would be strong enough to enact the laws making Russia a constitutional monarchy.

The revolutionary Socialist parties rejected the notion that Nicholas would bow to legislation restricting his power, but they differed on tactics for the Duma elections. The Mensheviks favored an active election campaign as an effective way of presenting their program to the people. And their deputies on the floor of the Duma, free to attack the regime by virtue of their parliamentary immunity, would use it as a tribune and the strategic center of battle.

Lenin, on the other hand, branded the Duma as a complete fraud and demanded boycott of the elections. Lenin's point of view won in the councils of all Socialist parties. He carried on a relentless campaign, speaking at scores of anti-Duma meetings. Declaring that the defeat of the Moscow insurrection had not terminated the revolutionary struggle, he attacked the Liberals for "haggling with Czarism over the dead bodies of the workers." He accused the Mensheviks of failing to grasp the lesson of the abortive revolt. But he also said that it was impossible to introduce Socialism in Russia.

A bourgeois revolution was needed to smash the remnants of feudalism and bring radical agrarian reforms, said Lenin. Within the framework of a democratic republic the working class would organize and grow strong. Proletarian revolution would come first in Great Britain and France. He was very firm on this point, stressing the Marxist axiom that such revolutions must begin in advanced capitalist nations.

With the Socialists carrying out their boycott decision, the first Duma returns indicated a victory for the Cadets. Also elected were more than a hundred radical peasants, who formed a separate group under the name of *Trudoviks* (Toilers), and a dozen independent workers who later formed a Social Democratic group.

Just before the Duma opened, the Bolsheviks and Mensheviks held a secret conclave in Stockholm. On the insistence of his followers, Lenin had agreed to seek a reconciliation. Pre-Congress maneuvers centered on the efforts of each side to arrive in Stockholm with a majority. Lenin frankly explained to Lunacharsky:

"If we have a majority in the Central Committee, we will demand the strictest discipline. We will insist that the Mensheviks submit to party unity. So much the worse for them if their petty bourgeois nature will not allow them to go along with us. Let them assume responsibility for splitting party unity."

"But what if we remain in the minority?" asked Lunacharsky. "Shall we be forced to submit to them?"

Lenin replied with a smile: "We won't permit the idea of unity to tie a noose around our necks, and we shall under no circumstances permit the Mensheviks to lead us by the rope."

Lenin's hopes of capturing a majority in the Central Committee were ill-founded. Outwardly, Lenin was bound by the Stockholm decisions and, on paper, party unity was achieved. In practice, however, Lenin was guided by what he had told Lunacharsky. By retaining his own Bolshevik Center he made certain that formal unity would not interfere with his plans.

During his stay in Stockholm, Lenin once more saw Elizabeth K. She had followed him there according to previous arrangements with a Swedish Social Democrat. When she reached the city she communicated with the Swedish intermediary who put through a telephone call to Lenin. He agreed to meet her the following day in the automat, with the warning that if other Russians were present she was to take no notice of him until they had left. At the appointed time she went to the automat. While waiting for Lenin, she noticed two Georgians struggling with one of the vending machines. When Lenin appeared they rushed to his side and one of them said loudly:

"Comrade Ilich, please show us how to use this infernal bourgeois mechanism. We want ham sandwiches and instead we get nothing but pastry."

Lenin had less difficulty with the "infernal bourgeois mechanism" and the two Georgians got their ham sandwiches. During this interlude Lenin and Elizabeth showed no signs of recognizing each other. After the two Georgians had gone, he told her: "Those were delegates of our Caucasian organization. Splendid boys but complete savages."

The Congress gave Lenin little leisure, but on at least one Sunday he was able to spend several hours with Elizabeth in the country near Stockholm. Along the shores of a lake they found a boat for hire. Lenin took the oars and was soon stroking with a powerful rhythm.

"You were not cut out for the role of a professional revolutionist," mocked Elizabeth. "You should have been a farmer, a fisherman, a sailor, or a tinsmith." Lenin laughed heartily. As the boat turned a bend and unfolded a scene of northern beauty, Elizabeth remarked that the setting reminded her of Knut Hamsun's novels.

"Yes indeed," replied Lenin. "Hamsun is an extraordinary writer. In *Hunger* he gives a remarkable picture of the physical and psychological symptoms of a person suffering from starvation—an unfortunate victim of the capitalist order."

Elizabeth shrugged her shoulders and laughed. She had been thinking of Hamsun's more romantic works, *Pan* and *Victoria*. Again, as when she had played the "Appassionata Sonata" for him, she realized that their worlds were far apart. As the Congress dragged on, Lenin found little opportunity to be with her; she grew restless and finally left Stockholm without notifying him of her departure.

Back in St. Petersburg several weeks later she received a note from Lenin to which she did not reply. She had decided to break off her relations with him forever, she thought at that time.

But two years later, when she was in Paris, she could not resist attending a meeting where Lenin spoke. During the intermission she went backstage to see him. He was surrounded by the usual crowd of admirers. When he saw her his eyes opened wide in amazement but he quickly checked himself and asked calmly, "What brought you here?"

"I came to hear your lecture," she replied; "besides which I have a commission to you from a certain person." Thereupon she handed him an envelope containing her address and telephone number with the hour at which she could be reached.

The next morning, instead of the expected phone call, Lenin himself appeared, looking somewhat sheepish.

"I thought you were no longer alive," he said, and as they shook hands he reached out to embrace her. But she stopped him with, "I'm sorry, my friend, all that is past."

"You are quite right." He laughed. "All that is past. But still you are an interesting woman. It's a pity you are not a Social Democrat."

Elizabeth's reply was quick. "You are an interesting man. It's a pity you are are *only* a Social Democrat." Lenin roared with laughter.

The atmosphere was cleared, and all tension vanished. They chatted pleasantly for several hours. She reminded Lenin of their excursion outside of Stockholm. "It was then I realized for the first time," Lenin remarked, "that you are not at all a Social Democrat. You had read all Hamsun's works except *Hunger.*"

"I, too, realized how far apart we were on that trip," Elizabeth replied. "It seemed to me that you had read only *Hunger.*"

They parted with the understanding that they would meet again in Switzerland.

On May 10, 1906, while Lenin was still in Stockholm, the Duma called for full political freedom; amnesty for political prisoners and religious dissidents; abolition of capital punishment; equality for the various national minorities; autonomy for Poland and Finland; a broader suffrage law; democratization of the organs of local self-government; expropriation of state lands and the estates of the nobility for the benefit of the peasantry; humane labor laws and comprehensive social legislation.

For a time the Czar wavered. At one stage he went so far as to enter into negotiations with Miliukov with a view toward establishing a constitutional government. While Miliukov himself was not convinced that these overtures were sincere, a determining factor in the Czar's shifty calculations was the degree of united popular support behind the Duma. If the Duma was not supported by the entire nation, and especially if the city workers were divided, there was little reason to bow to the Duma's will.

In this critical hour Plekhanov and the Mensheviks appealed to the laboring masses to put aside their differences and throw the weight of their support behind the Duma. Lenin and the Bolshevik newspaper, on the other hand, continued their unremitting war again the Duma, maintaining that the most urgent task of the Social Democrats was to "unmask the liberal counter-revolutionary Cadets," and calling the masses to prepare again for armed revolt.

After the Revolution of 1917 documents found among the archives of the secret police disclosed that the Okhrana had instructed its agents to give the Bolsheviks a free hand in their campaign against the Duma. Every important mass meeting had the tacit support and the devious cooperation of Okhrana agents. Bolshevik agitation for an armed uprising no longer frightened the government. The real danger to its power was in the Duma.

From the standpoint of the Czar, Lenin's campaign was a success. It helped undermine public confidence in the Duma to such an extent that seventy-two days after its opening it was possible for Nicholas to order its dissolution without risking another general strike. New elections were ordered six months hence.

After the dissolution of the Duma, the Bolshevik Center continued to work for an armed uprising. Krassin, a revolutionist since 1887 and a member of the Central Committee since the Second Congress, had wide contacts in the upper crust of society. As a friend of Maxim Gorky, he came in contact in 1903 with Savva Morozov, a Moscow millionaire textile manufacturer who dabbled in radicalism. While acting as Lenin's "finance minister" Krassin approached Morozov for a loan, beginning by expounding Lenin's virtues as a radical leader. Morozov cut him short: "I know all about that; I agree; Lenin is a man of vision. How much does he want?"

"As much as possible," replied Krassin.

"My personal yearly income," replied Morozov, "is about 60,000 rubles. A third of it goes for petty things, scholarships and the like. Shall we say 1,000 rubles a month?"

When Morozov committed suicide in 1905, he left a large

legacy to Gorky's wife for the use of the Bolshevik Party. The following year Krassin arranged a profitable American tour for Gorky, which raised considerable additional funds for the Party.

In addition Krassin personally supervised the underground ammunition plants set up by the Bolsheviks, and assisted his close friend "Papasha," later known as Maxim Litvinov, in smuggling arms from the Balkans.

To forestall a reactionary victory in the election campaign for the Second Duma, the Mensheviks wanted to fuse with local liberal candidates in districts where reactionary candidates appeared likely to win. To settle this issue, a conference of the Social Democratic organization of St. Petersburg was called early in January 1907. Led by Lenin, the Bolsheviks insisted that the main business on hand was to define the position of the Mensheviks on the issue of fusion. Feeling insecure, the Mensheviks tried to eliminate this from the agenda. When a clash arose between the forty-two Bolshevik delegates and the thirty-one Menshevik representatives over the question of mandates, the Mensheviks withdrew.

The remaining delegates heard Lenin advocate a policy of complete independence in the elections. To the young Bolsheviks his appeal was in complete accord with their slogans of "armed uprising" and "dictatorship of the proletariat and peasantry." A small group headed by Vladimir Woytinsky, however, argued that the Bolsheviks should fuse on a limited scale with the parties to the left of the Cadets.

On the appearance of this unexpected opposition Lenin abruptly reversed himself. After fifteen minutes of speculation he suddenly advocated fusion slates.

Although it was Lenin who had reversed himself completely, he charged the Mensheviks with treason in his pamphlet, *On the Hypocrisy of the 31 Mensheviks*. The Mensheviks insisted that Lenin appear before a party tribunal on charges of slander. At the hearing Lenin admitted that he had slandered the Menshevik leaders but claimed that he was right in resorting to calumny, in order to discredit the Menshevik policies before the masses: "I purposely chose that tone calculated to evoke in the hearer hatred, disgust, and contempt for the people who carry on such tactics. That tone, that formulation is not designed to convince, but to break the ranks, not to correct a mistake of the opponent but to annihilate him, to wipe him off the face of the earth. . . . It is not permissible to write about party comrades in a language that systematically sows hatred, repugnance, and contempt among the workers to those that think differently from us. It is *permissible* and it is *imperative* to write in such a language about an organization that split off."

Despite these internecine battles, the elections brought another defeat for the regime: Again the majority of the deputies were Liberals and Socialists. But in some districts members of the Black Hundreds, the Russian Ku Klux Klan organization supported by the Okhrana, were elected. They had not held a single seat in the First Duma.

Again the government was faced with either acceding to the popular demand for broad reforms or dissolving the Duma once more. Premier Stolypin began to look for an excuse to dissolve the Duma and the Bolsheviks furnished him with one. Lenin insisted that the deputies use their parliamentary immunity to agitate for an armed uprising. Unless they used their parliamentary status to organize a revolt, they were useless, he said. The Bolshevik Center began organizing delegations of soldiers and sailors who demanded that the Duma start "real work." These delegations, organized by Duma deputies together with their secret revolutionary military groups, attempted to show that the people were demanding "deeds" instead of speeches.

Years later it was discovered that these secret Bolshevik cells were infested with agents of the secret police. By keeping a sharp eye on the Social Democratic deputies, these stool pigeons were able to frame the deputies on the charges of inciting rebellion, thus giving Stolypin his excuse.

A woman agent named Shornikova, planted by the Okhrana in the Social Democratic military organization, confessed:

"I met every member of the Central Committee then in St. Petersburg, and all the members of the military organization; I knew all the secret meeting places and passwords of the revolutionary army cells throughout Russia. I kept the archives of the revolutionary organization in the Army; I was present at all the district meetings, propaganda rallies, and party conferences; I was always in the know. All the information I gathered was conscientiously reported to the Okhrana."

At the next Party Congress, called in London in April 1907, Lenin won control of the Central Committee. The sessions were attended by representatives of the Mensheviks, Bolsheviks, Jewish Socialist Bund, Polish, Latvian, and Lithuanian Social Democratic parties. All the leading lights were present, including Lenin, Plekhanov, Axelrod, Martov, Potresov, Trotsky, Bogdanov, Krassin, Rosa Luxemburg, Tseretelli, and Maxim Gorky. In addition, the Congress included many who were to be famous in the years to come: Zinoviev and Kamenev, who played leading roles in the early years of the Soviet regime; Tomsky, the future leader of Soviet trade unions; Yaroslavsky, chief of the militant atheists; Voroshilov, head of the Soviet army; David Zaslavsky, Moscow's top propagandist; Fuerstenberg-Ganetsky, who figured so significantly in the events of 1917, and Stalin.

Shortly after the Social Democratic Duma deputies returned to Russia from London, the Bolshevik military organization decided to make demands on them through a delegation of soldiers. Shornikova, the Okhrana agent, took part in the drafting of the resolution. While the police could have arrested the members of the military organization at will, their object was to establish collusion with the Social Democratic deputies. All the threads of this frame-up led directly to Premier Stolypin, who saw the text of the resolution before it reached the Social Democratic deputies. Shornikova had made two copies, leaving one with the military organization and sending the other to the secret police.

No sooner did the delegation present the resolution than gendarmes appeared. Their search for the document, however, was fruitless. A deputy placed it in his portfolio and since the police had no right to search him, the whole frame-up was in danger of collapse. The police, however, used the copy of the resolution forwarded by Shornikova, and submitted it as evidence at the trial of the Social Democratic deputies. The deputies were charged with high treason, and on June 16, 1907, the Duma was dissolved. Tseretelli and the majority of the Social Democratic deputies were sentenced to hard labor in Siberia. The Party belonged to the Bolsheviks.

According to Lepeshinsky, Lenin, in the summer of 1906, forecast defeat for the revolution and stressed the need of preparing for strategic retreat. Nevertheless he urged sustaining the "revolutionary mood" of the workers because he thought such a mood never did any harm. If there was any chance to score a half victory, according to Lenin, it was only by arousing the revolutionary instinct of the masses. If, on the other hand, retreat was inevitable, then at least it could be executed in military fashion, to frighten the forces of reaction.

Madame Krzhizhanovskaya, however, claims that Lenin still expected a successful armed uprising. Lenin, she asserts, hoped that the peasants would come to the rescue of the workers and that a new revolutionary wave would sweep the country. To lead the revolting peasants, Lenin proposed setting up trained units of five to ten determined men. He expected widespread peasant disturbances to begin in the fall of 1906. But the peasants failed to rise.

After the Shornikova affair, life for Lenin in St. Petersburg became hazardous.

When he fled one night as the police were closing in he was unable to inform Krupskaya. While she kept an all-night vigil for her husband, who was supposed to be attending a meeting, Lenin made good his flight to Finland.

It was in Finland that Lenin began to develop the headaches and insomnia which were to torture him intermittently for the rest of his life. Immediately after breakfast he would write for five and six hours without a break. Late at night he took long walks in an effort to tire himself to sleep. He arose late and morose after one of his sleepless nights.

Remaining in Finland was dangerous. With the police searching for him, he was forced to attempt escape to Stockholm. To board ship at the port of Abo was to invite certain arrest. Lenin therefore decided to cross the ice at night to a gulf island, where he would board a waiting vessel. Accompanied by two Finnish peasants, who acted as guides, he made his way at night along the ice toward the island. Suddenly the ice began to give way under their feet. They barely made the opposite shore. Lenin later recalled that when he heard the ice cracking, one thought flashed through his mind:
"What a silly way to die."

6   THE LOWER DEPTHS

LENIN NOW FACED PERHAPS THE MOST DIFFICULT PERIOD OF his career. The revolution had, for the time, spent itself, and prospects ahead were not bright. His capture of the party machinery had given him control of the Central Committee, but his majority was precarious. Moreover, the London Congress had voted to dissolve all party fighting units and strong-arm squads (*boyeviki*) and prohibited the raising of party funds by armed robberies, known as "expropriations."

Lenin had no intention of disbanding the fighting units and "expropriation" squads. More than ever he needed large sums of money to carry on under unfavorable conditions and until there was a new upward surge of revolutionary feeling among the masses. To keep the Bolshevik movement alive and vigorous required desperate measures. He could not allow squeamish men such as Plekhanov and Martov to tie his hands. The Bolshevik Center had to be maintained at all costs —and money had to be raised by any possible means.

By mid-1907 Lenin abandoned hope for an imminent armed uprising and called on his comrades in Russia to participate in the elections for the Third Duma. But the raids of his strong-arm men continued.

From the London Congress until 1910 the Bolshevik Center subsidized the Bolshevik-controlled St. Petersburg Committee of the Party to the extent of one thousand rubles a month and gave the Moscow Committee five hundred rubles a month —this at a time when the visible income of the United Central Committee did not exceed one hundred rubles a month.

Lenin secured these large sums from a number of sources. Maxim Gorky supported Lenin with donations. Garin-Mikhailovsky, another writer and wealthy engineer, gave Lenin tens of thousands of rubles. This was in addition to the 12,000-rubles-a-year subsidy given to the Bolsheviks by Morozov.

But the armed holdups of the Bolshevik *boyeviki* provided much more. The largest of these was staged in Tiflis in June 1907.

At ten-thirty on the morning of June 26 the Tiflis post office received a large consignment of cash. Soviet historians maintain the sum was 250,000 rubles; the Russian press placed the figure at 341,000 rubles. Officials loaded the sacks into a stagecoach and proceeded toward the bank, followed by a coach filled with soldiers. Both vehicles were escorted by armed Cossacks. As the convoy approached the heart of the city, a bomb was hurled into the street from the roof of a nearby house. It exploded with such force that windowpanes within the radius of a mile were shattered. Simultaneously bombs were hurled from the street at the Cossacks, while seemingly innocent pedestrians opened fire with revolvers. The sacks of money vanished.

Months later a number of prominent Bolsheviks were arrested in Berlin, Munich, and Paris, when they attempted to exchange five-hundred-ruble notes bearing the serial numbers of the money consigned to Tiflis. In January 1908 a woman was arrested in Munich when she tried to change one of these bills. At about the same time Maxim Litvinov was arrested in Paris with twelve bills in his possession.

All those discovered with the incriminating bank notes in their possession were arrested, but the French and German governments refused to turn them over to the Russian authorities.

Further investigation revealed that Leonid Krassin had supplied the boyeviki with necessary bombs.

The nucleus of the Caucasus strong-arm squad consisted of Kamo, Lomidze, and Tzintsadze. Kamo's superior, as Lenin's deputy in the Caucasus, was "Comrade Koba," also known as Josef Djugashvili, and later as Stalin. Kamo was the field commander of these operations; Stalin represented Lenin's supreme headquarters.

Since the London Congress of the Social Democratic Party had outlawed these strong-arm tactics, the members of the Caucasian boyeviki group, as well as Stalin, were expelled from the Party.

The adulation of the Caucasian partisans for Lenin was fostered by Stalin and other Bolshevik delegates from the Caucasus, who returned from the Stockholm and London congresses with word that Lenin personified the revolution; his word was law.

Shortly before the Tiflis robbery the Prussian police discovered a Berlin storehouse filled with watermarked paper to be used for counterfeiting three-ruble notes. Several Bolsheviks were arrested.

The German Social Democrats were furious because the paper to be used for counterfeiting had been shipped without their knowledge to the address of the Berlin *Vorwaerts*.

When Axelrod heard the news, he wrote to Martov: "If the affair is true, how can one remain in the same party with the Bolsheviks?"

And Plekhanov declared, "The whole affair is so outrageous that it is really high time for us to break off all relations with the Bolsheviks."

Lenin was not greatly disturbed by the indignant protests of Axelrod and Plekhanov.

"When I see Social Democrats," he declared, "announcing with pride and self-satisfaction that 'we are no anarchists, no thieves, no brigands, we are above that, we reject the partisan struggle,' then I ask myself—do these people understand what they are saying?"

Nevertheless many Bolsheviks demanded an investigation of the counterfeit plot. The Foreign Bureau of the Party appointed George Chicherin, later Soviet Foreign Commissar, to conduct the probe. Lenin was certain that all clues had been destroyed. Chicherin, however, showed photographs of leading Bolsheviks to the German manufacturer from whom the watermarked paper had been ordered. The latter identified Krassin as the man who had placed the order. Lenin, alarmed, induced the Central Committee to delegate the investigation to its foreign bureau. Here the Bolshevik majority buried the evidence.

Acting on Lenin's suggestion, the Bolshevik majority also restored to good standing in the Party the Caucasian strongarm men and Stalin. Moreover, they demanded that Martov be tried for appearing as a witness against the accused Bolsheviks at the party investigation.

A memorial volume published in Moscow after Krassin's death proudly described how the plans for the "expropriations" were formulated by Krassin and carried out by Kamo. When Krassin himself was arrested in Finland in 1907, Lenin was certain that the police of St. Petersburg had enough evidence to hang him. But while the Bolsheviks were working on a scheme to spring Krassin, the latter was suddenly released without explanation. He left for Berlin, where he obtained a position with the electrical firm of Siemens-Schuckert and also managed to cash in a batch of five hundred-ruble bills from the Tiflis haul by the chemical alteration of the serial numbers.

No sooner had the Krassin scandal died down than the Party was again thrown into an uproar by the Comrade Victor affair. Victor, whose real name was Taratuta, was admitted to the Bolshevik Center, although for three years he had been under suspicion as an Okhrana informer. But no investigation was made, and Victor's undertakings remained a secret from all but a handful of Bolshevik leaders. When these charges were leveled against Victor in the *Proletari* by Bogdanov, an investigation was finally ordered, but the findings were never made public. Although Victor had not been publicly exonerated, the Bolsheviks at the London Congress named him a member of the Central Committee of the Social Democratic Party, head of the important Foreign Bureau, as well as Financial Director of the Bolshevik Center. In this last capacity, Victor soon displayed remarkable talents.

A Moscow manufacturer named Schmidt had bequeathed a large sum of money to the Social Democratic Party. Lenin demanded that the money go to the Bolshevik Center. The executor, however, insisted that the Central Committee was the only recognized party center. A conference was called between the members of the Bolshevik Center—all of whom were also members of the Central Committee—and the executor and family heirs. Here the executor complained that Victor had tried to extort the money from him for the Bolshevik Center. The Bolshevik leaders promised to defer decision until the estate was fully settled and to investigate Victor's action.

The Menshevik and Bund members of the Central Committee knew nothing of the whole affair until much later, when the question was raised by chance at a Central Committee meeting. The Bolsheviks replied that since the estate was not yet settled, the matter should remain quiet "for reasons of conspiracy."

A year later it was discovered that Victor had already handed over a large part of the legacy to the Bolshevik Center.

But the Schmidt affair really went back further. Schmidt, his brother, and two sisters had inherited a furniture factory in Moscow. In January 1905, when his workers went on strike, Schmidt granted their demands and suggested that they persuade workers in other factories to follow their example. He also invested a large sum for a school in his factory and planned to make his men share-holders in the plant.

During the Moscow insurrection of December 1905 Bolshevik rebels barricaded themselves in the factory, whereupon the building was destroyed by artillery fire. Schmidt was arrested and jailed. After a year in prison he hanged himself. Before his death he willed most of his estate to the Social Democratic Party. His sisters, although they had Bolshevik sympathies, tried to delay the transfer of the money. When

Lenin, then in Switzerland, discovered what was going on, he
sent a Bolshevik named Andrekanis to Moscow with instructions to convince one of the sisters to relinquish her share to
the Bolshevik Center. Andrekanis persuaded one of them,
Catherine, to marry him. After the marriage, however, he
did not deliver the money until his Bolshevik comrades threatened to kill him. The Bolshevik Center finally collected 100,-
000 rubles on this transaction.

Lenin then sent Victor to get his hands on the other sister's
share. Victor followed Andrekanis's example. He married the
other girl, Elizabeth, but the money did not reach the Bolshevik coffers. Bogdanov, Lunacharsky, and other Bolshevik
leaders again charged that Victor was a Czarist spy. But Lenin
stood by Victor, refusing at first to have him tried. A party
court was finally convened and Vladimir Burtzev, the great
nemesis of *agents provocateurs,* was called in as an investiga-
tor. The court found no proof of Comrade Victor's guilt, but
ruled he was unfit to engage in party activities. He was dropped
from the party organizations.

That should have been the end of Victor's political career.
But it wasn't. After the Bolshevik Revolution, Victor was back
in Lenin's favor. Under his real name, Taratuta, he became
Mocow's representative of the Communist International in
France. Later he was given a high post in the Soviet Supreme
Economic Council. When he died in the twenties, the Soviet
press said very little about him.

Stanislav Volsky, a prominent old Bolshevik who later
edited Maxim Gorky's Petrograd newspaper, was one of those
surprised when Lenin nominated Victor, despite his reputation, for the Central Committee at the London Party Congress
of 1907. Lenin shrugged off these reproaches by saying:
"Quite simple! A Central Committee to be effective must be
made up of gifted writers, able organizers, and a few intelligent scoundrels. I recommended Comrade X [Victor] as an
intelligent scoundrel."

When Professor Rozhkov, an early Bolshevik leader, remarked that everybody knew Victor to be a scoundrel, Lenin
laughed.

"That is exactly why he is useful to us. Precisely because he
will stop at nothing. Now tell me frankly, would you consent
to be a gigolo? To live with a Moscow heiress for her money?
You would not! Neither could I bring myself to do it. But Victor did, and therefore he is a very useful man who cannot be
replaced."

His opinion of many close associates who were to play a
much larger role in Soviet history was no better.

Lenin's total disregard of "bourgeois prejudices" as evi-
denced by his support of Comrade Victor, the counterfeiting
scheme, and the continued underworld exploits of the Cauca-

sian boyeviki now boomeranged. A wave of desertions from the Bolshevik Center included some of its leadings writers and theoreticians, among them Maxim Gorky, Bogdanov, Lunacharsky, Professor Rozhkov, Alexinsky, Professor Po krovsky, and Stanislav Volsky. These men indicted Lenin for disregarding the majority will of his own faction, for illegal seizure of party funds and the party press, and for seeking to suppress all independent opinion. Krassin also deserted Lenin for reasons of his own. In later years some of these men were to return to the Bolshevik camp, but in 1908 Lenin stood almost alone. The two leading Bolsheviks who remained firmly at Lenin's side throughout this crisis were Gregory Zinoviev and Leo Kamenev—both of whom were to be executed by Stalin in 1936.

In Russia itself former professional revolutionists and students alike were losing their faith and enthusiasm. Under the firm hand of Premier Stolypin, the ablest reactionary statesman to win the Czar's confidence, the revolutionary tide was halted. With a revised election law imposing new class restrictions on suffrage, the Third Duma was far more conservative than its predecessors. And under Stolypin's iron-handed guidance, revolutionary and terrorist action was suppressed with ruthless efficiency. Intellectuals and workers alike deserted the revolutionary ranks.

Back in Geneva, Lenin occupied himself with editing various Bolshevik publications, especially the newspaper *Proletari*, but he was discontented with his existence.

"It's several days since we've landed in this damned hole," he wrote to his sister Maria on January 14, 1908, "but we can't help ourselves. We will have to get used to it. How are all doing? Are you freezing? Is Mother well? Please kiss her for me."

Walking one day along the deserted streets of Geneva in this period of doubt and pessimism, he remarked to his wife: "I feel as if I have come here to be buried."

In Switzerland, Lenin again met Elizabeth K. She lived not far from Geneva, and Lenin often visited her by bicycle. Sometimes he brought along a tiny chessboard to teach her the game, but she made little progress. With some impatience Lenin remarked, "I have yet to meet a single woman who can do these three things: understand Marx, play chess, or read a railroad timetable."

In the autumn of 1909 Lenin moved to Paris, where he was to spend probably the most difficult years of his exile. The Lenins rented a four-room flat on the outskirts of the city. The rooms were large and light, with mirrors over the mantels. One room was for Krupskaya's mother, another for Lenin's sister Maria who was studying in Paris, a third for the Lenins, the fourth a sitting room. The Bibliothèque Nationale was a considerable distance off and Lenin was forced to travel there by bicycle.

There was much red tape getting a book too. And the library closed during the luncheon period. Lenin was forever cursing the Bibliothèque Nationale and Paris.

In 1910 the Lenins moved to the quiet Rue Marie Rose, not far from the Boulevard Montparnasse, where they had two rooms whose windows faced a garden. Here Lenin instituted a strict regime. At eight o'clock in the morning he rose and went to the Bibliothèque, returning about two. Then he worked at home, Krupskaya making certain his comrades disturbed him as little as possible.

Lenin remained stubborn in his resolve not to seek reconciliation with his opponents. At the Congress of the Socialist International in Copenhagen in the summer of 1910, where the differences dividing the various factions were sharply revealed, general animosity was concentrated chiefly against Lenin. "He is one man against the whole Party. He is ruining the Party. How fortunate the Party would be if he disappeared, vanished, evaporated, died!" were the remarks Madame Krzhizhanovskaya heard on every side during meetings of the Russian section. When she asked one of Lenin's opponents how one man could ruin the entire Party, he replied: *"Because there is no other man who thinks and dreams of nothing but revolution—twenty-four hours a day."*

The revolutionary movement continued to lose ground in Russia. Police spies and agents provocateurs riddled its weakened ranks.

But although 1910 was ebbtide for revolutionary Socialism, Russia had moved forward considerably since 1905. Within the limits imposed by Stolypin there was more freedom of the press; from time to time Socialist periodicals appeared. When the censor banned a newspaper, it often reappeared under a different name the following day. Workers now exercised the right to organize trade unions and mutual-aid associations. As long as these organizations stayed out of politics the regime did not interfere.

The Mensheviks, realizing the potentialities of trade unionism, now devoted their main energies to this field. But Lenin regarded this new trend as a danger to the Social Democratic Party. He noted with alarm that workers were shying away from the underground and were less inclined to accept the leadership of the professional revolutionists. The Party was in danger of becoming an emasculated auxiliary of the legal trade-union movement. Lenin accused the Menshevik leaders in Russia of treason to the revolutionary cause, charging them with seeking to "liquidate" the Social Democratic Party.

As the trade-union movement grew in influence, however, Lenin launched a campaign to gain control of the strategic unions, while demanding that they be subordinated to the Party. One of the strongest labor organizations was the St. Petersburg Metalworkers' Union.

In 1906 a worker named Roman Malinovsky was elected its general secretary. His intelligence and zeal, as well as his oratorical ability, had won for him the following of his fellow metalworkers. In 1909 Malinovsky was arrested and expelled from St. Petersburg. He went to Moscow, where he joined the local Menshevik organization, but in April 1910 Malinovsky and a group of his comrades were arrested. He was soon released, although the Mensheviks seized with him remained in jail. His release aroused suspicion because all had been arrested for their revolutionary speeches at the same mass meeting and Malinovsky's oration had been the most inflammatory of all. A short time later Malinovsky joined the Bolshevik faction.

Soon thereafter came a wave of arrests among the Bolsheviks in Moscow. Among those rounded up was Nikolai Bukharin (destined to become one of the top Soviet hierarchs and to be executed by Stalin in 1938). Bukharin, then a member of the Moscow Committee of the Bolshevik Party, had distrusted Malinovsky from the start, despite the latter's assiduous attempts to win his confidence. For Bukharin had noticed several times that when he arranged a secret rendezvous with a party comrade, Okhrana agents would be waiting to pounce on him. In each case Malinovsky had known of the appointments, and the men whom Bukharin was to meet had been arrested.

When Bukharin himself was finally seized he was convinced that Malinovsky had betrayed him in order to eliminate him from the Moscow Committee. In jail Bukharin met several Mensheviks who also suspected Malinovsky of being responsible for their arrest. But there were no conclusive facts. With Bukharin and other Bolshevik leaders out of the way, Malinovsky began a meteoric rise in the party organization.

Despite the lull in revolutionary action, the labor movement was making impressive gains. Czarism was still firmly in control, but the workers staged effective strikes in St. Petersburg, Moscow, and a number of provincial cities. The tribune for the reviving labor movement was the Social Democratic delegation in the Third Duma. Soviet historians admit that these deputies contributed greatly toward stirring the Russian workers to resume the fight for political and economic rights.

The split in the Social Democratic Party, however, continued to grow. When the United Central Committee of the Party met in Paris in 1910, the Bolsheviks claimed control by virtue of their 1907 majority at the London Congress. But the Menshevik and Jewish Socialist Bund members refused to submit to Lenin's leadership.

The Bolshevik Center, then headed by Lenin, Zinoviev, and Kamenev, used the large funds at its disposal for overt as well as underground activity in Russia. Through his agents in Russia, Lenin founded a large weekly in St. Petersburg called *Zvezda* (Star). The paper acquired added prestige when Plekhanov consented to contribute articles. The condition he laid down was that *Zvezda* represent all Social Democratic groups opposed to liquidating the underground Party organizations. The first issue appeared late in 1910, with the official support of the Social Democratic delegation in the Duma. The editorial board included one Duma deputy, one Bolshevik, and one Plekhanovite Menshevik. The newspaper suspended publication in June 1911. When it reappeared in the fall Plekhanov and the other non-Bolsheviks were out. *Zvezda* became Lenin's personal organ and its main contributors were Zinoviev, Kamenev, and Krupskaya.

Lenin was now forty years old, at the very prime of his powers, but the structure he had spent years to perfect was still quite feeble. The strain was telling. He looked worn, was harassed more than ever by headaches and insomnia, but continued to work with furious energy.

By the end of 1911 Lenin was occupied with new plans for gaining control of the party machine, hoping to win a new Congress majority which would sanction his supremacy. In his own ranks there were still some who advocated reunion with the Mensheviks, and representatives of the two groups negotiated once more in Paris, but Lenin would have no part in these talks. To forestall the opposition, he sent his agents into Russia to mobilize a "general party convention" of his sympathizers.

The conference of Bolsheviks was scheduled to open in Prague in January 1912. After Lenin had left for that city two Bolshevik delegates arrived in Paris on their way to Prague. One of them was Brendinsky, whose chief work was distributing illegal literature in Moscow. He had been arrested in Vilna just before his departure for western Europe but was released after ten days in prison.

Krupskaya had received word that the Bolshevik publications were not being distributed in Moscow. When she asked Brendinsky to whom he delivered his literature in Moscow he became confused, declaring that it went to workers. She asked for their names and addresses. His stumbling reply showed he was lying. Under further questioning, Brendinsky broke down. It was discovered that all the literature he received from abroad had gone directly to the Okhrana.

Many years later the Great Soviet Encyclopedia in its account of the Prague Conference admitted that two of the thirteen voting delegates were Okhrana agents.

Lenin's hand-picked delegates in Prague proclaimed that they represented the entire Social Democratic Party and denounced the "liquidators" and other anti-Leninists. A Central Committee was elected consisting of Lenin, Zinoviev, Ordzhonikidze, Spandarian, Goloschokin, Schwartzman, and—Malinovsky.

Malinovsky was appointed chief of the Russian Bureau of the Bolshevik Central Committee, with the right to add such new members to the Central Committee as he saw fit. On the suggestion of Lenin, Malinovsky appointed Stalin, who had escaped from exile in the Vologda province in February 1912.

The Prague Conference put the final stamp on the division between the two factions. Thereafter the Bolshevik Party maintained a completely separate existence from the Mensheviks, except for their limited collaboration in the Duma. But this, too, was soon to end.

Lenin had told his sister Anna when she visited him in Paris a few months before, "I do not know whether I'll live to see a revival of the Party." But now he felt confident that the turning point had been reached.

Stalin, for the short time that he was free, played a leading role in reorganizing the Bolshevik cells in Russia. Living under the assumed name of Ivanov in a small St. Petersburg hotel, he wrote to Lenin on February 10, 1912: "Things are going rather well. I hope they will be going very well. The frame of mind of our crowd is reassuring."

Less than two months later a political crisis shook the Russian Empire. It started with a strike by miners in the Lena gold fields of northern Siberia. When the miners' delegates were arrested, the men gathered in a throng to demand their release. Without warning, troops opened fire and hundreds were shot down. This was on April 4, 1912. A week later, when the news reached European Russia, it produced violent reverberations. In the course of a few days spontaneous strikes swept nearly all the great industrial cities of Russia; more than 215,000 workers walked out in protest. It was the greatest demonstration of unrest since the general strike of 1905. Arrests quickly followed. Stalin, who was working in the St. Petersburg office of Lenin's weekly newspaper, was seized once more and exiled to Siberia.

At about this time Burtzev charged that Dr. Zhitomirsky, one of the leaders of the Foreign Bureau of the Bolshevik Party and a close friend of Lenin, was an agent provocateur. Greatly disturbed, Lenin ordered Malinovsky to investigate where Burtzev got his evidence. But Burtzev was suspicious of Malinovsky and refused to divulge any information to him.

After the Revolution of 1917, when the State Police records were opened, it was disclosed that Dr. Zhitomirsky had served as an Okhrana agent from 1902 to 1917.

The Prague conference had also decided to turn out a popular daily newspaper in St. Petersburg to be called *Pravda*, and Malinovsky was entrusted with publishing it.

The Mensheviks, despite their large trade-union following, were not only unable to finance a daily newspaper, but even had trouble supporting their weekly. The Bolshevik Center, however, drawing on the large funds obtained by armed expropriations, legacies, and political marriages, was in a position to foot the bill. The first issue of *Pravda* appeared in May 1912, a few weeks after the protest strike that followed the Lena massacres. In this fresh current of revolutionary agitation, *Pravda*, as the only labor daily newspaper in Russia, gained a large circulation. For some time the paper carefully avoided controversy with other Socialist groups, thereby gaining a solid reputation among the workers of St. Petersburg. Only after *Pravda* had gained considerable prestige and influence did Lenin begin to blast his Socialist opponents in its pages.

In July 1912 Lenin, Zinoviev, and Kamenev moved from Paris to Cracow, Galicia. Their purpose was to be close to the frontier in order to facilitate the editing of *Pravda* and the direction of Bolshevik action. The arrangements which permitted Lenin to live in Cracow were made with the Austrian Government by Fuerstenberg-Ganetsky, a man who was to appear many times in the crucial years ahead, when Lenin needed his services most.

Most of the *Pravda* editorials and policy articles were written by Lenin, although in St. Petersburg the publisher was Roman Malinovsky and the official editor was Chernomazov.

At this time Bukharin fled from exile, crossed the Russian frontier, and reached Lenin in Galicia. As soon as he arrived, he warned Lenin against Malinovsky.

Despite Bukharin's suspicions, both Lenin and Zinoviev defended Malinovsky vigorously. Bukharin was not convinced. In the meantime Malinovsky had become the leader of the Bolshevik organization in Russia. He was, in fact, Lenin's deputy inside Russia. He sat in the Fourth Duma as the leader of the Bolshevik faction of five deputies and as the vice-chairman of the combined Social Democratic delegation, headed by Nikolai Chkheidze, an old Menshevik from the Caucasus. In the previous three Dumas the Social Democratic delegation had voted and acted as a unit, and had built up wide popularity among the Russian masses.

In December 1912, at a party council held in Cracow, Bolshevik delegates decided to organize revolutionary street demonstrations, strikes, and secret shop and factory committees. The council was attended by Lenin, Kamenev, Zinoviev, Krupskaya, the Bolshevik Duma deputies, including Malinovsky as well as Stalin, who had made good another escape from exile.

Another delegate was Alexander Troyanovsky, later Soviet Ambassador to the United States.

In February 1913 Troyanovsky's wife, who had just returned from Austria, was arrested in Kiev. She had been asked to become secretary to the Bolshevik group in the Duma. Important secret documents were found in her possession.

Very few people had known of her arrival. Both Bukharin and Troyanovsky suspected Malinovsky's hand in her arrest.

Convinced that his wife's arrest was the work of an agent provocateur, Troyanovsky investigated the details of her trip to Russia. All the evidence pointed strongly to Malinovsky.

After discussing the matter with Bukharin, both wrote to the Central Committee demanding that Malinovsky appear before a party court. In reply, they received a severe rebuke from Lenin, who, speaking for the Central Committee, forbade them to spread these rumors about Malinovsky. Lenin called their action worse than treason, and threatened to have them expelled from the Party if they persisted. Bukharin obeyed, but Troyanovsky soon parted company with Lenin and did not rejoin the Bolsheviks until 1921. But fresh evidence against Malinovsky continued to accumulate.

Late in the summer of 1913 Sverdlov fled from Siberia to St. Petersburg, and hid in the apartment of Badaiev, a deputy to the Duma. A few days later the janitor asked Badaiev whether he was harboring a man answering to Sverdlov's description. Badaiev realized that Sverdlov was no longer safe with him. After consulting Malinovsky, he decided to move Sverdlov elsewhere. He was taken to the home of Petrovsky, another member of the Duma. That very night he was arrested and sent back to Siberia. And still no action was taken to investigate Malinovsky.

A few days after Sverdlov's arrest the Bolsheviks organized a concert and ball to raise income for *Pravda*. Such concerts were held frequently in St. Petersburg, and served as fairly safe meeting places for revolutionaries, including those living under false passports. Among those present were Stalin, who was living illegally in St. Petersburg, and Malinovsky.

Before Stalin had time to warm his feet he found himself surrounded by police agents. The organizers of the concert took him into a dressing room to change his clothes and furnish him with a disguise, but agents of the secret police broke into the dressing room. He was taken away to prison and again exiled to Siberia, where he remained until the revolution.

After these new arrests the conviction grew that there was

an agent provocateur in the Bolshevik higher councils who was delivering party members to the police. But no one could name him.

In August 1913 the Bolshevik leaders were summoned to a new Central Committee Conference in a village near Zakopane in Galicia. There were twenty-two Bolsheviks present, including Lenin, Zinoviev, Kamenev, Shotman, Ganetsky, Malinovsky, and the other Bolshevik deputies in the Duma. Five of these men later proved to be Okhrana agents. Lenin pushed through his resolution to split the Social Democratic delegation in the Duma and Malinovsky was charged with the task of establishing a separate Bolshevik caucus.

Two weeks later the six Bolshevik deputies presented the seven Menshevik deputies with an ultimatum to accept Lenin's program. When the Mensheviks refused, Lenin's followers formed their own caucus with Malinovsky as chairman.

Immediately *Pravda* began a campaign to discredit Chkheidze and the Mensheviks. Most of the *Pravda* editorials continued to be written by Lenin and Zinoviev, but local policy was set up by Malinovsky, who took every occasion to attack the Menshevik Duma deputies and trade-union leaders. In the Duma itself Malinovsky delivered fiery revolutionary speeches accusing the entire liberal and radical opposition of cowardice and treason to the people.

The Bolsheviks succeeded in gaining the upper hand in several major unions, when the government suddenly began to round up all the Menshevik leaders and prominent Menshevik workers. At the time these arrests seemed part of the general policy of repression. Later they were revealed as a plan conceived by Malinovsky.

Malinovsky's bold speeches made him very popular among the workers. He became Lenin's alter ego in Russia, often journeying to Cracow for instructions.

In April 1914 the Czarist government made an attack on the parliamentary immunity of the members of the Duma. The Czar had removed Premier Kokovtsev for alleged liberal tendencies, and replaced him with the incompetent old reactionary, Goremykin, who was ordered to stamp out the revolutionary movement. Goremykin started by bringing charges against Chkheidze for a radical speech he had made in the Duma. As Goremykin began to address the Duma, the Left-wing deputies pounded on their desks and shouted: "Freedom of speech for members of the Duma!" Goremykin could not continue. Rodzianko, the Speaker, after trying unsuccessfully to restore order, apologized to Goremykin, and moved that the Social Democrats and Alexander Kerensky's Trudovik group be excluded for fifteen sessions. The motion was carried.

When the suspended deputies returned on May 7, 1914, Kerensky, on behalf of the entire Left, read a statement condemning the government. The Speaker interrupted him several times and finally ruled him out of order. Malinovsky followed Kerensky, but he, too, was ruled out of order. Malinovsky, however, continued to speak from the rostrum until the Speaker called the sergeant-at-arms, who ordered him to return to his seat.

Malinovsky demanded that all Left-wing deputies resign from the Duma, charging that their continued presence there merely enhanced the prestige of reaction. When his proposal was rejected, he went to the Speaker in his chambers and delivered a sealed envelope to him with the words, "Good-by, Mr. Rodzianko."

Malinovsky went home. When Rodzianko opened the Duma he informed the members that he had just received Malinovsky's resignation from the Duma. The statement caused a commotion and everyone looked at Badaiev, the only Bolshevik member present at the session. No less amazed than the rest, he immediately telephoned to *Pravda,* where the editorial workers were thunderstruck by the news.

Badaiev explained that no one in the Bolshevik delegation had had an inkling of Malinovsky's plans. They considered it a flagrant breach of party discipline. Petrovsky was sent to Malinovsky to demand that he appear before the Bolshevik deputies with a satisfactory explanation.

Petrovsky found Malinovsky, half dressed, pacing the floor of his room.

Petrovsky said, "Without permission from the Party you have taken a step which borders on treason. I was sent by the Party to demand that you come immediately to the delegation's office to explain your unprecedented action."

"I'm not in a position just now to give any explanations," Malinovsky answered curtly.

"Does that mean that you refuse to abide by the decision of the Party?"

"Take it any way you like!" Malinovsky shouted. "But I tell you again I am in no position to explain."

When Petrovsky reported to the Bolshevik Duma group they sent him back to Malinovsky with the message that unless he came immediately they would take strong measures against him.

Threatened with a Party trial, Malinovsky became hysterical, and ran up and down the room, shouting, "Try me! Bring your charges! Do what you like! I won't give any explanations, do you hear? No explanations!"

Badaiev declared that Malinovsky's act was not only a violation of Bolshevik discipline, but that it supplied their enemies with effective ammunition. Rumors spread of a split within the Bolshevik delegation, and the affair created a tremendous sensation.

What Badaiev did not say was that the Menshevik newspaper *Rabotchaya Gazeta* demanded that a commission of all the Left-wing parties investigate the whole Malinovsky affair. This demand came when Vice-Speaker of the Duma, Prince Volkonsky, a Conservative deputy, was reported to have told a Left-wing deputy that he had been informed that Malinovsky had been a police spy all along.

The Mensheviks set about investigating Malinovsky's record and came across other evidence that he was indeed an agent of the Okhrana. Their newspaper then published an editorial demanding that he face a tribunal.

Pravda, however, published a statement signed by Lenin and Zinoviev condemning the Mensheviks as slanderers and cowards, who were afraid to come out with an open charge against Malinovsky, but were seeking to stab the Bolshevik Party in the back. Martov and Dan, the two top Menshevik leaders then in St. Petersburg, published a signed statement reiterating their charges and their demand. Exposing a police agent was a penal offense, so Martov and Dan, by their signed statement, risked arrest.

Lenin, Zinoviev, and Kamenev, writing in the *Pravda*, replied that they refused to allow "liquidators" and representatives of "Stolypin's Workers' Party" to sit in judgment over a spokesman of the revolutionary proletariat. *Rabotchaya Gazeta*, meanwhile, continued to print resolutions and letters demanding that Malinovsky face a revolutionary tribunal.

Malinovsky had gone to Lenin in Galicia from St. Petersburg. On May 25, 1914, the following letter signed by Malinovsky appeared in *Pravda*: "Although for personal reasons I have discontinued my political activities, I remain a Bolshevik adherent. I shall bring those reactionaries Martov and Dan to court in a free country if they have the effrontery to accuse me over their signatures."

Along with Malinovsky's letter, *Pravda* received this telegram from Galicia signed by Lenin, Zinoviev, and Ganetsky: MARTOV AND DAN ARE FILTHY SLANDERERS WHO ALWAYS SPREAD SINISTER RUMORS ABOUT THEIR OPPONENTS. WE DEMAND OF THEM A DIRECT ACCUSATION WITH THEIR SIGNATURES. HAVING INVESTIGATED THE RUMORS, WE ARE ABSOLUTELY CONVINCED OF MALINOVSKY'S POLITICAL HONESTY.

Editorially, *Pravda* announced that these statements by Malinovsky and Lenin put an end to the dastardly slander and called on its followers "to march forward with closed ranks against the enemies outside and the slanderers and traitors like the Martovs and the Dans."

In 1915 Lenin's émigré paper *Sozialdemokrat* carried an item that Malinovsky had been killed in the war. An obituary was published mourning the premature death of "this great proletarian leader." But Malinovsky was not dead by any means, nor was his case closed.

The attitude of the non-Bolshevik factions to Lenin at this time was succinctly expressed by Charles Rappaport, the Russo-French Socialist, who later became an important Communist. Rappaport compared Lenin's position in the revolutionary movement to that of Stolypin in the Czarist regime. No party could exist under Lenin's autocratic rule, said Rappaport in 1914:

We recognized Lenin's achievements. He is a man of iron will and incomparable organizer of groups. . . . Whoever opposes him is forever condemned by him. . . . He sees in capital punishment the only means of assuring the existence of the Social Democratic Party. . . . Instead of combating his opponents . . . by Socialist methods; i.e., by argument, Lenin uses only surgical methods, those of "bloodletting." No party could exist under the regime of this Social Democratic Czar, who regards himself as a super-Marxist, but who is, in reality, nothing but an adventurer of the highest order. I do not belong to any of the contending factions, but the experience of many years led me to the conviction that Lenin's victory would be the greatest menace to the Russian revolution. Lenin will hold it in his embrace so tightly that he will choke it.

In a letter to Chkheidze, the leader of the Mensheviks in the Duma, Trotsky had previously written:

One cannot but deplore as a devilish brew the party squabble which is systematically fomented by the master of such affairs, Lenin, that professional exploiter of backwardness in the Russian workers' movement. . . . The entire edifice of Leninism at present rests on lies and falsifications and carries within itself the poisonous seeds of its own disintegration.

On July 16-17, 1914, a special conference of the International Socialist Bureau was held in Brussels. Its agenda was to include the problem of unity in the Russian labor movement.

The International Socialist Bureau had long been concerned by the split in the Social Democratic Party and the aggressive role of Lenin and his lieutenants. Still it avoided interfering in the Party's affairs. However, the scandal had become too great to be overlooked any longer. Lenin did not wish to submit to a reprimand by the Socialist International. Neither he, Zinoviev, nor Kamenev appeared at the Brussels Conference. Instead, minor representatives were sent to report Lenin's rejection of a new united party. They delivered prepared speeches, declaring that the best way of assuring the unity of the movement was to recognize Lenin's committee as the Central Committee of the entire Party. Plekhanov declared that unity was impossible without curtailing Lenin's influence in the Party. Alexinsky charged that Lenin had blocked the un-masking of agents provocateurs. The members of the Interna-tional Bureau were shocked at these charges, and, since the Bolshevik delegates avoided discussion, Vandervelde, sec-onded by Kautsky, proposed that the question of the schism in the Russian Social Democratic Party be put before the Congress of the International in Vienna at the end of August. That Congress, however, was fated not to convene.

But although Lenin was not popular among the older lead-ers of the Social Democratic Party, his influence among fac-tory workers of St. Petersburg, Moscow, and other industrial centers mounted. His simple and direct slogans for revolution-ary action appealed more strongly to the average Russian worker than the complicated theories of western European Marxism and the Menshevik policy of moderation.

In June 1914 the Bolshevik Central Committee was meeting in Cracow to discuss the steps for convening a new Bolshevik congress. But these preparations were interrupted by the out-break of war.

7 FROM WAR TO REVOLUTION

LENIN HAD SEEN THE RUSSO-JAPANESE WAR DRIVE THE ENTER-ing wedge for the Revolution of 1905; he expected another war to be the prologue to a new revolution. In 1913 he had written to Maxim Gorky: "War between Austria and Russia would be very useful to the cause of the revolution in western Europe. But it is hard to believe that Franz Josef and Nicholas will grant us this pleasure."

A year later they did. When news of the German declara-tion of war on Russia reached Lenin in Cracow the first ques-tion he asked Zinoviev was:

"How will the Second Socialist Internationl react?"

"You will see," predicted Zinoviev. "The Social Democratic gentlemen of Germany will not dare to vote against the Kaiser's government on the question of the war credits. They will abstain."

"No," replied Lenin. "They are not so cowardly as all that. Without doubt they will not oppose the war. But to appease their conscience they will vote against it, if for no other reason than for fear the working class will rise up against them."

The Conference of the International Socialist Bureau, held in Brussels late in July 1914, condemned Austria and Russia. And in Germany the Social Democrats tried hard to stave off the impending conflict. Tremendous demonstrations were staged in all the German cities, and on July 25 the Executive

Committee of the German Social Democratic Party proclaimed:

"No German soldier's blood must be spilt to gratify the murderous intentions of the Austrian tyrant. We call upon you, comrades, to express at once by mass meetings the unshakable desire of the class-conscious proletariat for peace."

Nevertheless, when the pleas of German workers were not heeded, the Social Democrats were faced with the reality of a war they had fought against so long. Arguing that they had tried to prevent the Kaiser's government from aggression and that to oppose the war now could mean a victory for the Czar, the German Social Democrats confounded both Lenin and Zinoviev by voting in favor of the first war credits. When Lenin picked up the Berlin *Vorwaerts* he refused to believe the news.

"It is impossible!" he cried out. Convinced at last, he exclaimed with finality: "The Second International is dead!"

With the outbreak of war the Austrian police began a spy hunt throughout Galicia. On the rainy night of August 7, 1914, Lenin called on Ganetsky.

"A search has just been made of my living quarters," he said. "It was conducted by the *Wachtmeister* of the local gendarmerie. He has ordered me to meet him in the morning at the railroad station and go with him to Nowy Targ. . . . What do you think? Will they arrest us tomorrow in Nowy Targ or will they let us go? . . ."

The Cracow police, according to Ganetsky, were all aware that Lenin was an irreconcilable enemy of Czarism. They had kept a continuous watch over him and knew that he did not concern himself with Austrian affairs. That was the attitude of Cracow. But Nowy Targ was another story. Here the worst could be expected.

Ganetsky therefore communicated with Dr. Marek, the Austrian Social Democratic deputy who had helped obtain permission for Lenin to settle in Cracow. Lenin himself wired to the police director of Cracow:

The local police suspects me of espionage. I have been living in Cracow for the past two years at 57 Lubomirszca Street in the Zwenschintz district. Personally gave information to the police commissioner of Zwenschintz. I am an émigré, a Social Democrat. I beg you to wire the proper officials of Nowy Targ in order to prevent a misunderstanding.

The next day the local gendarmerie received a telegram from the police commissioner of Cracow stating that there were no reasons to hold Lenin. In the meantime, however, Lenin and Zinoviev had been arrested. Ganetsky then telegraphed the Austrian Social Democratic leader, Victor Adler, and the Galician Socialist deputy, Ignatz Daszynski. The Socialists in Austria, like their comrades in Germany, were generally supporting the war effort and therefore were in better standing with their government than usual. Adler went to the Foreign Minister to intercede on Lenin's behalf. He assured the Minister that, in view of Lenin's attitude toward Czarism, freeing him would be most useful to the Austro-German cause.

The Austrian Ministry of the Interior then issued this order:

It is the opinion of Dr. Adler that under the present circumstances Ulianov could be of great service. The police authorities are requested also to inform us, as soon as possible, what military court has jurisdiction over Ulianov.

Lenin was released from prison on August 19, 1914, with permission to go to Switzerland.

In Zurich and Geneva sharp differences of opinion on the war were already developing among the Socialist émigrés. Martinov, a Menshevik leader, gave a series of lectures which started a debate lasting several evenings. Then a number of Germans spoke. They were followed by Karl Radek, Trotsky, Alexinsky, and finally by Lenin, Zinoviev, and Martov.

Trotsky, who at that time was still not close to Lenin, held that the prowar stand of most Socialist parties stemmed from objective causes. Despite the assumed community of interest among capitalists of all countries he maintained that the world economic structure was still largely national rather than international. And the workers believed, according to Trotsky, that if their country conquered new colonies and markets they would enjoy higher living standards. In time of war, therefore, the workers still identified themselves with the cause of their exploiters.

Trotsky's slogan in 1914 was "peace without indemnities and annexation, peace without victors and vanquished." The only radical step he advocated was the dismemberment of the Austro-Hungarian Empire. His "internationalism" was then directed primarily against Germany. During the first few weeks of the war, when German victory seemed likely, even the "internationalists" were afraid of the possible consequences. But by the time Trotsky left for Paris the fortunes of war had changed. It was clear that Wilhelm would not get the kind of peace he wanted. In France, Trotsky was soon fighting against the patriotism of the French Socialist Party as he had previously attacked the German Social Democrats.

Martov, Martinov, and a number of Bolsheviks then in Switzerland shared the same "internationalist" viewpoint. But it was generally agreed that internationalism was still too weak to overcome the new flush of national patriotism which the war had produced.

At a meeting of the Bolsheviks, held the morning after his

arrival, Lenin outlined his views on the war. A resolution was adopted branding the conflict as imperialist and the conduct of the leaders of the Second International as a betrayal of the proletariat. The Bolshevik Duma deputy Samoilov was instructed to take this resolution back to St. Petersburg to the Central Committee and the Bolshevik Duma group.

At a debate in Zurich, Lenin called Trotsky's slogan of peace "a pious platitude." Not peace but civil war was Lenin's program. To go into the trenches and create revolutionary cells was the correct tactic, he maintained.

"Take your rifles and turn them against your officers and the capitalists," he said. And he quoted Engels to the effect that the workers should let the bourgeoisie shoot first. Now that the world bourgeoisie had begun shooting it was time to reply. Pounding his fist, he repeated, "You shot first, gentlemen of the bourgeoisie."

Word that Plekhanov was advocating support of the Allied war effort infuriated Lenin. He was anxious to meet Plekhanov face to face. Plekhanov maintained that if Germany won, she would deprive Russia of her littoral provinces and turn her into a virtual German colony. Russia's industry would decline, and with it the Russian working class. The landowners would gain dominance, thus strengthening Czarism and turning back the clock for Russia by decades.

"We learned in Lausanne," relates Bukharin, "that Plekhanov was to make a speech at the Maison du Peuple and we immediately sent a wire to Lenin, who was then in Berne. Ilich arrived with the speed of the wind. The hall crowded to suffocation. . . . Plekhanov, noticing Lenin, remarked jestingly that he felt 'decoyed into a trap.' "

His eyes flashing under his silvery brows, Plekhanov eloquently defended the Socialists of the Allied countries for their patriotism. When Plekhanov criticized the German Social Democrats, Lenin joined in the general applause. But when Plekhanov argued that the Socialist parties of France, Belgium, and England had to give full support to their governments against German militarism, Lenin was furious. As soon as Plekhanov finished talking, Lenin rose, holding a glass of beer in his hand, and walked to the platform. His face was as white as a death mask.

"Never before or after did I see such a deathly pallor on Ilich's face," Bukharin writes. "Only his eyes were burning brightly, when, in a dry, guttural voice, he started to lash his opponent sharply and forcefully."

"He spoke calmly," relates Krupskaya, "and only his paleness betrayed his emotion. Ilich said that the war which had broken out was not an accidental one, that it had been prepared by the entire character and development of bourgeois society. The International Socialist congresses in Stuttgart, Copenhagen, and Basle had decided the attitude of the Socialists toward the coming war. The Social Democrats would carry out their duty if they conducted a fight against chauvinistic fog in their own countries. The war must be transformed into a resolute conflict between the proletariat and the ruling classes. Ilich spoke only ten minutes, he touched only the essentials. Plekhanov, with his well-known barbs, answered him. The Mensheviks, who were in the majority at the meeting, applauded him. It was the impression that Plekhanov had won."

In a letter to Shliapnikov, a prominent Bolshevik, on October 17, 1914, Lenin wrote:

In Russia chauvinism is hiding behind the phrases of *la belle France*, unfortunate Belgium, and enmity to the Kaiser and Kaiserism. Therefore it is our absolute duty to fight against this sophistry, and in order that this fight travel along a clear and straight path, a slogan is necessary to summarize the entire question. The slogan should show that from the standpoint of the interests of the Russian working class there is little doubt that the defeat of Czarism is the lesser catastrophe, because Czarism is a hundred times worse than Kaiserism. The slogan "peace" is not the right one at this moment. This is a slogan of priests and the petty bourgeoisie. The proletarian slogan should be "civil war." . . . We cannot <u>promise</u> a civil war and we cannot <u>decree</u> a civil war, but our duty is to conduct all our work, if necessary for a long time, <u>in that direction.</u> [Lenin's underscoring.]

When a Bolshevik named Shklovsky attempted to argue that unless Germany was defeated, democracy in France would be destroyed, Lenin replied:

"Let them destroy it. France is nothing but a backward republic of usurers and *rentiers* fattening on their gold. . . . For us revolutionary Marxists it makes no difference who wins. . . ."

Above all he despised the pacifists and conscientious objectors who wanted a premature end of the war, thereby destroying the bright prospects of revolution. "War is no accident and no 'sin,' as the Christian reverends think," he wrote on November 11, 1914. "They, like all opportunists, preach patriotism, humanitarianism, and pacifism. War is an inevitable part of capitalism. It is just as much a legitimate form of capitalism as is peace. . . . It is simply insane to talk about abolishing capitalism without a frightful civil war or without a succession of such wars. . . . The only duty of the Socialists, when an imperialist war breaks out between the bourgeois classes of different nations, is to transform this war between nations into a war between classes. Down with the sentimental, hypocritical slogan: 'Peace at Any Price!' Long Live the Civil War!"

Active among the "internationalists" in Switzerland was Karl Radek, who arrived from Germany in August 1914. His paper on imperialism, delivered in Zurich, was received with considerable interest.

Radek had much to say about Parvus, a Russo-German Social Democrat, who had a bad reputation because of his corrupt dealings with women and money. He had been expelled from the German Social Democratic Party for misappropriation of funds. But Radek spoke of Parvus with a great deal of warmth and with indulgence toward his faults. Parvus had a brilliant mind, Radek said, but could not stick to one thing for any length of time. At the moment, however, Parvus was serving the Central Powers. Turkey and Germany were trying to recruit Georgian war prisoners to fight the Russians on the Caucasian front as special units in the Turkish Army. They maintained an affiliated organization in Bulgaria where many Georgian deserters had fled. Unofficially, Parvus, who had lived in Constantinople for several years before the war, was the organizer of this scheme.

Now Parvus was both an ardent German patriot and a contractor for the German Army. Speculation during the war added to his earnings. One of the men who worked for him was Ganetsky. Radek, who remained in constant contact with both Parvus and Ganetsky, had no part in Parvus's commercial and financial affairs, but the Parvus-Ganetsky link and Parvus's ties with Berlin were to play an important role in Lenin's later actions.

Lenin had sent word to Kamenev, in St. Petersburg, to have the Bolshevik deputies make a declaration from the floor of the Duma that the Russian working class hoped for Russia's defeat. At a secret joint conference of the Bolshevik organization and the Bolshevik Duma deputies, Kamenev moved for the adoption of Lenin's declaration.

While Kamenev was urging the Duma deputies to accept Lenin's declaration, the police raided the conference and arrested all those present. All the participants, including the Duma deputies, were convicted of high treason and sent to Siberia.

Lenin's propaganda found sympathetic response at this stage among émigrés who shared his hopes that Russia's defeat would hasten the revolution. Some of his supporters were pacifists who considered Lenin an apostle of peace and did not take his summons to civil war seriously.

The Mensheviks had split into two factions. The majority, led by Potresov in Russia and Plekhanov in Switzerland, favored support of the war; the minority, headed by Martov and Axelrod, sided with the "internationalists," taking the same position as the left-wing Socialists of Germany, Italy, and France. The Socialist Revolutionary ranks were split along the same lines. While the group headed by Victor Chernov joined the "internationalists," a second led by Nikolai Avksentiev favored the Allies.

Despite great difficulties Lenin carried on correspondence with the St. Petersburg Bureau of the Bolshevik Central Committee and succeeded in establishing communications with Stalin, Sverdlov, and other Bolshevik exiles in Siberia. He also managed to send them his "thesis" on the war.

Lenin delivered a policy report to the Bolshevik groups abroad, and the conference adopted his resolution which formulated the main Bolshevik slogans for the duration. Lenin proposed that the "opportunists" be presented with the following ultimatum: "Here is the manifesto . . . of our Central Committee on the war. Are you willing to publish it in your language? No? Then, good-by, our ways part!"

The war was straining Russia's badly integrated economy, exposing the weak spots of agriculture, industry, and the transportation system. On the already heavily overtaxed nation fell the added burden of war. The government was forced to obtain foreign loans and the external debt mounted rapidly.

Eighteen million men, nearly half of the adult working population, were called up. Manufacturers were compelled to petition for the return of workers from the front. Skilled laborers disappeared and were replaced by untrained hands from the villages. The Russian industrial plant was badly equipped and little machinery was coming from abroad. In addition the importation of raw materials decreased, while the output of coal shrank.

After some initial victories, the poorly equipped Russian armies suffered costly defeats and were heavily bled in ill-planned operations. For the inefficient conduct of the war and the shortsighted approach to domestic affairs the responsibility fell squarely on the shoulders of Czar Nicholas.

Contrary to the regime's expectations, the war did not relegate the agrarian question to the background. Indeed the peasants firmly believed that ownership of the land would be their reward for bearing arms for the Czar.

At the outset of the war the Duma had been called together for a one-day session to demonstrate that Russia was united. A "civil peace" had been concluded between the government and the Liberals. "Let us forget our internal quarrels," said the Cadets. "Let us not give the enemy the slightest opportunity to hope for dissension among us, and let us remember that the first and foremost duty before us is to support the nation's defenders who are fighting for our just cause."

But Czar Nicholas II was a weak and stubborn man who, instead of drawing on the support of the Liberals, relied on his German consort and Rasputin. Compared with Nicholas II, the Empress Alexandra had both brains and will power.

Rasputin's hold over the Empress came not only from his hypnotic gifts, which enabled him to check the bleeding of the haemophilic heir to the throne, but from his alleged powers as a clairvoyant. He became intermediary between Alexandra and God and played the same role for Nicholas. Rasputin had no program but he was always consulted when political appointments were made. This was his favorite domain. Here he filled his pockets without arousing the Czar's suspicion. The popular rumors that Rasputin was a German spy were never proved. Both Rasputin and the Empress did, however, wage a vicious campaign against the Duma, as the challenger to imperial power.

"As now decided, the Duma will convene in August, whereas our Friend asked you several times to postpone the opening to a later date," the Empress wrote to her husband in the summer of 1915.

Major defeats on the Galician front forced the Czar to reconvene the Duma on June 19, 1915. But on September 3 it was adjourned once more. These sporadic sessions did not improve the temper of the deputies, who were demanding the removal of Rasputin from the court. The so-called Progressive Bloc, formed in 1915, tried to reconcile the interests of the middle class, the nobility, and the court party. Miliukov, the organizer of this alliance, acknowledged that the initiative had come from certain Czarist Ministers. Including six conservative and liberal Duma groups, the bloc's program called for broad political and social reforms and the creation of a united government, but it did not venture to demand a cabinet responsible to the Duma. Final authority would still rest with the Czar. This excellent program, however, proved to be nothing more than a catalogue of pious wishes. No reforms were enacted.

Lenin wrote in the summer of 1915:

Much has been left in the world that must be destroyed by fire and iron for the liberation of the working class. And if bitterness and despair grow in the masses, if a revolutionary situation is at hand, prepare to organize new organizations and *utilize* these so useful weapons of death and destruction against your own government and your bourgeoisie.

This is not easy, to be sure. It will demand difficult preparatory activities. It will demand great sacrifices. This is a *new* species of organization and struggle that *one must learn,* and learning is never done without errors and defeats. The relation of this species of class struggle to participation in elections is the same as storming a fortress is to maneuvering, marching, or lying in the trenches.

On September 5, 1915, a conference of all European anti-war Socialist groups who called themselves "internationalists" opened in Zimmerwald, Switzerland. Earlier, in Berne, Lenin had proposed creating a new International and appealing to the soldiers and workers of all belligerent nations to lay down their arms and go out on strike against the war.

When Italy entered the conflict in May 1915, the Italian Socialists took the lead in the international anti-war organization. The Italian Socialist Party sent Angelica Balabanoff and Morgari to Berne to negotiate with the Internationalists.

Lenin's proposals had a hostile reception. Merrheim, one of the French left-wing syndicalist leaders, argued that the proposed manifesto to the workers and soldiers would be a futile gesture. Other delegates pointed out that the men who signed this appeal would face the death penalty as traitors when they returned to their homes, while Lenin himself remained safely in neutral Switzerland. After an eight-hour conference, the Berne session had broken up without results.

Robert Grimm, a Swiss journalist and Socialist leader, moved to create a permanent liaison between the various anti-war groups. The Italian Socialist Party had invited all groups that accepted the principle of class struggle and voted against military appropriations. But the organizers of the Zimmerwald Conference also wanted to invite the so-called "Centrists" of the German Social Democratic Party.

At a pre-conference meeting Zinoviev, representing the Bolsheviks, had spoken against inviting the German "Centrists." A few weeks earlier Kautsky, Bernstein, and Haase had published a manifesto demanding peace without annexations. When Axelrod, representing the Menshevik "internationalists," declared that if the "Centrists" were not invited he would not participate either, Zinoviev's recommendation was voted down.

Later it developed that the Kautsky group preferred to deal directly with the powerful French Socialist Party rather than with the splinter groups assembled at Zimmerwald.

Germany was represented by ten delegates, of whom the majority, headed by Ledebour, took a middle position between Kautsky and the extreme Left. Only the followers of Karl Liebknecht sided with Lenin.

The Bolsheviks were represented by Lenin and Zinoviev, the Menshevik-internationalists by Axelrod and Martov. Trotsky spoke for his own small group. The internationalists of the Russian Socialist Revolutionary Party were represented by Chernov and Bobrov; Poland by Karl Radek, Varsky, and

Lapinsky (all three acting for splinter groups). There were also two delegates of the fictitious Balkan Federation, Kolarov (now President of Bulgaria) and Christian Rakovsky. Also present were delegates from splinter groups in Sweden, Norway, and Holland. From France came the syndicalist Merrheim and the Socialist Bourderon, neither speaking for his organization. Only two large western European organizations were represented, the Italian and Swiss Socialist parties. In all there were 35 delegates.

The majority statement condemned the war as imperialist and called for a fight against war and for Socialism. But the Bolsheviks insisted on a more militant resolution, urging an open civil war and the organization of a new revolutionary International.

With the French and German delegations equally opposed to Lenin's proposed manifesto, the conference was on the verge of breaking up. At this point, however, Rakovsky stepped into the breach with a compromise proposal. The manifesto which was finally adopted called on the proletariat of Europe to fight for "peace without indemnities and without annexations" on the basis of the "self-determination of peoples." Lenin voted against the compromise proposal when it was offered in committee and when the final vote was taken.

Out of this conference emerged the so-called Zimmerwald Union, a loose grouping of anti-war Socialists which lasted until the formation of the Communist International.

While these great issues were being fought over, Lenin was having trouble paying for his room and board.

A month after Zimmerwald, Lenin wrote in his *Sozial-demokrat:*

The social content of the next revolution in Russia can only be a revolutionary democratic dictatorship of the proletariat and the peasantry. The revolution cannot emerge victorious without overthrowing the monarchy and the feudal landowners, and it is impossible to overthow them without the peasantry supporting the proletariat. The aim of the proletariat in Russia is to lead the bourgeois democratic revolution to its end, in order to kindle the Socialist Revolution in Europe.

* * *

In January 1916 Lenin and his wife moved from Berne to Zurich.

Lenin's efforts to organize a following among the mixed radical groups in Zurich met with little success. A gathering was called in the Café Zum Adler, not far from Lenin's living quarters. The audience included a few Russian and Polish Bolsheviks, some Swiss Socialists, and a handful of young Germans and Italians. When Lenin outlined to them his attitude toward the war and toward Europe's Socialist leaders as a whole, he met a cool reception. One young Swiss radical told Lenin that he was beating his head against the wall in vain. Others agreed, and the gathering fizzled out. At later meetings the audience continued to shrink in size. At the final session in the Café Zum Adler, attended only by Russians and Poles, Krupskaya reports that "we exchanged some funny stories and went home." Never was Lenin's isolation so complete as in Zurich in 1916.

* * *

As the war continued on with no end in sight, the Zimmerwald International Socialist Committee called another conference. Held in the Swiss town of Kienthal on April 24, 1916, the forty-three delegates included three Socialist members of the French Chamber of Deputies.

At Kienthal the Zimmerwald Left, headed by Lenin, was much stronger than a half year before and pushed through a resolution censuring the International Socialist Bureau of the Second International. While this was no clear-cut Bolshevik victory, Lenin was satisfied with the tactical gain.

But Lenin attacked also some of his own supporters for their attitude toward war, peace, and revolution. He was particularly stern with their "pacifist illusions."

"There was nothing more pernicious," said Lenin, "than the clerical, petty-bourgeois, pacifist argument that war could be abolished under capitalism. Imperialism necessarily gives rise to fierce rivalry among the capitalist states for the division and redivision of the world. Consequently, under capitalism, wars are inevitable. . . ."

Lenin poured withering scorn on those who suggested that the proletariat should refuse to bear arms. "Our slogan," said Lenin, "must be: Arm the proletariat in order to vanquish, expropriate, and disarm the bourgeoisie!"

Chafing because political action was impossible, Lenin plunged into writing. In the fall of 1916 he buried himself in the library from nine to six every day collecting the material to complete his book *Imperialism, the Highest Stage of Capitalism.*

Lenin emphasized the newer role of financial monopolies in world economy. He laid down the thesis that capitalist states, in their pursuit of new markets and colonies, would always settle their competitive differences by war.

But he went still further. Until Socialism was established everywhere, it was false to advocate disarmament. Socialism could come only through revolution, according to Lenin and revolutions could not be made by unarmed men. Before the victory of Socialism could be accomplished a war to the finish between the bourgeoisie and the proletariat was inevitable.

Guns would decide that revolution, and guns in the hand of revolutionary troops spelled victory for the proletariat.

The year 1916 was darkened by the death of Maria Alexandrovna. Lenin had not seen his mother since their last meeting in Stockholm in 1910. It was there that she had heard him speak before an audience for the first time. Maria Alexandrovna's death hit Lenin hard.

Isolated from events in Russia, deserted by many of his early followers, struggling to pay his modest living expenses, seeking in vain to rally Socialists of other lands to his slogans of international civil war, Lenin, at the end of 1916, was hitting the bottom rung of his ladder. Never did his words seem to attract fewer followers. Many looked on him as a crackpot.

When he returned from a political meeting in Geneva, he complained because he was receiving no word from the few men he had sent to Russia. One of his disciples, Comrade Filia, then suggested calling a congress of some fifty to sixty Bolsheviks in Russia to issue an anti-war manifesto in the name of the Party.

Lenin replied: "Why fifty or sixty? That's too many. Four or five are sufficient. One from the Caucasus, one or two from Siberia, one from the Urals, one from Moscow, and one from Petrograd. If these four or five men, representing the laboring classes, came together from these centers, declared themselves delegates to a conference called in the name of the Party, and came out strongly against war, that would be a great historic event and would be a tremendous spur to the development of the revolutionary movement in Russia."

Filia looked at Lenin with astonishment.

"Around these four or five men calling themselves a party conference," Lenin continued, "in the tense revolutionary atmosphere that would be created, there would crystallize the will of tens of thousands of workers hoping for a revolution."

But even these four or five were not available as the year 1916 drew to a close. Where were they to be found? Where was the Bolshevik from the Caucasus? He was in Siberian exile, together with the Bolshevik members of the Duma and the members of the Central Committee of the Bolshevik Party.

Lenin had few adherents among the Bolsheviks who were still in European Russia on the eve of the Revolution. When his friend Solomon heard he was badly in need of money, he tried collecting funds among Lenin's former friends in Petrograd. He approached Krassin, who then had an excellent job as an engineer. The future Soviet diplomat shrugged his shoulders when Solomon asked him to contribute money for Lenin's support.

"George," he said, "you're wasting your time. You don't know Ilich as well as I do. Let him go to the devil. Let's go out to lunch instead."

While they were dining, Solomon renewed his plea. "All right," replied Krassin, "I'll do it as a favor to you." And he reached into his wallet for two five-ruble notes.

Angrily, Solomon threw back the ten rubles. "We'll do without your contribution," he told Krassin.

"That's excellent," Krassin calmly replied, slipping the two notes back into his wallet. "But don't be angry, George. Lenin doesn't deserve help. He is a destructive type and you can never tell what wild scheme will suddenly emanate from his Tartar skull. To hell with him."

Krassin wasn't the only Bolshevik who had grave doubts about Lenin in those days. In a Paris émigré newspaper *Our Echo,* in July 1916, Viacheslav Menzhinsky, later chief of the Soviet secret police (in an article signed S.D.), wrote:

Lenin is a political Jesuit who over the course of many years has molded Marxism to his aims of the moment. He has now become completely confused. . . . Lenin, this illegitimate child of Russian absolutism, considers himself not only the natural successor to the Russian throne, when it becomes vacant, but also the sole heir of the Socialist International. Should he ever come to power, the mischief he would do would not be much less than that of Paul I [the half-mad Czar who preceded Alexander I]. The Leninists are not even a faction, but a clan of party gypsies, who swing their whips so affectionately and hope to drown the voice of the proletariat with their screams, imagining it to be their unchallengeable right to be the *drivers* of the proletariat.

On January 22, 1917, Lenin told an assembly of young workers in Zurich:

"The present gravelike stillness in Europe must not deceive us. Europe is charged with revolution. The monstrous horrors of the imperialist war and the suffering caused by the high cost of living engender everywhere a revolutionary spirit; and the ruling classes, the bourgeoisie and their lackey governments, are moving more and more into a blind alley from which they can never extricate themselves without tremendous upheavals."

The "gravelike stillness" was about to end.

Events inside Russia were heading rapidly toward the explosion that was to bring Lenin from exile in Switzerland to the limelight in Petrograd. The years of uphill struggle were drawing to a close. In January 1917 Lenin's name was still only vaguely known in Russia except among professional revolutionists. To the Socialists of western Europe he was still the café conspirator, the Russian with large theories and few followers. Three months later, installed in the palace of the Czar's favorite ballerina, he was to become the thundering voice of a revolutionary movement such as the world had not seen since the days of the Jacobins.

8 "THE FREEST COUNTRY IN THE WORLD"

LONG QUEUES LINED UP IN FRONT OF FOOD STORES IN EVERY Russian city and town. In many cities electric powerhouses and waterworks ceased to operate.

The head of the Moscow Political Secret Service Bureau advised the State Police Department in October 1916: "Privation is so great that many people . . . are actually starving. . . . To permit these lines when there is a shortage of food is as harmful in its influence as the holding of revolutionary meetings and the scattering of tens of thousands of revolutionary leaflets. I am sure that sure bitterness and exasperation have never been witnessed before. Compared with conditions in 1905 the present state of affairs is of far graver portent to the government."

In January 1917 the Police reported: "If the populace thus far has not engaged in food riots, that does not mean that it is not going to do so in the near future. The exasperation of the people is growing by leaps and bounds. Every day more and more of them demand: 'Either give us food or stop the war.' And they are the most suitable element among which to conduct anti-government propaganda. They have nothing to lose from a disadvantageous peace. Just when the thing will happen and how, it is hard to tell. But events of the greatest importance and fraught with the most dangerous consequences are most certainly close at hand."

The government chose to ignore these warnings.

The continued drafting of workers and the requisitioning of horses greatly diminished the areas of sown land. By January 1917 the price of commodities in Petrograd had increased sixfold. In Moscow signs reading "No bread today, and none expected," were a common sight. Moscow was compelled to cut in half its consumption of electricity.

Among the peasants still ran the thread of hope that after the war they would be given land. As the war continued and new classes were mobilized, these expectations dimmed. Soldiers wrote of being compelled to fight without guns and on short rations. And, as casualty lists mounted, crippled veterans began to fill the villages. The second-class military reserves, the last bulwark of the peasant countryside, were called to the colors.

Ugly rumors of Rasputin's power reached the villages. The front subsisted on rumors and reports from the village, the village on tidings from the front. The peasants in the ranks reacted as did the peasants at home, but with greater intensity. Their resentment took more resolute forms.

The Police were forced to report: "The Army . . . is full of elements, some of whom may become an active force of rebellion, while others may refuse to participate in punitive measures against the mutineers. Should the former succeed in organizing themselves properly, there would hardly be enough units in the Army to constitute a strong counter-revolutionary force to defend the government. A whole people in arms is permeated with revolutionary elements. . . ." All this inflammable material was rapidly approaching the point of spontaneous combustion. The government was disintegrating. No such pitiful assembly ever headed the government as during the last year of Romanov rule. The only more or less able personality was Protopopov, the Minister of Interior. But even he picked the day for summoning the Duma by consulting his horoscope.

The other Ministers were opportunists, grafters, and old men placed in high office to cover up corruption. There was Stuermer, a dotard "fit to be led by a string," as Rasputin expressed it. Khvostov was an embezzler who had purchased his office through Rasputin. There was Shcheglovitov, whom Rasputin called a "brazen-faced Cain"; Kurlov, a debauchee and grafter; Dobrovolsky, who made decisions of state at spiritualist séances.

Even the Empress called them "fools and idiots."

In the last month of the monarchy the real ruler of Russia was the Empress.

The Duma was powerless to influence events. Yet by the latter part of 1916 the parties of the Progressive Bloc had to make a determined bid for power. New leadership and a new command were needed to save Russia's economic structure and the Army. Alexander Guchkov, former president of the Duma, urged a coup d'état. Someone suggested that the Empress be invited aboard a warship and taken to England. Guchkov and General Krimov favored seizure of the imperial train, forcing Nicholas to abdicate in favor of his young son Alexis, with the Grand Duke Mikhail (the Czar's brother) as regent, and arresting the members of the government.

On November 7, 1916, Grand Duke Nikolai had an intimate talk with his nephew the Czar and warned him that his throne was tottering.

On December 30, 1916, members of the court attempted to save the dynasty by killing Rasputin. The elimination of Rasputin, however, came too late to help Nicholas.

From all quarters the Duma was bombarded with demands

that it assume full control. To those who demanded that the Duma seize the reins of government, Rodzianko, its president, replied, ". . . I am neither able nor willing to rouse the people against the Czar."

In January 1917 General Krimov described the critical situation along the fighting line. He declared that the Army was ready to support the Duma in a palace revolution.

But the Duma was not ready to act. Opinion was divided.

"The general is right—a coup d'état is necessary," argued Deputy Shingarev, "but who will dare to undertake it?"

Deputy Shidlovsky angrily exclaimed, "We cannot waste pity on the Czar if he ruins Russia."

This sentiment was echoed by many members of the Duma, who subscribed to the words of General Brusilov, the commander on the Southwestern Front, "If it comes to a choice between the Czar and Russia, I will take Russia."

On February 3, 1917, Grand Duke Mikhail asked Rodzianko point-blank: "Do you think there is going to be a revolution?" Rodzianko replied that it was still possible to save the country by removing the Empress from politics and appointing Ministers in whom the country had confidence. He warned, however, that revolution was inevitable if the Empress remained in power.

The Grand Duke agreed: "Sir George Buchanan [the British Ambassador] said the same thing to my brother. Our family realizes how harmful the Empress is. She and my brother are surrounded by traitors. . . . But what to do?"

"Describe the exact situation to the Czar," Rodzianko suggested. ". . . Tell him . . . that the people regard her as a Germanophile, working against the interests of Russia."

The Grand Duke promised to try.

Two weeks later, on February 15, Rodzianko warned the Czar: "Your majesty must find a way to remove the Empress from politics."

He pleaded with Nicholas to appoint a responsible Prime Minister. "The idea spreads that everything is done that harms Russia and benefits the enemy. . . . There is not one honest man in your entourage: all decent people have either been sent away or have left. . . ."

Nicholas replied: "Produce your facts. You have no evidence to support your words."

On February 27, 1917, the Duma was convened. At the opening session Kerensky declared: "There are people who assert that the Ministers are at fault. . . . The country now realizes that the Ministers are but fleeting shadows. The country can clearly see who sends them here. To prevent a catastrophe the Czar himself must be removed, by force if there is no other way. . . ."

When the Empress read Kerensky's speech she demanded that he be hanged as a traitor.

At a secret meeting in Petrograd of all Left parties, the Bolshevik spokesman Shliapnikov declared that his group could not back the liberal demand for the creation of a ministry responsible to the Duma. The Bolsheviks would not oppose the planned demonstration, he said, but they would conduct their propaganda with other slogans.

In the demonstration on February 27 a large number of officers joined the students. The wall between the barracks and the street had begun to totter.

The Duma had been in session a week when Rodzianko heard that the Czar was about to announce the creation of a responsible Ministry. Premier Golitsyn and other members of the Cabinet had been summoned and Nicholas himself promised to appear before the Duma the following day.

Golitsyn's joy was brief, for in the evening the Emperor told him that he was leaving for Headquarters.

"But Your Majesty, what about the responsible Ministry? You planned to go to the Duma tomorrow."

". . . I have changed my mind. . . ."

While Nicholas was floundering, events resolved themselves with sudden speed. On March 8 the workers of Petrograd went on strike. On March 10 General Khabalov, commander of the Petrograd garrison, sent a wire to the Czar informing him that workers in many factories were on strike and that the populace had become unruly.

The Czar replied: "Stop the disorder . . . at once." Khabalov ordered wholesale shooting of the rioters.

To the Empress these rumblings represented nothing more than minor disorders. On March 9 she wrote her husband:

Yesterday there were riots on the Vasiliev Island and on Nevsky, when the poor raided the bakeries. They demolished the Filipov bakery and Cossacks were sent against them. All this I learned from unofficial sources. The riots increased by ten o'clock, but by one they subsided. Khabalov is now in control of the situation.

The next day she wrote:

The strikers and rioters in the city are now in a more defiant mood than ever. The disturbances are created by hoodlums. Youngsters and girls are running around shouting they have no bread; they do this just to create some excitement. If the weather were cold they would all probably be staying at home. But the thing will pass and quiet down, provided the Duma behaves. The worst of the speeches are not reported in the papers, but I think that for speaking against the dynasty there sould be immediate and severe punishment.

On March 11 she confided to her husband that idlers were causing this contretemps:

The whole trouble comes from these idlers, well-dressed people, wounded soldiers, high school girls, et cetera, who are inciting others. Lily spoke to some cabdrivers to find out about things. They told her that the students came to them and told them if they appeared in the streets in the morning, they would be shot to death. What corrupt minds! Of course the cabdrivers and the motormen are now on strike. But they say that it is all different from 1905, because they all worship you and only want bread.

On the very eve of open revolution the Empress wrote: ". . . I think everything will be all right. The sun is shining so brightly and I feel so calm and at peace at His grave. He died to save us." "He" was Rasputin.

While the Empress was dispatching these letters of comfort, Rodzianko on March 11 wired the Emperor:

The situation is serious. The capital is in a state of anarchy. The government is paralyzed; the transport service has broken down; the food and fuel supplies are completely disorganized. Discontent is . . . on the increase . . . troops are firing at each other. It is urgent that someone enjoying the confidence of the country be entrusted with the formation of a new government. There must be no delay. Hesitation is fatal.

This he followed the next day with another wire:

The situation is growing worse. Measures should be taken immediately. . . . The last hour has struck, when the fate of the country and dynasty is being decided.

"Dissolve the Duma!" replied the Czar.

Rodzianko's wire advised: "By your Majesty's order, the sessions of the Imperial Duma have been adjourned until April. The last bulwark of order has been removed. The government is powerless to stop the disorders. The troops of the garrison cannot be relied upon. The reserve battalions of the Guard regiments are in the grip of rebellion, their officers are being killed . . . they are marching on the offices of the Ministry of Interior and the Imperial Duma. Civil war has begun and is spreading. Order immediately the formation of a new government. . . . Revoke your recent order and command the legislative chambers to reconvene. Announce a manifesto to these measures. . . . Should the agitation reach the Army, Germany will triumph and the destruction of Russia along with the dynasty is inevitable. In the name of Russia, I beg Your Majesty to carry out the above recommendation. The hour which will decide your own fate and the fate of Russia has arrived. Tomorrow it may be too late."

General Khabalov sent a wire to the Czar reporting mutiny in Petrograd and asking for new units to suppress the rebellion.

Nicholas, however, continued to follow his wife's advice. By dissolving the Duma he destroyed the last barrier between himself and the revolution.

By general agreement an unofficial meeting of the deputies was called on March 12 to decide on a course of action following the Czar's dissolution order.

Deputies came to the Duma, reporting the fast-moving events. Workers were holding an election. A regiment has revolted; apparently the Volinski. They've killed their commanding officer. The Cossacks fraternize with the people. Barricades have been thrown up on the Nevsky. No one knows anything about the fate of the Ministers. An army of some 30,000 workers, students, soldiers, and women is marching on the Duma.

Later there was a meeting of the leaders of all parties in the office of the president of the Duma. Rodzianko presided. To remain in session after the order of dissolution meant proclaiming revolution. Rodzianko and the majority did not dare take this step. It was decided to go through the motion of obeying the decree, to meet at once in an informal session. From all sides came excited speeches. Someone proposed that the Duma refuse to disperse, proclaim itself the acting government, or declare itself a Constituent Assembly. Another demanded that the Duma declare whether it stood with Nicholas or with the people. Just then there was a commotion at the door, shouts were heard, and an officer rushed into the room.

"Gentlemen of the Duma, I implore your protection," he cried. "I am the head of the guard, your guard, the guard of the Duma. Some unknown soldiers have forced their way in. They tried to kill me. I barely escaped. Help me."

At this moment Kerensky spoke up: "What has just happened proves that we must not delay. . . . I am now going to visit the regiments. I must know what to say to them. May I tell them that the Duma is with them, that it assumes all responsibility, that it will stand at the head of the movement?"

"I do not recall," writes Shulgin, "whether he received an answer—probably not. But from that moment his figure stood out. He spoke with positiveness, as one having authority. . . .

" 'He is the Dictator!' I heard a whisper near me."

The 30,000 marching men and women, soldiers, workers, and students arrived at Tauride Palace. Kerensky addressed the first wave of soldiers as "the first revolutionary guard." The Duma and the revolution were fused in a turbulent union as the people took possession of the building.

On the same day—March 12—the workers of the Petrograd

factories organized a Soviet of Workers' Deputies, modeled after the Petrograd Soviet of 1905 and elected Chkheidze chairman, with Kerensky as vice-chairman.

The revolting regiments and workers freed the political prisoners, then marched to the Palace. Here the outstanding figures of revolutionary Petrograd were already assembled. By two o'clock most of the trade-union and co-operative leaders had arrived. Banding together with the Leftist Duma deputies, the leaders of the Labor Group of the War Industries Committee organized the Provisional Executive Committee of the Soviet of Workers' Deputies. It consisted of Socialist Duma Deputies Chkheidze and Skobelev and five other members.

Immediately the committee went into action, calling the first meeting of the Petrograd Soviet of Workers' Deputies for seven o'clock that evening. The appeal was distributed by truck to all factories in the city. Within a few hours the proletariat of Petrograd was organized in a revolutionary assembly.

Long before seven o'clock the delegates began to pour in by the hundreds. They were registered by a crew grouped around a long table outside the hall.

At the chairman's table, awaiting the arrival of the Provisional Executive Committee, sat Khrustalev, who had headed the 1905 Soviet, and Sokolov. The latter opened the meeting at nine o'clock and asked for the election of a presidium. When the session began there were two hundred and fifty delegates present, but more and more groups continued to arrive carrying all sorts of mandates and credentials.

The delegates discussed the food situation, measures against developing anarchy, and preparations for the final fight against Czarism. They then elected a permanent presidium, consisting of Chkheidze as chairman, Kerensky and Skobelev as vice-chairmen, and Gvozdiov, Sokolov, Grinevich, and the Left Menshevik Pankov as secretaries.

When a group of soldiers asked for the floor, their demand was granted with enthusiasm. The soldiers reported what was taking place in their regiments. The assembly listened with rapt attention, for their recital spelled the end of Romanov rule.

"We are from the Volinsky regiment . . . from the Pavlovsky regiment . . . from the Litovsky . . . from the Finlindsky . . . from the Grenadiers . . ."

As the names of the regiments that had turned the bread riots into a revolution rang out, they were greeted by tremendous bursts of applause.

"We are assembled . . . we were told to say . . . the officers are in hiding . . . in the Soviet of Workers' Deputies we were told to say that we don't want to serve against the people . . . we join our brothers, the workers, in order to defend the cause of the people together . . . we'll give our lives for it . . . our meeting decided to greet . . . Long live the Revolution!"

In a matter of a few moments the delegates decided to unite the revolutionary army and workers in one organization. The assembly now became the Soviet of Workers' and Soldiers' Deputies.

While the Soviet was discussing the situation, a young soldier, waving his rifle above his head, ran in and shouted, "Comrades and brothers, I bring you the comradely greetings of all the soldiers of the Semionovsky Guards. All of us, to the last man, have decided to join hands with the people. . . ."

Once more the meeting was thrown into a frenzy of enthusiasm. Every member of the audience knew that the Semionovsky Guards had suppressed the Moscow uprising of 1905. As more and more units rushed representatives into the hall, revolutionary Petrograd knew that Czar Nicholas no longer could command the forces to halt the revolution.

The Soviet published a proclamation telling the people to maintain order. The proclamation ended with the summons for an elected Constituent Assembly.

The document was published in the first issue of *Izvestia*, organ of the Petrograd Soviet, which appeared the next morning.

The elections to the permanent Executive Committee which followed were largely non-partisan, because the position of each party was not yet clearly defined or familiar to the delegates.

During the first few weeks not one of the future central figures of the Revolution belonged to the Executive Committee. Some of them were in exile, others still abroad.

In the early days the Soviet set for itself the task of spreading and consolidating the revolutionary gains. The Soviet was not a conventional parliamentary body. It functioned from day to day, without set rules. Its membership soon reached 2,000; by the middle of March it had 3,000 delegates.

It was to the Soviet that Rodzianko appealed for permission to secure a train to see the Czar; it was the Soviet that stopped the general strike, reopened the factories, and restored streetcar traffic.

At the Duma the situation was still chaotic. No one knew what would happen next. Kerensky and Chkheidze took a bold chance. They appeared on the streets and made a direct appeal to the soldiers to join the rebellion. The soldiers responded.

With their mandate from the Petrograd Soviet, Kerensky and Chkheidze now persuaded the majority to elect a Provisional Committee to take over the government. Both became members of this committee.

The walls of the city were plastered with the first issue of *Izvestia*, calling on the people to complete the overthrow of the Czarist regime.

The Czar's Council of Ministers now offered to disband. Frantically Grand Duke Mikhail telephoned Chief of Staff General Alexeiev, asking him to make an eleventh-hour appeal to the Emperor to grant a responsible Ministry. The Czar replied that he would do nothing of the kind.

In his imperial train at General Headquarters, near Moghiliev, Nicholas still did not realize what had happened. He would show a firm hand. He would appoint a dictator to put down the uprising. General Ivanov was chosen for the job. On the night of March 13 Ivanov left for the capital at the head of a detachment of presumably loyal troops. Nicholas gave orders for the imperial train to return to Tsarkoye Selo near Petrograd.

At two o'clock in the morning the train pulled into the station of Malaya Vishera, where an anxious group was waiting on the platform. "We've been ordered to reroute your train straight to Petrograd where there is some kind of a Provisional Government in power."

Quickly the imperial train started back for Pskov, where Geenral Ruzsky had his headquarters. Perhaps Ruzsky would help.

Nicholas had not yet renounced hope that Ivanov's troops would crush the rebellion.

The Empress meanwhile was in Tsarkoye Selo. She wrote to her husband: "Things are rotten. I don't know where I can reach you but I firmly believe, and nothing can shake my belief, that everything will be all right. Not knowing where you are, I tried to get in touch with you through Headquarters, as Rodzianko pretended that he did not know where and why you were detained. It is clear that they are trying to prevent you from seeing me before they make you sign some paper, a constitution or some other horrid thing, I suppose. And you, without the support of the Army, caught like a mouse in a trap, what can you do? It is the greatest meanness and vileness, unheard of in history, to detain someone's Emperor. Perhaps by showing yourself to the troops in Pskov and in other places you will rally them around yourself. If you are forced to make concessions, you don't have to feel bound to live up to them because they have been obtained under duress."

Ruzsky advised him to bow to the will of the Provisional Duma Committee. After more than an hour of argument the Czar agreed to the formation of a responsible Ministry, headed by Rodzianko. Ruzsky, then returned, asked the Emperor to countermand General Ivanov's orders. Nicholas capitulated.

The Czar made these concessions at half-past three on the morning of March 14. Ruzsky immediately notified Rodzianko. But Rodzianko was furious when he received the Czar's instructions. Had he not recommended this action weeks earlier, when it had been possible? The people now demanded the Czar's abdication.

At ten-fifteen in the morning Ruzsky once more appeared in the imperial car. Ruzsky placed before Nicholas the text of his conversation with Rodzianko. Nicholas asked Ruzsky to read it to him. Then he rose from his chair and walked over to the window. There was a moment of silence. At last Nicholas regained his self-control.

His voice did not betray excitement, but his words were almost incoherent: "If it is necessary that I step aside for the good of Russia, I am ready, but I am afraid the people will misunderstand . . . Why, the Cossacks will accuse me of quitting the firing line . . . I was born to be unhappy. I bring unhappiness to Russia. . . . But the Old Believers will never forgive me for violating the oath I gave on coronation day. . . ."

At this point a telegram arrived from General Alexeiev, the chief of staff, stating that the war could be continued only if the Czar abdicated in favor of his son, under the regency of Grand Duke Mikhail. Every moment lost would lead to further demands by the revolutionists.

Ruzsky read Alexeiev's telegram.

"What do you think about it, Nikolai Vladimirovich?" the Czar asked.

"The matter is so important," the general replied, "that I shall have to ask Your Majesty for a little more time to consider it. Let us hear what the commanding generals on the other fronts have to say."

At two o'clock Ruzsky called again, this time accompanied by two other generals.

Ruzsky reported the latest news. The Czar's own bodyguards had deserted and marched to the Duma to offer their services; the Empress had expressed a desire to confer with Rodzianko; Grand Duke Cyril Vladimirovich, heading a detachment of troops, had pledged loyalty to the Duma; the military governor of the Moscow District had accepted the authority of the Provisional Duma Committee; the Czar's Ministers were under arrest.

At half-past two came Alexeiev's wire with the answers of the commanding generals at the various fronts. All favored abdication.

There was a moment of silence. "I have made up my mind," stated the Emperor. "I am abdicating," and made the sign of the cross. The generals did the same.

On telegraph blanks he wrote two messages. One, to Rodzianko, read: "There is no sacrifice that I would not be willing to make for the welfare and salvation of Mother Russia.

Therefore I am ready to abdicate in favor of my son, under the regency of my brother Mikhail Alexandrovich, with the understanding that my son is to remain with me until he becomes of age."

The other, addressed to General Alexeiev, declared: "For the happiness and salvation of our beloved Russia I am ready to abdicate the throne in favor of my son. I request everyone to serve him faithfully and honestly."

At five o'clock in the morning of March 15, 1917, Duma Deputies Guchkov and Shulgin set out from Petrograd for Pskov with a document of abdication for the Czar's signature. Shulgin writes:

We arrived at ten o'clock at night. We stepped out on the platform. . . . Someone came up to say that the Emperor was waiting. He led us across the tracks . . . to the car of the Emperor. He appeared in a few minutes. . . . We bowed. . . . He shook hands with us in a friendly way . . . motioned us to a seat. Guchkov began to speak. . . . He was quite excited. . . . He related what was taking place at the capital. . . . He painted things as they were in Petrograd. The Emperor sat there quite composed. . . .

When Guchkov had finished, the Emperor said in a calm and matter-of-fact manner:

"I have decided to abdicate the throne . . . Until three in the afternoon I thought that I would abdicate in favor of my son Alexei. . . . But at that time I changed my mind to abdicate in favor of my brother Mikhail. . . ."

We did not expect this. It seems to me that after Guchkov raised some objections I asked for a quarter of an hour to advise with Guchkov . . . but this did not take place . . . we agreed. . . . What else could we do?

The Czar rose . . . and we all stood up. . . . Guchkov handed him his outline of the abdication act which the Emperor took, and walked out. After a little while he returned with the text of the abdication, which he handed to Guchkov.

It was then twenty minutes before midnight. The Emperor bade us good-by, shaking us by the hand . . . and his attitude was, if anything, warmer than when we arrived. . . . We returned to our car . . . and in the morning reached Petrograd.

In Petrograd, the Duma Committee and the Executive Committee of the Soviet had, in the meantime, appointed the members of the new Provisional Government. Heading the Cabinet was Prince George Lvov, President of the All-Russian Union of Zemstvos and Municipalities; Professor Paul Miliukov, leader of the Cadet Party, was named Foreign Minister; Alexander Guchkov, Minister of War, and Alexander Kerensky, Minister of Justice.

Nicholas's abdication came too late. The Soviet of Workers' and Soldiers' Deputies refused to recognize the continuation of the dynasty.

On March 16, at six o'clock in the morning, Kerensky telephoned the Grand Duke to inform him that the members of
the Duma Committee, headed by Rodzianko, wished to talk
with him. The committee, with the exception of Miliukov, all
agreed that the Grand Duke should be persuaded to decline
the throne.

Rodzianko presented the view of the majority. Miliukov
then argued that the establishment of order required a suitable
symbol of power to which the Russian people were accus-
tomed; namely, a monarch.

After several hours of deliberation, the Grand Duke decided to waive his right to the throne.

Alexandra meanwhile still hoped for a repetition of 1905
when Nicholas, after granting a constitution and civil liberties, had revoked his promise and crushed the Revolution.
She wrote on March 16:

I quite understand your action, my hero. I know that you could
not have signed anything that was contrary to your oath given at
the coronation. We understand each other perfectly without words,
and I swear, upon my life, that we shall see you again on the
throne, raised there once more by your people, and your army,
for the glory of your reign. You saved the empire for your son
and the country, as well as your sacred purity, and you shall be
crowned by God himself on earth in your own land.

The Petrograd Soviet of Workers' and Soldiers' Deputies
was now the most important body in Russia. It recognized the
authority of the Provisional Government, after the latter
pledged itself to carry out eight basic recommendations,
framed by the Duma Provisional Committee and the Soviet
Executive Committee. These provided full and immediate
amnesty for all political prisoners and exiles; freedom of
speech, press, assembly, and strikes; the abolition of all class,
group, and religious restrictions; the election of a Constituent
Assembly by universal secret balloting to determine the form
of government and adopt a constitution for Russia; the sub-
stitution of the police by a national militia, subject to the local
authorities; democratic elections of officials for municipalites
and townships; the retention in Petrograd, fully armed, of the
military units that had taken part in the Revolution; the exten-
sion of civil liberties to the soldiers subject to military discipline while in the performance of duty.

For the moment, the popular idol was Kerensky. Although
the only Socialist in the first revolutionary government, he
also represented the Soviet of Workers' and Soldiers' Deputies.
He was known as an eloquent defense attorney at political
trials. His investigation into the massacre of the strikers at the
Lena gold mines had added to his reputation. He had entered

the Duma as a champion of labor and became one of the leaders of the moderate Socialist wing.

Although the first Provisional Government was largely "bourgeois," it had to bow to the Soviet, whose majority were Mensheviks and Socialist Revolutionaries. Most of these men regarded the Provisional Government as a regime of the propertied classes. The Soviet was determined to steer the Revolution along a course that would bring major social changes as well as political freedom. On March 15, 1917, the Petrograd Soviet issued an order which instructed the troops not to obey orders of their officers unless countersigned by the Petrograd Soviet, and to organize local Soviets in every army unit. This order dealt a deathblow to military discipline.

Kerensky at first served as the link uniting the moderates of the Duma and the radicals of the Soviet. He traveled through the country rallying the people to the support of the new government.

"I see," he said, at a meeting of army units in Odessa, "the great enthusiasm which has swept the entire country. Such miracles as the Russian Revolution which transform slaves into free men happen but once in a century.

"We have suffered enough. And the hearts of all the people of Russia throb with one feeling. Let us throw all our energies into the struggle for peace for the whole world. We believe in the happiness and the glorious freedom of all nations."

Professor Eugene Trubetskoy, a moderate liberal, wrote:

This revolution is unique. There have been bourgeois revolutions and proletarian revolutions, but I doubt if there has ever been a revolution so truly national, in the widest sense of the term, as the present Russian one. Everybody made this revolution. Everyone took part in it—the workers, the soldiers, the bourgeois, even the nobility—all the social forces of the land.

This was the spirit that animated the March Revolution which overnight transformed Russia into what Lenin, in *Pravda* of April 20, 1917, called "the freest country in the world."

9 LENIN'S ROAD TO PETROGRAD

THE ACTUAL NEWS OF THE RUSSIAN REVOLUTION CAME AS A surprise to Lenin. In March 1917 the majority of the Bolshevik leaders were either abroad or in Siberian exile. Zinoviev, Semashko, Lunacharsky, Litvinov, Chicherin, Ganetsky, Radek, Riazanov, Madame Kollontai, and Larin had been living abroad for years, some in Switzerland, others in London and Paris. Bukharin was in New York, editing an émigré newspaper with Trotsky. Stalin, Kamenev, and Sverdlov were in Siberia.

When Bronsky, an old comrade, rushed into Lenin's room with the breathtaking report from Petrograd, Lenin refused to believe him until the Zurich newspapers confirmed the news. From that moment his whole energy was directed toward one objective: to reach Petrograd as fast as possible. Every hour mattered; out of fragmentary accounts he had already begun to piece together the new alignment of revolutionary forces. He could see the outlines of the battles ahead, inside his own party and against the others. And he had little faith in the ability of his Bolshevik lieutenants in Russia to steer the right course.

From all parts of Europe and America, from the wastelands of Siberia and Asiatic Russia, all roads led to Petrograd in the spring of 1917. The army of returning expatriates included men and women of every brand, veteran revolutionists, liberals, Socialists, peasants, students, and radical intellectuals; men who had spent years in Czarist prisons and at Siberian hard labor; thousands of students and workers who had been swept almost by chance into the earlier maelstrom of 1905.

All roads led to Petrograd, for the amnesty granted by the Provisional Government was universal. This was Russia's hour of supreme liberty, and Petrograd, shedding its last thin blanket of snow, was the festive tribune of the liberated Russian people.

The first important Bolsheviks to reach Petrograd were Stalin, Kamenev, Muranov, and Sverdlov, who completed the journey from Siberia before the end of March. They arrived while the political honeymoon was still on, and they became infected with its spirit. But in the offices of *Pravda*, the organ of the Bolshevik Party, which had resumed publication immediately after the fall of the Czar, they found a different attitude. Molotov and Shliapnikov, the provisional editors of the paper, were attacking the Provisional Government.

Quickly Stalin, Kamenev, and Muranov superseded the acting editorial board, the first issue under their direction appearing on March 28. Under the new triumvirate *Pravda* adopted a conciliatory attitude toward the government and the other Socialist parties. While Lenin and Trotsky, independently of each other, were summoning the proletariat to war against the Provisional Government, and demanding immediate action to halt the war, Stalin adopted a very cautious position.

On March 27 the Petrograd Soviet unanimously adopted a manifesto addressed to "the people of the whole world," which interpreted the March Revolution as a step toward a democratic peace based on the defeat of Imperial Germany. This manifesto was a far cry from Lenin's interpretation of the war as a purely imperialist struggle between two contending evils. Of this manifesto Stalin wrote in *Pravda* of March 28:

The mere slogan: "Down with the war" is absolutely impractical. As long as the German Army obeys the orders of the Kaiser, the Russian soldier must stand firmly at his post, answering bullet with bullet and shell with shell. . . . It is impossible not to greet yesterday's manifesto of the Soviet of Workers' and Soldiers' Deputies issued to the masses of the world, urging them to compel their governments to call a halt to this wholesale slaughter. . . . Our slogan is pressure on the Provisional Government with the aim of compelling it . . . to make an attempt to induce all the warring countries to open immediate negotiations. . . . And until then every man remains at his fighting post!

According to Shliapnikov, the new *Pravda* threw consternation into the Bolshevik ranks. The Tauride Palace buzzed with news that "the moderate reasonable Bolsheviks have been victorious over the extremists in their own Party!" In the Executive Committee of the Soviet the Bolsheviks were received "with poisonous smiles."

In various Bolshevik headquarters workers met to demand that Stalin, Kamenev, and Muranov be expelled from the Party. The following day, March 29, Stalin told the Petrograd Conference of the Bolshevik Party:

"The Provisional Government, unwilling though it may be, and with wavering and faltering footsteps, has taken upon itself to fortify the gains already won by the revolutionary masses. Such a situation has both its negative and positive aspects. It is not to our advantage to force the march of events and quicken the process of sifting from our midst the bourgeois elements which must later leave our ranks. To the extent that the Provisional Government fortifies the march of the Revolution, we must support it. To the extent that it is counter-revolutionary, we cannot support it."

The official conference minutes read: "On the agenda of the day is Tseretelli's proposal for unity."

"Stalin: We must agree to this. It is necessary to decide upon our propositions on the question of unity. Unity is possible on the platform of Zimmerwald."

When Molotov arose to voice his dissent, Stalin replied: "It is not necessary to anticipate and prevent differences of opinion. As members of one Party our small differences of opinion will fade away." That was Stalin's position in March 1917. It was shared by many Left Mensheviks and Bolsheviks. But not by Lenin.

On March 20, still in Zurich, Lenin wrote the first of his *Letters from Afar*. When it appeared in *Pravda* on April 3 it signalized a complete break with the conciliatory line adopted by Stalin and Kamenev.

According to Lenin the apparent ease with which the dynasty was overthrown was owing to the "conspiracy of the Anglo-French imperialists who were pushing Miliukov, Guchkov and Co. to seize power in order to prolong the imperialist war, in order to wage it more ferociously and tenaciously, in order to slay fresh millions of Russian workers and peasants, so as to obtain possession of Constantinople for Guchkov, Syria for the French, and Mesopotamia . . . for the British capitalists, et cetera."

On the same day Trotsky wrote in his New York newspaper *Novy Mir:*

"The Czar's government is no more," the Guchkovs and Miliukovs are telling the people. "Now you must pour out your blood for the all-national interests." But by national interests the Russian imperialists mean the recovery of Poland. the conquest of Galicia, Constantinople, Armenia, Persia. In other words, Russia now takes her place in the joint ranks of imperialism with other European states, and first of all with her allies, England and France.

On March 24 Lenin wrote another *Letter from Afar* summoning the proletariat to organize a militia, 750,000 strong, to combat "the Guchkovs and Miliukovs, the landowners and capitalists." He called for the repudiation of Russia's treaties with the Allies, the publication of all secret agreements, and the proclamation of new peace terms, including the liberation of all colonies and the summons to workers of all countries to depose their governments and transfer all power to Councils of Workers' Deputies.

These letters went to Ganetsky in neutral Stockholm. Ganetsky forwarded them to Lenin's sister Maria in Petrograd.

Lenin was still in Zurich and there were obstacles delaying his return to Russia. The Provisional Government offered no objection to the homecoming of its sworn enemy, but the British and French were reluctant to grant him a transit visa and travel facilities.

But Lenin was not in Switzerland for long. If the Allies would not help him return to Russia for the purpose of overthrowing the Provisional Government and concluding peace with Germany, Berlin would.

Ironically enough, it was Martov who first proposed that Russian Revolutionists should return via Germany in exchange for German prisoners of war.

Shortly after Martov made his proposal for a Russo-German exchange, Robert Grimm, the Swiss Social Democrat, volunteered his services. He dropped out of the picture, however, when the Mensheviks refused to act without the consent of the Executive Committee of the Soviet. Lenin had told Grimm that "his party had decided unconditionally to accept the proposal for the passage of the Russian émigrés and to organize that journey immediately."

At this point only ten émigrés were willing to go along without the consent of the Petrograd Soviet. "The Mensheviks," Lenin cabled Ganetsky in Stockholm, "demand the approval of the Executive Committee of the Soviet."

When Grimm refused to continue negotiations on this basis Fritz Platten, another Socialist "internationalist," entered the picture. "Platten," said the official Bolshevik statement, "concluded a definite agreement with the German Ambassador in Switzerland, of which the main points were the following: First, that all the émigrés should go, irrespective of their attitude toward the war; second, that the train in which they were to travel was to be an extraterritorial one; finally, that all passengers should agitate in Russia for the subsequent exchange of an equal number of Austro-German prisoners interned in Russia."

That is as far as the official version goes. General Hoffmann, chief of the German General Staff on the Eastern Front, described the German objective in concrete terms:

"We naturally tried, by means of propaganda, to increase the disintegration that the Russian Revolution had introduced into the Army. Some man at home who had connections with the Russian revolutionaries exiled in Switzerland came upon the idea of employing some of them in order to hasten the undermining and poisoning of the morale of the Russian Army.

"He applied to Deputy Erzberger and the deputy of the German Foreign Office. And thus it came about that Lenin was conveyed through Germany to Petrograd in the manner that afterward transpired."

Who was the *"man at home who had connections with the Russian revolutionaries exiled in Switzerland"*? It was Parvus who had suggested that the admission of Lenin and the Socialist extremists into Russia could be put to good use by Germany. Parvus's proposal was supported by Count von Maltzan and Erzberger, then the chief of German military propaganda. They convinced Chancellor Bethmann-Hollweg, who accordingly advised the General Staff of Parvus's "brilliant maneuver."

While Parvus was completing the arrangements through the Wilhelmstrasse, Paul Levi, a German anti-war Socialist who belonged to the Spartacist Union (the forerunner of the German Communist Party), was handling the Berne-Zurich end of negotiations. After conferring with Lenin and Radek in Zurich, Levi requested the Berne correspondent of the *Frankfurter Zeitung* to take up the matter with the German Ambassador in Switzerland. The Ambassador promised to check with Berlin.

The following evening, while Levi was in the People's House, he was called to the telephone. The voice at the other end of the line was the German Ambassador's:

"I've been looking for you all over town," he said. "How can I get in touch with Lenin? I expect final instructions any moment regarding his transportation."

From the tone of his voice he realized that Berlin considered the matter most urgent. When he conveyed the Ambassador's message to Lenin, the latter feverishly began to jot down the terms on which he—Lenin—would agree to travel through Germany! Lenin dictated the conditions. All of them were accepted. The road to Petrograd was open.

When news leaked out that Lenin had agreed to travel through Germany, without awaiting the approval of the Petrograd Soviet, it caused an uproar among Socialists in Switzerland and France. At meetings of the Russian émigrés Lenin and his followers were denounced.

At the station two days later, a large crowd of Russian émigrés and Swiss and Italian workers came to see Lenin and his companions off. In his immediate party were Zinoviev, Radek, Krupskaya, Karpinsky, and several other Bolsheviks. But the party also included some twenty non-Bolsheviks. Lenin had insisted on their traveling with him in order to offset the unfavorable impression produced by his trip under German auspices. Lenin's supporters milled around the waiting train carrying revolutionary banners and singing the "Internationale"; his enemies, a group of anti-German Socialists, shouted, "Spies! German spies! Look how happy they are—going home at the Kaiser's expense!"

Lenin stood at the window of his compartment, supporting his chin on the ledge, and shaking his head with a smile.

On April 13, Ganetsky received this telegram from Lenin:

TRELLEBORG AT 6 P.M. TODAY.

Ganetsky met Lenin at Malmö. As they embraced each other, there were tears in Ganetsky's eyes. A few hours later they were in a special car bound for Stockholm. In Lenin's compartment sat Ganetsky, Krupskaya, and Zinoviev. They talked late into the night, Lenin pumping Ganetsky for the latest news from Petrograd.

Parvus did not meet Lenin, but conveyed the message that it was urgent to begin working for peace negotiations at once. Lenin replied that his business was revolutionary agitation, not diplomacy.

10 SPRING THUNDER

A GREAT CROWD GATHERED IN THE TWILIGHT OF THE FINLAND
Station in Petrograd on April 16, 1917. Workers, soldiers,
sailors, and representatives of various revolutionary organizations, carrying red banners, made up the milling throng.
At last the resounding clang of the first bell was heard. A moment later the brilliantly illuminated cars glided into view.

Lenin was the first to alight. A group of workers quickly
hoisted him on their shoulders and carried him into the
"People's Room" (formerly the Czar's Room) of the Finland Station. From all sides the crowd surged forward, shouting greetings to the revolutionists who had returned to the
liberated capital.

Lenin strode quickly to the middle of the room, and stopped
short before Chkheidze, the chairman of the Petrograd Soviet.

"Comrade Lenin," said Chkheidze, "we welcome you to
Russia in the name of the Petrograd Soviet and the Revolution. . . . But we believe that the chief task of the revolutionary democracy at present is to defend our revolution
against every kind of attack both from within and without.
. . . We hope that you will join us in striving toward this
goal."

Lenin stood there as though Chkheidze's words did not concern him in the least. His eyes traveled from one side of the
room to the other, taking in the crowd; and finally, turning
away from Chkheidze and the members of the Executive Committee of the Soviet, he addressed the crowd:

"Dear comrades, soldiers, sailors, and workers, I am happy
to greet you in the name of the victorious Russian Revolution,
to greet you as the vanguard of the international proletarian
army. . . . The hour is not far off when, at the summons of
our Comrade Karl Liebknecht [the German Spartacist leader],
the people will turn their weapons against their capitalist exploiters. . . . The Russian Revolution, achieved by you, has
opened a new epoch. Long live the world-wide Socialist Revolution!"

From the Finland Station Lenin was escorted to the Bolshevik Headquarters in the palace of Kshesinskaya.

Outside, a throng of soldiers and sailors was waiting. Speaking from the second-story balcony, Lenin assured them that
the Russian Revolution marked the beginning of an international uprising by the toiling masses everywhere.

Lenin then returned to the salon where the leaders of the
Bolshevik Party were assembled. With a faint smile of contempt, he listened to their speeches. Then he rose and bitterly

assailed them for having given tentative support to the government during his absence in Switzerland.

"No support for the Provisional Government," were practically his first words. His complete break with the line taken by Stalin and Kamenev and his uncompromising tone left his lieutenants gasping.

After lashing out at his own followers, Lenin disassociated himself from the non-Bolshevik majority in the Soviet, consigning them to the enemy camp.

"Only the Zimmerwald Left stands guard over the proletarian revolution!" cried Lenin. "The rest are the same old opportunists speaking pretty words but in reality betraying the cause of Socialism and the working masses."

While the Bolshevik high command was still reeling under his merciless attack, Lenin restated the basic points of his program. He minced no words. Kamenev, who presided, summed up the general Bolshevik reaction to Lenin's speech.

"We may agree or disagree with Lenin's view," he said. "We may not follow him in his evaluation of this or that particular situation, but in any case in the person of Lenin there has returned to Russia the recognized leader of our Party and together with him we shall move forward to Socialism."

Lenin himself paid his first visit not to the Tauride Palace but to his mother's grave. No sooner had he settled in the Kshesinsky Palace than he phoned for a car and drove out to the cemetery.

When the circumstances of Lenin's return became generally known, it caused resentment among large segments of Petrograd's sailors, soldiers, students, and workers. On April 17 the sailors of the Second Baltic Fleet passed a resolution condemning Lenin for accepting German help. In the barracks of the Volinsky regiment the question of Lenin's arrest was discussed. Many other soldiers' meetings demanded that the Provisional Government investigate the facts behind Lenin's trip through Imperial Germany.

The union of gymnasium students staged a demonstration against Lenin outside the Kshesinsky Palace, and a delegation of wounded soldiers and sailors appeared with placards reading "Lenin and company—back to Germany!"

The condition of Russia upon Lenin's arrival was far from a stable one. With the fall of the monarchy Russia experienced a profound psychological shock. The entire population was suddenly swept, in Kerensky's words, by a "sense of unlimited freedom, a liberation from the most elementary restraints essential to every human society." At the same time, the people were overcome by a terrible weariness, an utter exhaustion after the strain of three years of war. The reaction expressed itself in a general paralysis of the will. The workers in the factories ceased to work, the soldiers at the front ceased fighting.

"The people lost the capacity to obey. The authorities were no longer capable of giving directions and issuing commands. . . . In the factories the workers began to roll out in wheelbarrows the especially hateful directors and engineers. In many places the peasants seized the land without waiting for government action. At the front, desertions reached disastrous proportions. The soldiers held meetings from morning till night, and the entire officer corps fell under suspicion. On March 13 the sailors in Kronstadt had killed the commander of the Baltic fleet and a number of officers. Other officers were arrested and incarcerated. In the cities a wave of lynchings, robberies and lawlessness broke out as the apparatus of local government ceased to function." It required tremendous effort on the part of the new authorities to prevent collapse.

On the morning following Lenin's return to Petrograd a general Social Democratic conference was held in the Tauride Palace to discuss for the last time the possible union of all factions into a single party. Here Lenin delivered an uncompromising speech, echoing the hard line he had already laid down to his Bolshevik comrades, and putting a quick end to any hope of unity.

When Lenin concluded his speech, Joseph Goldenberg, a former member of the Bolshevik Central Committee who had just returned from exile, took the floor. He knew Lenin well, had worked with him, and had enjoyed his respect. Containing his anger with difficulty, he declared:

"The place left vacant by the great anarchist, Bakunin, who for many years had no worthy successor, is now occupied. Everything we have just heard is a complete repudiation of the entire Social Democratic doctrine, of the whole theory of scientific Marxism. We have just heard a clear and unequivocal declaration for anarchism. Its herald, the heir of Bakunin, is Lenin. Lenin the Marxist, Lenin the leader of our fighting Social Democratic Party, is no more. A new Lenin is born, Lenin the anarchist." Goldenberg exhorted his audience to fight against the new danger caused by the arrival of Russia's "friends from abroad." George Steklov, who was to become the editor of *Izvestia* under Lenin's regime, spoke in much the same spirit.

These unfavorable reactions to Lenin's return and to his first words before the Soviet lulled the leaders of the Provisional Government into a false sense of security. They believed that the very fact that Lenin had been "imported" into Russia with German assistance would destroy the power of Bolshevik propaganda. On April 17 Skobelev assured the Cabinet that Lenin was a "has-been who stands outside the ranks of the movement."

This complete miscalculation of Lenin's strength was perhaps best illustrated in the diary entry made by Maurice

Paleologue, the French Ambassador to Petrograd, on April
18, 1917. "This morning," he wrote, "[Foreign Minister]
Miliukov told me . . . that 'Lenin had completely failed at
the Soviets yesterday. He went to such an extreme, so in-
solently and clumsily defended his thesis on immediate peace,
that the hissing forced him to step down and leave. From this
he will never recover.' " To which Paleologue wisely added:
"Let us hope so, I told him, but I am afraid lest Miliukov once
more be punished for his optimism."

According to Vladimir Zenzinov, a Socialist Revolutionary
member of the Central Executive Committee of the Soviet,
only one man—Alexander Kerensky—dissented sharply from
the general opinion that Lenin represented no threat to the
March Revolution. He recalls that within a few days after
Lenin's arrival Kerensky told him, "This man will destroy the
Revolution."

A few days after the stormy meeting in the Tauride Palace
Lenin summoned a council of his former Bolshevik colleagues,
men who had once stood with him, but whose present attitude
was ambiguous.

"Lenin," says Sukhanov, "called in his old marshals, not to
discuss the situation and convince them. He wanted to know
whether they believed in his new truth, whether they were in
accord with his plans and would be useful to him. The marshals spoke. Not one of them expressed his support. . . . Not
one proved himself useful for his needs. Lenin silently heard
the 'traitors' and let them go their way."

Two days later *Pravda* published Lenin's famous *April
Theses*. In this sharp outline of his program for action Lenin
frankly called for civil war as a means of ending the war
between nations.

"How shall we end war?" he asked, and replied:

. . . The war was caused by the development of world capital
for the last fifty years, the millions of threads and filaments that
enter into its fabric. You cannot get away from the imperialistic
character of the war. It is impossible to make a democratic peace,
one that is not imposed by force, without destroying the power of
capitalism. It is only by breaking through this front that the
proletariat can advance its own interests as a class.

In order to bring permanent end to war, it was essential that
the proletariat take power. In Russia, the weapon for waging war
against capitalism existed in the form of the Soviet of Workers'
and Soldiers' Deputies.

The Russian Revolution of March 1917 was the beginning of
that process which was to change the imperialistic war into a civil
war. This revolution made the first step toward stopping the war.
But then a second step is necessary to make the cessation of war
permanent, and that is for the proletariat to take the reins of
power. This will serve as the beginning of the world-wide "break-

ing through" the front of capitalist interests, and only by breaking through this front can the proletariat free mankind from the horror of war and secure for it the blessings of a lasting peace.

He now supported the Soviet instead of the parliamentary democracy which he had advocated until the March Revolution. To emphasize his complete break with the past, Lenin urged dropping the name Social Democratic Party in favor of Communist Party.

"The majority of the 'Social Democratic' leaders . . . of the 'Social Democratic' parliamentarians and the 'Social Democratic' papers which are the means of influencing the masses, have betrayed Socialism, have proved unfaithful to Socialism, and have deserted to the side of their 'own' national bourgeoisie.

"The broad masses of the people are indignant over it and feel that they have been deceived by their own leaders.

"What we want is to build the whole world over again. We want to end the imperialist war and save the hundreds of millions of people who have been drawn into it and in which billions of dollars have been invested and which cannot be terminated by a general democratic peace without a proletarian revolution—the greatest in the history of mankind!"

Lenin's *Theses,* in the words of an old Bolshevik, had the force of an "exploding bomb." A few days after their publication the editors of *Pravda* wrote:

"As for Lenin's general scheme, it seems to us unacceptable in that it starts from the assumption that the bourgeois revolution is ended, and counts on an immediate transforming of this revolution into a Socialist revolution."

The *Theses* met considerable opposition among Lenin's most intimate party comrades. Lenin answered his opponents point by point, driving home his views in many articles, pamphlets, and speeches. His vigorous line gradually won an increasing number of adherents in the Bolshevik Party.

Adding to Lenin's initial difficulties, the Malinovsky affair now came back to life. For when the Provisional Government opened the secret files of the Okhrana, the facts were only too clear. Malinovsky worked for the Okhrana under the name of Portnoy. He reported all important Bolshevik meetings, disclosed the identity of Bolshevik leaders who carried false passports, and gave the location of underground party presses. He was directly responsible for the arrest of the Bolshevik Central Committee in 1910. He furnished detailed reports on the activities of the editorial offices of *Pravda* and supplied Beletsky with a list of *Pravda's* financial supporters and subscribers. He was responsible for the arrest of Stalin and Sverdlov, as well as Troyanovsky's wife.

When Malinovsky was installed in the Duma, Beletsky, the

Okhrana chief raised his pay from five hundred to seven hundred rubles a month, in addition to paying him generous bonuses for particularly valuable information. He had a direct wire to Beletsky and met him regularly in the private rooms of the better restaurants of St. Petersburg. Malinovsky also furnished the Okhrana with the confidential memoranda of the Social Democratic Duma caucus, as well as advance proof sheets of all *Pravda* articles, which Beletsky personally edited. Chernomazov, the nominal editor of *Pravda*, was no obstacle to these operations. He, too, was an Okhrana agent!

Confronted with these nasty facts, Lenin admitted that Malinovsky was an Okhrana agent, but explained:

"Malinovsky could and did destroy a number of individuals. But as for the growth of the Party in the sense of increasing its importance and influence on the people by the tens and hundreds of thousands, that growth could not be stopped, controlled, or directed by Malinovsky."

In the light of Lenin's ferocious attacks on Martov and others, this was a lame apology, but the concluding chapter was still to be written.

Despite the storms, large and small, that raged about him, when the All-Russian Bolshevik Party Conference met from May 7 to 12, 1917, Lenin was in complete command and the main resolutions that were adopted followed his *April Theses*.

Although for the Party as a whole this settled the big issues in Lenin's favor, some of the Bolshevik leaders continued to oppose him. Dzerzhinsky, the coming chief of the Soviet secret police, demanded that a dissenting report be heard from the "comrades who along with us have had the practical experience of the Revolution." Kamenev delivered a dissenting report in defense of the "bourgeois" democratic state. Kalinin continued to advocate a coalition with the Mensheviks against the Duma Liberals. Smidovich, a Moscow Bolshevik, complained that "every time we speak they raise against us a bogy in the form of Comrade Lenin's *Theses*." Stalin remained silent.

Notwithstanding these reservations by leading Bolsheviks, the conference branded the Provisional Government as a "government of landowners and capitalists," and rejected the proposal of unity with the "patriotic Mensheviks." At the same time the conference denied that the Bolsheviks sought or would seek a separate peace with Germany.

After this declaration of principles there were some resignations from the Party, including Lenin's old comrade in arms, Vladimir Woytinsky. Kamenev, despite his opposition, did not leave the Party.

The rank and file did not quite understand what Lenin meant by the slogan "All Power to the Soviets." To the masses, the Soviets elected by the workers, peasants, and soldiers, represented the will of the democratic revolution. To Lenin, however, the slogan "All Power to the Soviets" was brilliant cover for his real objective: the dictatorship of the Bolshevik Party. While the Petrograd Soviet was packed with Kronstadt sailors and Bolshevik troops, he could hope for that momentary advantage which he would pursue to power. But Lenin not only concealed his aim from the masses, but from his own general staff as well.

After the conference, the Bolsheviks stepped up their propaganda. By the end of May a large proportion of the workers' section of the Petrograd Soviet was pro-Bolshevik, and a number of units of the Petrograd garrison were also veering toward Lenin.

Lenin's cause was aided by the major blunder of Foreign Minister Miliukov. On May 1 Miliukov instructed the Russian diplomatic representatives to transmit a note in which he promised that the Russian people would fight on together with their Allies until a "decisive victory" over Germany had been won.

Miliukov's note immediately aroused a storm of protest. Demonstrations were held demanding Miliukov's resignation.

The Soviet called on the people to rally around the regional Soviets which were springing up all over the country. The Soviet leaders firmly believed that the peoples of all the belligerent nations could compel their governments to begin negotiations for peace without annexations or indemnities.

On May 8 the Executive Committee of the Soviet voted to summon an International Socialist Conference representing all parties and factions of the working class that accepted the proposed peace platform of the Soviet. A delegation representing the Soviet Executive Committee was to go abroad at once to establish contacts in neutral and Allied countries and to meet with delegations of Dutch and Swedish Socialists in Stockholm in order to prepare for the International Conference.

But the storm provoked by Miliukov's declaration of Russian war aims made it clear that there were two governments in Petrograd. And the result of dual power was mounting demoralization at the front and at home. A coalition representing the Provisional Government and the Soviet was essential. On May 12 Guchkov resigned as Minister of War; six days later Miliukov left the Provisional Government. Premier Lvov then called on the Soviet leaders to join in the Cabinet.

On May 17 a coalition was formed by Lvov with Kerensky as Minister of War and Navy, and five Socialists in the cabinet. Included among them were Victor Chernov, leader of the Socialist Revolutionary Party, and Tseretelli, leader of the Mensheviks.

This coalition gave Russia a far more representative regime.

The new Cabinet reflected the rising anti-bourgeois tide. But it did not command the strength or authority to govern with a firm hand. The floodgates of revolution were still wide open. Promises to strive for a peace without indemnities or annexations, while at the same time honoring Russia's obligations as an ally of France, Great Britain, and the United States (which had just entered the war), did not appease the restless troops of Petrograd, some 150,000 strong. The mere hint of dispatching these units to the front to relieve the pressure on their hard-pressed comrades was enough to start a new insurrection.

The Socialist and liberal leadership, and some of the veteran skilled workers of Petrograd, formed the slender dyke of moderation and restraint. Pounding against this dyke was a tidal wave of discontented soldiers, turbulent sailors of Kronstadt, and the peasant masses. They responded to the promise of immediate salvation through still more revolution. The Revolution's need for violence had not spent itself. The Socialist leaders of the Provisional Government and of the Petrograd Soviet were trying vainly to mold the furious emotional drive of the revolutionary mass into a pattern of placid democratic faith. After three hundred years of Romanov rule and three years of war and privation they addressed the Russian people in language that would have been more appropriate before an audience of British trade unionists.

In Lenin's battle slogans the restless mass heard its own voice, expressing its piled-up resentment against the whole bourgeois world.

Nowhere was the irrepressible conflict between these crosscurrents in the Russian Revolution more vividly expressed than in the debate between Lenin and Kerensky at the All-Russian Congress of the Soviets which opened in Petrograd on June 16, 1917.

It was at this Congress that the fatal dualism inherent in Russian revolutionary Socialism, since the days of Herzen, Lavrov, and Bakunin, found its most articulate expression.

Lenin addressed this assembly on June 17. After acclaiming the Soviet as the modern counterpart of the French Revolutionary Convention of 1792, Lenin demanded that the Soviet act at once to wrest all power from the Provisional Government.

Then Kerensky replied. He warned his audience that the road which Lenin recommended would lead to the end of the Russian people's newly won liberties and to the dismemberment of the country:

"You recommend that we follow the road of the French Revolution of 1792. You recommend the way of further disorganization of the country. . . . When you, in alliance with reaction, shall destroy our power, then you will have a real dictator. It is our duty, the duty of the Russian democracy, to say: Don't repeat the historic mistakes. You are asked to follow the road that was once followed by France, and which will lead Russia to a new reaction, to a new shedding of democratic blood."

But it was Lenin, not Kerensky, who received an ovation from the soldiers and sailors who made up the bulk of the audience. A few days later, however, the Bolsheviks overshot their mark.

While the Congress was in session Bolshevik posters were plastered on walls of the working-class districts of the capital summoning the proletariat to demonstrate on the afternoon of June 23 against the "counter-revolution."

On the morning of June 22 Chkheidze told the Soviet Congress that the demonstrations scheduled for the following afternoon had been secretly planned for days; that a number of military units, including the First Machine Gun Regiment, would participate; that unless the demonstrations were called off there would be bitter fighting in the streets of Petrograd.

Krylenko protested against any action by the Soviet Congress in the absence of the Bolshevik leaders. Nevertheless the Soviet voted to rush its delegates to the factories and barracks to cancel the demonstration. The delegates spent the entire night making the rounds of factories and military installations.

When the Soviet Congress convened at eight o'clock on the morning of June 23, they learned that the Central Committee of the Bolshevik Party had decided, after a night-long discussion, to call off the march. *Pravda* appeared that morning with large white spaces on page one; the Bolshevik proclamation calling on the workers to demonstrate had been pulled out at the last moment.

Trotsky put in an appearance at the morning session of the Soviet, but, despite the demand of many delegates, refused to state his position. It was Kamenev's unpleasant job to speak in the name of the Bolshevik Party. Nervously he protested that the Bolsheviks had had no intention of starting a revolt and claimed that the Party had bowed to the will of the Soviet majority.

Tseretelli, however, rose to deliver an impassioned attack against the Bolshevik Party. For the first time this Socialist leader spoke of the Bolsheviks as conspirators.

On June 26 *Pravda* ran a story headlined "The Truth about the Demonstration," labeling Tseretelli's charges against the Bolsheviks a complete lie. Nevertheless, when the details of the proposed demonstration were later revealed, it was learned that the Bolsheviks had actually planned a march on the Mariensky Palace, headquarters of the Provisional Government, led by Bolshevik workers' battalions and pro-Bolshevik troops. Picked groups were to invade the offices of the Ministers, while party orators outside would work up the fury of the crowd. At the proper psychological moment the members of the Provisional Government would be arrested. The Central Committee of the Bolshevik Party, acting in the name of the Soviet, would then proclaim itself the new government of Russia.

The full facts of this abortive Bolshevik plot did not become known until much later. In June 1917 they played the role of offended innocents.

The effect of the June fiasco was to give the Mensheviks and the Socialist Revolutionaries the temporary upper hand in the Soviet. For the moment Lenin's prestige was damaged; his Party had to fall back in retreat under a smoke screen of alibis and countercharges. On the other hand the Socialists were not prepared to take energetic action against their former comrades. And this was a vital lesson.

Before regrouping his forces for the next move, Lenin left Petrograd for a vacation at the home of his old friend, Vladimir Bonch-Bruyevich, who lived in the village of Neivola on the Finnish railroad. The last three months had exhausted him completely. After ten years as a political émigré, the feverish pace of revolutionary Petrograd and the excitement of battle had sapped his strength.

In this quiet countryside Lenin would lie on a blanket for hours in the shade without reading. Sleep and rest gradually restored his health.

But on July 17, at about six in the morning, there was a rap on the window. Bonch-Bruyevich looked out and saw the smiling face of his party comrade, Saveliev.

"What has happened?"

"There is an uprising in Petrograd."

Crowds of demonstrators were marching on the Duma and the Tauride Palace, Saveliev reported; shots were heard in the streets; there were rumors that the government was mobilizing troops and an armed clash was awaited at any moment.

Lenin was aroused from his sleep with difficulty.

"I must go," he said, as soon as he heard the news. Perhaps the decisive hour had come.

11 THE JULY UPRISING

FOR WEEKS PRECEDING THE JULY UPRISING BOLSHEVIK AGITATORS were working feverishly among front-line troops, sailors of the Baltic fleet, the garrison troops in the main cities, and among the peasants. Soldiers were urged to fraternize with the Germans, peasants to seize the land without waiting for the Constituent Assembly. Bolshevik Army newspapers (*Soldat-*

skaya Pravda, Okopnaya Pravda, et cetera), distributed at the front and read in the trenches, told the troops to lay down their rifles and go home to their villages.

On June 29 Kerensky, as Minister of War, called on the officers and soldiers of the Russian Army to strike hard at the enemy in a grand offensive on the southwestern front; the Central Executive Committee of the Soviets supported Kerensky with an appeal to the armed forces. On July 1, 1917, General Brusilov launched an attack on the Galician front. For a short time the Russians scored impressive gains, but the offensive soon spent itself. By July 19 the Germans were counterattacking on a large scale and meeting only half-hearted resistance.

Among the troops of Petrograd and the Kronstadt sailors the Kerensky offensive was unpopular from the start, and new revolt was in the air before Brusilov's drive petered out.

On the night of July 15 the Central Committee of the Bolshevik Party held a stormy meeting. The situation was similar to that of June 23. An uprising was already under way, and the question was whether to give it full Bolshevik support or yield once more to the Soviet.

The Central Committee debated all night whether the Bolshevik Party should officially assume command of the uprising. In the evening the question was decided in the affirmative and a proclamation to that effect was drafted for publication in *Pravda.* But as incoming reports from various parts of the city indicated that the Provisional Government was taking energetic steps to quell the uprising, the Bolshevik leaders backed down. The *Pravda* proclamation, which had not only been set up in type but also cast, was cut from the matrix. On the following day *Pravda* again appeared with a large blank space on its front page.

Although the Central Committee decided to back down, orders for the mobilization of Kronstadt, issued earlier that day, were not canceled. Armed sailors landed in Petrograd, formed ranks, and marched to the headquarters of the Bolshevik Party.

The arrival of the Kronstadt sailors changed the atmosphere of the capital. Again it seemed that the Provisional Government might fall. Lenin, who had quickly returned to Petrograd, began to waver when he saw the mass of revolutionary sailors outside the Kshesinsky Palace. He went out and addressed them, but his words were noncommittal. He did not summon them to revolt, did not tell them in so many words to continue their demonstration. Instead, he delivered a tirade against the Provisional Government and the leaders of the Soviet, whom he called "social traitors." He called on the sailors to "defend" the Revolution and to remain devoted to the Bolsheviks.

At this point Lenin caught sight of Lunacharsky, who was popular at Kronstadt, and told him to speak to the sailors. Lunacharsky, taking his cue from Lenin, addressed them in about the same language, then placed himself at the head of their column and marched them off to the Tauride Palace.

As the sailors, some 20,000 strong, marched toward the headquarters of the Soviet, they were joined by armed workers; the revolt which the Bolshevik Central Committee had not dared give official sanction gathered momentum.

At about five o'clock the Kronstadt sailors finally reached the Tauride Palace. Belligerently, they demanded to see the Socialist Ministers of the Provisional Government. Victor Chernov, the Socialist Revolutionary leader, was the first to emerge. As soon as he showed himself, cries came from the mob:

"Search him! See if he has weapons!"

"In that case I have nothing to say," Chernov told the crowd, turning to re-enter the palace. The noise then subsided and Chernov delivered a short address, attempting to pacify the rebels. When he had finished, he was seized by a few strong sailors, forced into an automobile, and placed under arrest as a hostage.

This action threw the crowd into confusion. A group of workers rushed into the palace and warned the Soviet leaders:

"Comrade Chernov has been arrested by the mob! They will tear him to pieces! Save him!"

Pandemonium broke out; the chairman, barely restoring order, quickly told Kamenev, Martov, and Trotsky to go out and rescue Chernov from the mob. When Trotsky tried to speak, the mob did not calm down.

Trotsky himself became alarmed at the ugly temper of the crowd. After complimenting the sailors for coming to "rescue" the Revolution, he shouted above the din:

"You have come here to express your will and to show the Soviet that the working class no longer wants the bourgeoisie in power. Why stain your cause through small outbursts of violence against chance individuals? They are not worthy of your attention. Every one of you is ready to sacrifice his head for the Revolution. I know it. Give me your hand, brother, give me your hand, comrade."

And he held out his hand to one of the Kronstadt stalwarts. But the latter refused to shake Trotsky's hand. The sailors, however, were somewhat pacified by Trotsky's words and Chernov was finally released. Arm in arm with Trotsky, he returned to the safety of the Tauride Palace.

Raskolnikov stood outside the headquarters of the Soviets, at the head of the Red sailors of Kronstadt, not quite knowing what to do next. From the Bolshevik Central Committee his orders were to act as circumstances indicated. His was still the power to arrest the Executive Committee of the Soviet, but he had no direct orders, and the Trotsky-Chernov episode had confused him. To do nothing was also dangerous, because the men of Kronstadt were in a nasty mood; they might turn against him at any moment.

After an uneasy pause the sailors began to disperse of their own accord. No sooner were they gone, however, than there appeared the pro-Bolshevik 176th Reserve Regiment. Their orders, too, were to "defend" the Revolution. But the Bolshevik leaders were not on hand to give them further instructions. It was now seven o'clock in the evening. The first two Bolshevik waves had spent themselves.

A short time thereafter the third wave stormed toward the Tauride Palace—this time a great mass of workers from the giant Putilov factory. Some of the workers broke into the palace, demanding to see Tseretelli. One of them, armed with a rifle, mounted the tribune and began to shout. Chkheidze, who presided, listened calmly to his speech, then handed him the appeal issued by the Soviet to the workers of Petrograd, asking them to return peacefully to their homes. The worker read the document, then stood for a moment in confusion until he was pushed from the tribune. His comrades left the assembly.

The July uprising was over. It had failed chiefly because of hesitation on the part of the Bolshevik leadership and poor co-ordination among the Kronstadt sailors, the 176th Reserves, and the Putilov workers. Whether the Bolsheviks could have exploited the initial success in July remains a moot question. Within the next few months the Bolsheviks were to gain strength they did not possess in July. For the moment, however, they were badly defeated, and not the least consequential factor in their defeat was the support of the Government by Cossacks and other local troops.

On July 19 the Provisional Government ordered the arrest of Lenin, Zinoviev, Kamenev, Lunacharsky, Raskolnikov, and Madame Kollontai. The charge: incitement to armed insurrection, with the financial support of the German Government. The Bolshevik headquarters were occupied by government troops.

"Now they will shoot us," Lenin told Trotsky.

"Fortunately," commented Trotsky, "our enemies . . . were not consistent enough and did not have the courage to do it."

The Provisional Government, as always, vacillated between a policy of resolute action and fear of offending the non-Bolshevik Socialists.

On July 21 Prince Lvov resigned as Prime Minister and was succeeded by Kerensky.

When the Provisional Government ordered Lenin's arrest on July 19, he and Zinoviev took refuge in the home of an old Bolshevik worker, Aliliuev, the future father-in-law of Stalin. On the twentieth of July Lenin's sister Maria and Krupskaya visited him there. Lenin hesitated whether to flee or stand trial, and finally decided to escape.

That evening Lenin's room was searched. On the twenty-fourth a squad of cadets ransacked Lenin's apartment, and arrested his sister Anna, her husband, and Krupskaya. But they were released within a day.

Lenin and Zinoviev remained in the house of an old Bolshevik in a suburb of Petrograd. Two days after his escape the Bolshevik Kronstadt newspaper *Proletarskoie Delo* ran a letter from Lenin and Zinoviev in which they explained:

"To give ourselves into the hands of the Pereverzevs and Miliukovs would mean to give ourselves up to the enraged counter-revolutionists, who do not wish to know about such constitutional guarantees which exist in the more or less orderly bourgeois countries. . . . Only the Constituent Assembly will have the right to pass on the order to arrest us."

The next day Trotsky published a letter declaring his solidarity with Lenin's party. He said that his delay in joining the Bolshevik Party was "explained only by the historical past that has lost all its meaning now."

Following Lenin's flight, the Bolsheviks momentarily vanished from the scene. Feeling against them ran so high that for a time Bolshevik leaders who remained in the capital feared to show themselves at public meetings. Steklov, the future editor of *Izvestia*, who was arrested at the home of Bonch-Bruyevich on July 23, at once declared that he had "absolutely nothing in common with the Bolsheviks."

On the same day Shotman met several members of the Bolshevik Central Committee, who instructed him to move Lenin and Zinoviev to a safe place.

Finally it was decided that Lenin and Zinoviev would cross the Finnish border disguised as workers from Sestroretsk, many of whom lived on the Finnish side and carried special permits. Documents were easily obtained. Lenin shaved off his mustache and beard, and put on a wig, while Zinoviev grew a beard and cropped his bushy hair short. Photographs taken in the disguise were then pasted on their false papers.

Lenin, according to the plan, was to travel to Finland, while Zinoviev was to remain in the home of a Finnish worker at Lesnoye on the Finnish railroad.

With the aid of a member of the Finnish Diet, Shotman arranged for Lenin to live in the home of the Helsinki Police Commissioner. No safer place could be desired.

12   THE TIDE TURNS

FROM THE MIDDLE OF JULY, WHEN THE UPRISING FAILED, UNtil September the Bolshevik Party steadily lost ground.

But the wane in Bolshevik influence was about to be offset. On July 30 Kerensky appointed Boris Savinkov deputy Minister of War, at the same time naming as commander in chief General Kornilov, characterized by General Brusilov as "a man with the heart of a lion and the brains of a lamb." Kornilov had distinguished himself during the retreat of the Eighth Army in Galicia. After the Revolution, he had briefly commanded the Petrograd garrison. Transferred to the southwestern front, he took command once more of the Eighth Army. On July 19 the Executive Committee of the southwestern front had wired Kerensky requesting that the armies of the front "be placed under the command of a leader capable of uniting and inspiring all the wavering elements and securing a victorious offensive by the sheer force and determination of his will." The next day Kornilov received the appointment.

Three days later Kornilov demanded an immediate cessation of the offensive on all sectors and the introduction of the death penalty for deserters at the front. Within another week Kornilov was commander in chief of all the Russian armies.

Kornilov and Kerensky saw eye to eye in military matters, although neither man trusted the other. Both felt that demoralization at the front and growing unrest in the rear would ultimately bring defeat and total chaos for Russia. Kornilov, in addition, wanted to eliminate the influence of the Soviets and "Bolshevik Petrograd." For the businessmen and Cadets, who stood on the right fringe of the Revolution, Kornilov represented "the salvation of the motherland."

On August 19 Kornilov ordered the transfer of the Third Cavalry Corps and the Savage Division to within striking distance of Moscow and Petrograd, and still another Cossack division to a region in Finland forty miles from Petrograd. Two weeks later he explained the purpose of this move to his chief of staff, General Lukomsky, as follows:

"It's time to hang the German supporters and spies, with Lenin at their head, and to disperse the Soviet of Workers' and Soldiers' Deputies so that it will never reassemble. I am shifting the cavalry corps mainly so as to bring it up to Petrograd by the end of August, and, if a demonstration of the Bolsheviks takes place, to deal with these traitors as they deserve. I want to commit the leadership of this operation to General Krimov. I am convinced that he will not hesitate, if need arises, to hang every member of the Soviet."

On August 28 the All-Russian State Conference, called by Kerensky, met in Moscow. About 2,400 delegates of all classes and parties, as well as of the armed forces, were present. Included were 488 deputies of the four Dumas. Despite the demand of the Bolsheviks and Martov's Left Mensheviks that these proceedings be boycotted, the Soviet Central Executive Committee voted to send its delegates to Moscow.

On the day the conference opened, the local Bolshevik organizations called a protest strike. The strike, although not completely successful, was enough to indicate that the conference did not enjoy complete public confidence.

In his keynote address, Kerensky warned all enemies of the Revolution that the government would suppress any attempt to overthrow the regime. General Kornilov then delivered a pessimistic report on the Army and demanded that energetic steps be taken to prevent Russia's military collapse. He asked for the suppression of political meetings among combat troops, the dissolution of soldiers' committees at the front, and the restoration of military discipline.

Despite much excellent oratory and expressions of good will, the Moscow Conference accomplished nothing. The Left was alarmed by Kornilov's demands; the Right insisted that it was "fed up with Kerensky's flowery promises."

On September 3 the Germans took Riga, threatening the approach to the capital. Immediately Kornilov asked for direct control over the Petrograd garrison. It was agreed that the Petrograd military district be turned over to Kornilov, but Kerensky insisted that the city itself remain under the control of the Provisional Government. The Prime Minister also asked for the liquidation of the reactionary Union of Officers and the Headquarters political department. Finally, Kerensky requested the despatch of a cavalry corps to enforce martial law in Petrograd, and "to defend the Provisional Government against any attacks whatsoever, especially from the side of the Bolsheviks." Kerensky indicated, however, that he wanted neither the Savage Division, with its Caucasian tribe components, nor General Krimov to be sent to the capital.

On September 7 Kornilov demanded the resignation of the Cabinet and the surrender of all military and civil authority to the commander in chief. On the ninth Kerensky dismissed Kornilov and ordered him back to Petrograd. Kornilov replied by moving his cavalry on Petrograd. It was a bold bid for power, but it collapsed overnight, when the Petrograd Soviet summoned its soldiers and workers to defend the Revolution. Railroad workers refused to transport Kornilov's troops, telegraph operators did not transmit his orders, agitators convinced Kornilov's Cossacks not to fight. The workers of Petrograd formed a militia that was to become the Red Guard of the Bolshevik Revolution. Actually no fighting took place. Kornilov's troops dissolved before they reached the city.

On September 12, 1917, Kerensky became Supreme Commander and Kornilov was arrested. On September 14 Russia was proclaimed a republic, but on the previous day, the Petrograd Soviet passed a Bolshevik-introduced resolution for the first time.

The Kornilov affair caused the final break between Kerensky and the army leadership as well as the conservative elements. Thereafter Kerensky was at the mercy of the Petrograd Soviet. He had no reliable military forces at his disposal. Under the new conditions, the Bolshevik leaders who had been arrested in July were released. For the Bolshevik cause, Kornilov's unsuccessful Putsch was a godsend which more than recouped their July losses. Bolshevik influence among workers, soldiers, and peasants began to mount swiftly.

From Finland Lenin wrote on September 12 to the Central Committee of the Party:

The Kornilov revolt was . . . an incredibly abrupt turn in the course of events.

Like every abrupt turn in events, it calls for a revision and alteration of tactics.

We must change the *form* of our struggle against Kerensky. While not relaxing our hostility toward him one iota, while not withdrawing a single word we uttered against him, while not renouncing the aim of overthrowing Kerensky, we say: We must *reckon* with the present state of affairs; we shall not overthrow Kerensky just now; we shall adopt a *different* method of fighting him; namely, we shall point out to the people (who are fighting Kornilov) the *weakness and vacillation* of Kerensky. That was done *before* too. But now it has become *the main thing.* That is the change.

News of the Kornilov uprising brought in its wake an outbreak of reprisals against officers in many cities. The military section of the Central Executive Committee of the Soviets described such events in Viborg as follows: "The picture of the lynching was dreadful. First three generals and a colonel, just arrested by the combined Executive Committee and the Army Corps Committee, were dragged from the guardhouse, thrown off the bridge, and shot in the water. . . . About eleven officers were killed in this manner."

According to one observer: "The Kornilov revolt had a most unfortunate effect on the military strength of the Army; it also served to attach a final stigma of counter-revolution to the entire officer corps. If the officers had hitherto still managed somehow to retain their position, the rebellion spelled their end. The soldier masses saw clearly that their way diverged from that of their commanders and turned away from them finally and completely.

"The inevitable end was coming. The soldier masses turned

away from their commanders, ceased to trust their committees, especially the more important ones, as well as the agents
of the government in the person of the military Commissars.
Having turned from these, they could no longer be stopped
and rapidly followed those who had already long called them
to land and freedom and promised to end the hated war."

The mood of the Petrograd working masses was already
crystallized long before November. It was predominantly pro-
Bolshevik.

In the remaining interval before the general elections to the
Constituent Assembly—now scheduled for November 25—
the Provisional Government decided to organize a Preliminary
Parliament to function until the Assembly met. This was
Kerensky's final effort to reconcile the forces represented in
the Soviet with the non-Socialist democratic elements and the
peasantry.

When Lenin learned that his party was participating, he
sent this angry letter from Finland to the Central Committee:

"You will be traitors and scoundrels if you do not at once
assign the entire Bolshevik faction to factories and plants, and
do not surround the 'democratic conference' and arrest all the
scum."

The letter was couched in very strong terms, according to
Bukharin, "and threatened us with dire punishment. . . . We
were all astounded. . . . At first everyone was perplexed.
Then, after some discussion, we reached a decision. This was
perhaps the only occasion in the history of our Party when
the Central Committee unanimously decided to burn Comrade Lenin's letter. This incident was given no publicity at the
time."

But Lenin continued to press for the seizure of power. In
two letters to the party leaders, in Petrograd and Moscow, he
outlined his strategy:

Having obtained a majority in the Soviets of Workers' and
Soldiers' Deputies of both capitals, the Bolsheviks can, and must,
take over the power of government.

Why must Bolsheviks assume power *now*?

Because the impending surrender of Petrograd will render our
chances a hundred times less favorable.

And while the Army is headed by Kerensky and Co. It is not in
our power to prevent the surrender of Petrograd.

Neither can we "wait" for the Constituent Assembly, for by sur-
rendering Petrograd, Kerensky and Co. can always *frustrate* the
convocation of the Constituent Assembly. Our Party alone, having assumed power, can secure the convocation of the Constituent
Assembly; and, having assumed power, it will accuse the other
parties of procrastination and will be able to substantiate its ac-
cusations.

It would be naïve to wait for a "formal" majority for the Bolsheviks; no revolution ever waits for that. . . . The wretched vacil-

lations of the Democratic Conference are bound to exhaust the patience of the workers of Petrograd and Moscow. History will not forgive us if we do not assume power now.

There is an apparatus: the Soviets and the democratic organizations. The international situation just now, *on the eve* of the conclusion of a separate peace between the British and the Germans, is in *our favor*. If we propose peace to the nations now we shall win.

Power must be assumed in Moscow and in Petrograd at once. . . .

In order to treat insurrection in a Marxist way, *i.e.,* as an art, we must, without losing a single moment, organize a *general staff* of the insurrectionary detachments; we must distribute our forces; we must move the loyal regiments to the most important strategic points; we must surround the Alexandrisky Theater; we must occupy the Fortress of St. Peter and St. Paul; we must arrest the general staff and the government; against the military Cadets and the Savage Division we must move such detachments as will rather die than allow the enemy to approach the center of the city; we must mobilize the armed workers and call upon them to engage in a last desperate fight; we must occupy the telegraph and telephone stations at once, quarter *our* general staff of the insurrection at the central telephone station, and connect it by telephone with all the factories, regiments, points of armed fighting, et cetera.

On October 3 the conference gave the Provisional Government a vote of confidence and endorsed the calling of the Preliminary Parliament. On October 8 the Provisional Government was reorganized for the last time with Kerensky as Premier and all Socialist and Liberal parties represented.

The same day Trotsky was elected chairman of the Petrograd Soviet, and Chkheidze, the retiring chairman, Tseretelli, the Menshevik leader, and Gotz, leader of the Socialist Revolutionaries, resigned from the Soviet presidium.

As reports of the pro-Bolshevik surge reached Lenin in Helsinki, he insisted on getting to Petrograd at once, but the Bolshevik Central Committee voted to postpone Lenin's return.

Impatiently Lenin proceeded to Viborg, intent on reaching Petrograd. Shotman found Lenin at the home of the Finnish writer Latukk. His first question was whether it was true that the Central Committee had vetoed his return to the capital. When Shotman explained that the committee had acted in the interest of his safety, Lenin demanded written confirmation. Taking a sheet of paper, Shotman wrote:

"I, the undersigned, hereby certify that the Central Committee of the Russian Social Democratic Labor Party (Bolshevik faction) resolved that V. I. Lenin shall be forbidden to come to the city of Petrograd until further notice."

Lenin took the paper, folded it carefully, put it in his pocket and, with his thumbs in his vest, paced up and down the room, repeating angrily: "I shall not let it go at that."

When he had calmed down, he began to show Shotman his figures on the increase in Bolshevik strength among the workers and the lower middle class. Kerensky's complaints about agrarian disorders, argued Lenin, indicated that the countryside was openly veering to the Bolsheviks. The time was ripe for the seizure of power.

Shotman argued that the Bolsheviks lacked the experts to run the machinery of state.

"Any worker can learn to run a ministerial office in a few days," Lenin replied. "No special ability is needed; the technical part of the work can be handled by the functionaries whom we shall compel to work for us."

As Shotman continued to quibble over details, Lenin, with more patience than usual, provided the answers.

The basic thing, said Lenin, was to enact the decrees that could convince the Russian people that the power was theirs. As soon as they felt that, they would support the new regime. His first act would be to end the war, thereby winning the support of the front-weary army. The lands of the Czar, the aristocracy, and the church would be confiscated and turned over to the peasants. The factories and plants would be taken from the capitalists and given to the workers. Who would then remain to oppose the Bolsheviks?

At the end of September Lenin sent a letter to the Central Committee urging immediate preparations for an armed uprising. Comparing the situation before and after the Kornilov affair, he explained that this time the uprising would not fail.

Furthermore, Lenin did not consider it advisable to wait for the All-Russian Congress of the Soviets. In a letter on October 12 he wrote:

"To wait for the Congress of Soviets is idiocy, for it would mean losing weeks at a time when weeks and even days decide everything."

First defeat Kerensky, then call the Congress, Lenin advised.

"The success of the insurrection is now *guaranteed* for the Bolsheviks: (1) we can (if we do not wait for the Soviet Congress) launch a *sudden* attack from three points—from Petrograd, from Moscow, and from the Baltic fleet; (2) we have slogans that guarantee us support: 'Down with the government that is suppressing the revolt of the peasants against the landlords!' (3) we have a majority *in the country;* (4) the disorganization among the Mensheviks and the Socialist Revolutionaries is complete; (5) we are technically in a position to seize power in Moscow (where the start might even be made, so as to catch the enemy unawares); (6) we have *thousands* of armed workers and soldiers in Petrograd who could *at once* seize the Winter Palace, the general staff, the telephone exchange, and the large printing establishments. Nothing will be able to drive us out of these positions, while agitational work *in the Army* will be such as to make it impossible to combat this government of peace, of land for the peasants, and so forth."

An attack at once, from Petrograd, Moscow, and the Baltic fleet, would succeed with smaller sacrifice than in July, Lenin said, because the troops will not advance against a government of peace.

In October Lenin completed his pamphlet entitled *Can the Bolsheviks Retain State Power?* More revealing than the contents was the title. The question in his mind was no longer whether the Bolsheviks could seize control but whether they would remain at the helm.

On October 20 the Preliminary Parliament began its sessions, with the Socialist Revolutionary leader Nikolai Avksentiev, chairman of the Soviet of Peasant Deputies, presiding. Under Lenin's pressure the Central Committee of the Bolshevik Party passed a boycott resolution. Trotsky read the declaration announcing the Bolshevik withdrawal.

"The bourgeois classes," said Trotsky, "while apparently non-political, have set themselves the aim to frustrate the Constituent Assembly *(Clamor from the right, exclamations! "A lie")*. . . . We, the Bolshevik Social Democratic faction, declare: We have nothing in common with this government of national treason. *(Much noise from the right and center, cries of "scoundrel.")* . . . Long live the Constituent Assembly!"

To Smilga, the Chairman of the Regional Committee of soldiers, sailors, and workers in Helsingfors, Lenin assigned the role of organizing the military and naval forces in Finland for the uprising:

> Now as to your role, it seems to me that the only thing which we can completely have in our hands and which is of military importance is the army of Finland and the Baltic fleet. . . . Give all your attention to preparing the army in Finland and the fleet for the overthrow of Kerensky. Form a secret committee of MOST DEPENDABLE military men; examine with them the question from all sides; collect (and personally verify) accurate information about the composition and disposition of the troops near and in Petrograd, about the possibility of bringing the army in Finland to Petrograd and regarding the movements of the fleet, et cetera.
>
> Beautifully worded resolutions and Soviets without power make us ridiculous losers. I think that you are in a position to bring together reliable and military men. Go to the Ino [fortress] and other important points; make a really careful and serious study of the situation; do not be carried away by the boastful phrases which we are too much in the habit of making.

Work among the soldiers and sailors on leave, he urged, and form a bloc with the Left Socialist Revolutionaries.

"Soldiers and sailors are given leaves of absence. Organize

those who have leave to go to the country into propaganda
units for systematic agitation. Let them visit villages and
counties to agitate in general and for the Constituent Assembly. You are in an exceptionally good position. You can
begin at once to form a bloc with the Socialist Revolutionaries
of the left wing. Only this move can put real power in our
hands in Russia and secure for us a majority in the Constituent Assembly. . . . At the present moment the Socialist
Revolutionaries 'firm' is doing a thriving business, and you
should take advantage of your good luck (for you have Left
Socialist Revolutionaries) to form in the villages in the NAME
of this firm a bloc of Bolsheviks and Left Socialist Revolutionaries, peasants with workmen, but not with the capitalists."

Agitation should begin immediately for the transfer of
power from the Provisional Government to the Petrograd
Soviet, he advised.

"In my opinion, in order to prepare people's minds properly
there should be circulated at once this slogan: The power
should immediately be placed in the hands of the Petrograd
Soviet, which should hand it over to the Congress of Soviets.
Why endure three more weeks of war and the Kornilov preparations of Kerensky?"

For his own protection, Lenin instructed Smilga:

"Send me . . . an identification paper (the more formal the
better), on the stationery of the Regional Committee, signed
by the chairman, with the seal; have it typed or written in a
very clear hand, made out to Konstantine Petrovich Ivanov.
Have the certificate read that the chairman of the Regional
Committee vouches for this comrade and asks all Soviets,
Viborg Soviet of Soldiers' Deputies as well as others, to have
full confidence in him in every possible way. I need it in case
ANYTHING should happen—a 'conflict' or 'meeting.' . . ."

Shortly afterward Shotman, en route to Lenin in Viborg,
met Rakhia at the station. There was no need to go to Viborg,
said Rakhia with a broad grin. Lenin was back in Petrograd.

13   LENIN SEIZES POWER

PROMPTLY UPON HIS ARRIVAL IN PETROGRAD LENIN TOOK OVER
the task of preparing the armed uprising. At a secret meeting
of the Bolshevik Central Committee on October 23, 1917, attended by Zinoviev, Kamenev, Stalin, Trotsky, Sverdlov, Uritsky, Dzerzhinsky, Kollontai, Bubnov, Sokolnikov, and Lomov,
Lenin insisted that the Bolshevik uprising could not wait for
the convocation of the Constituent Assembly.

"The international situation is such that we must make a
start," Lenin said. "The indifference of the masses may be ex-

plained by the fact that they are tired of words and resolutions. The majority is with us now. . . . To wait for the Constituent Assembly, which will surely be against us, is nonsensical because that will only make our task more difficult."

A long and bitter discussion followed Lenin's summons to insurrection.

In the early hours of the morning Lenin finally won his victory.

"Hastily, with a stub of a pencil, on a sheet of graph paper torn from a child's exercise book, he wrote: 'The Party calls for the organization of an armed insurrection,' " Trotsky recorded in his reminiscences. The resolution was put to a vote. The official minutes record: "Votes in favor—10; against —2."

A few days later Lenin again warned that further delay might be fatal.

"The agrarian disorders are increasing, the government is using the most savage measures against the peasants," he wrote. "Sympathy for our cause in the Army is growing. Ninety-nine per cent of the soldiers in Moscow are with us. The Army and the fleet in Finland are against the government.

"In Germany, it is now clear that the revolution has already begun, especially after the shooting of the sailors. In the elections to the Moscow Soviet the Bolsheviks received 47 per cent of the votes. Together with the Left Socialist Revolutionaries we shall surely command a majority of votes in the country.

"Under the circumstances to 'wait' is simply criminal. The Bolsheviks have no right to wait for the Congress of the Soviets. They must seize power immediately. In that way they will save the world revolution, otherwise there is danger that the imperialists of all countries will enter into an alliance against us. . . ."

Meanwhile Lenin continued stirring the workers and soldiers against Kerensky. Again and again he promised that when Kerensky was overthrown, the Bolsheviks would "at once give the land to the peasants, reconstruct democratic liberties and institutions which were maimed and ruined by Kerensky, and set up a government that *nobody* will ever overthrow."

Some members still wavered. The majority, however, decided on immediate action. On Trotsky's initiative the Petrograd Soviet organized a Military Revolutionary Committee to carry out the coup d'état. The Central Committee of the Party, on November 5, also elected a Political Bureau of seven to make the final technical preparations. But the real leadership in the insurrection was carried out by the Military Revolutionary Committee.

In order to gain control of the garrison, the Military Revolutionary Committee appointed a commissar for every army unit in Petrograd and its environs. On the night of November 3 the commissars of the Committee were sent to the Petrograd garrison. The Committee issued an order that "henceforth all power in Petrograd passes into the hands of the Military Revolutionary Committee." According to this order, the troops were to obey only the instructions and orders of the Committee, which would be transmitted to them through the regimental commissars; all other orders, whatever their origin, were declared counter-revolutionary. This order was in effect the beginning of the armed insurrection, since it brought out into the open the conflict between the Provisional Government and the Military Revolutionary Committee.

In the meantime Lenin, on November 6, addressed a letter to the members of the Central Committee in which he wrote:

The matter must be decided unconditionally this very evening, or this very night.

History will not forgive revolutionaries for procrastinating when they can be victorious today (will certainly be victorious today), while they risk losing much, in fact, everything, tomorrow.

If we seize power today, we seize it not in opposition to the Soviets but on their behalf.

The seizure of power is a matter of insurrection; its political purpose will be clear after the seizure.

It would be a disaster, or a sheer formality, to await the wavering vote of November 7. The people have the right and duty to decide such questions not by a vote, but by force; in critical moments of revolution the people have the right and duty to give directions to their representatives, even their best representatives, and not to wait for them.

The bold challenge showed that the Provisional Government had very small forces at its disposal. The Military Revolutionary Committee thereupon decided not to wait to be attacked but to overthrow the government with the means at its command. A plan was developed for the occupation of the Winter Palace and the arrest of the members of the government. If the government refused to surrender, it was to be forced to yield by fire from the cruiser *Aurora* and from the Fortress of St. Peter and St. Paul.

General direction of the operations was entrusted to Antonov, Chudnovsky, and Podvoisky. The Palace was to be attacked on the night of November 7. Headquarters for operations were to be the Fortress of St. Peter and St. Paul. At the last conference it was also decided that before the assault a delegation be sent to the government with the demand to vacate the palace, yield all arms, and surrender. If no answer came within twenty minutes, the *Aurora* would open fire, the sailors would disembark, and the Red Guards would storm the Winter Palace.

On the morning of November 6 Kerensky declared he had incontrovertible proof that Lenin had organized an insurrection. The Government, he said, was adopting measures for its suppression. It would unhesitatingly resort to armed force, but success in the struggle required the immediate co-operation of all parties and groups and the help of the whole people. He requested from the Pre Parliament "all measures of confidence and co-operation."

The Provisional Government did not have a secure majority in the Pre Parliament. The leading figure among them was Theodore Dan, a Left Menshevik. He offered a resolution which sharply criticized the Bolsheviks, but at the same time argued that successful action required decisive measures in the struggle for peace, an immediate transfer of landed estates into the hands of the peasants, and the speediest possible convocation of the Constituent Assembly. The projected revolt of the Bolsheviks, declared Dan, undoubtedly would lead the country to a catastrophe, but the revolutionary democracy would not fight against it by armed force, for "if the Bolshevik movement is drowned in blood, then the real triumph will belong to a third force, which will sweep away both the Bolsheviks, the Provisional Government, and the entire democracy." Dan's resolution placed the responsibility for the impending insurrection both on the Bolsheviks and the Provisional Government, and proposed to entrust the defense of the democratic Revolution to a Committee of Public Defense.

After the adoption of his resolution, Dan departed for the session of the Provisional Government to demand the immediate publication and posting, that very night, of leaflets throughout the city declaring that the government: (1) appealed to the Allied powers that they propose to all belligerent powers the immediate cessation of military action and the opening of general peace negotiations; (2) issued telegraphic orders placing all landed estates under the jurisdiction of local land committees until the final disposition of the agrarian problem; (3) decided to hasten the convocation of the Constituent Assembly.

At the same time, Dan told Kerensky that he exaggerated the danger, under the influence of the "reactionary headquarters." He said further that the resolution of the Pre Parliament was extremely useful for a "break in the mood of the masses," and that the influence of Bolshevik propaganda would henceforth rapidly decline. On the other hand, he said, the Bolsheviks themselves, in their negotiations with the leaders of the Mensheviks and Socialist Revolutionaries, expressed their willingness to "bow to the will of the majority in the Soviets."

According to Dan, Kerensky responded to these arguments with extreme irritation, declaring that "now is the time for action, not talk."

In the meantime, the Bolsheviks continued to claim that all assertions concerning "some alleged Bolshevik plot" were an invention of the "counter-revolutionaries" and "the Kornilovist, Kerensky."

Kerensky had barely finished his conversation with Dan when a delegation from the Cossack regiments stated that the Cossacks wished to know what forces the government had at its disposal for the suppression of the uprising. Then they declared that the Cossack regiments would defend the government only if he, Kerensky, personally gave them assurances that this time Cossack blood would not be spilled in vain, as it was in July, when the government did not take sufficiently energetic measures for the total liquidation of the Bolsheviks. Finally, the delegation insisted that the Cossacks would fight only at his personal command. Kerensky at once signed an order to the Cossacks to place themselves immediately at the disposal of the district military headquarters and to obey its commands implicitly.

While Kerensky was holding this midnight conversation with the delegates of the Cossack regiments, the Council of Cossack Troops, headed by right-wing Cossack officers, which met all through the night, expressed itself in favor of non-intervention in the struggle.

On November 7, 1917, the very day the Bolsheviks struck, *Izvestia*, the official organ of the All-Russian Central Executive Committee of the Soviets, carried an editorial entitled "Madness or Adventure," warning that a Bolshevik victory would lead to chaos and a civil war.

On the morning of November 7 Rakhia told Lenin that the government was planning to open the drawbridges across the Neva. "Yes, today the thing is going to start," was Lenin's response.

"Vladimir Ilich," Rakhia relates, "was pacing the room. . . . Presently he remarked: 'It's time to go to the Smolny Institute' [the new Bolshevik and Soviet headquarters . . .]. I urged him not to go, pointing out the dangers to which he would be exposing himself. Brushing all arguments aside, he declared: 'We are going to Smolny.'"

Lenin changed his clothes, bandaged his cheek with a soiled handkerchief, and put on his wig and an old cap. When they reached Smolny, Lenin sent for Trotsky and Stalin, and the four men retired to a separate room, where Lenin heard Trotsky and Stalin report on the situation.

The newspapers had reported that the negotiations of the Military Revolutionary Committee with the staff of the Petrograd Military District concerning the further fate of the garrison were approaching a favorable end. "Are you agreeing to a compromise?" Lenin asked Trotsky, with a piercing glance.

Trotsky answered that he purposely had given this calming news to the papers, and that it was only a temporary stratagem before the beginning of a general attack.

"That is good!" said Lenin, rubbing his hands and pacing the room. "That is v-e-r-y good!" he repeated.

The insurrection spread with incredible speed. Red Guards occupied the central telegraph office, the post office, and other government buildings. Armed Bolsheviks surrounded the buildings of the Winter Palace and the Military District Headquarters in an ever-tightening ring. Kerensky, accompanied by Vice-Premier Konovalov, proceeded to Headquarters. It was clear that only the immediate arrival of military reinforcements from the front could still save the situation. Consulting with Konovalov and another Minister, Kishkin, as well as with certain officers at Headquarters, Kerensky decided to break through the Bolshevik lines and personally meet the troops which, they thought, were coming to Petrograd from the front. In an open automobile he drove past Bolshevik patrols, recognized by passers-by and soldiers. The military snapped to attention, from habit. A second later none of them would have been able to explain to himself how this had happened. The automobile now sped on to Gatchina.

The other Ministers were assembled at the Winter Palace. "After a brief exchange of views," writes ex-Minister of Justice Maliantovich, "we reached the conclusion that the situation was so serious that the Provisional Government would not be true to its duty if it did not remain at the Winter Palace in full force, meeting in continuous session until the final solution of the crisis."

According to Maliantovich, the general mood of the soldiers could be described approximately as follows: "Rather unsympathetic to the Bolsheviks, but also without enthusiasm for the government. A position of neutrality. Will join the victor. . . ."

The All-Russian Congress of Workers' and Soldiers' Deputies was scheduled to open that evening and the Bolsheviks were racing to seize power in order to confront the Congress with a *fait accompli*. Night fell, and the Winter Palace, with Kerensky's Ministers, had not yet been captured. Smolny was in a state of intense agitation.

Meanwhile in the Petrograd City Council a strange meeting was taking place. The councilmen knew that the fighting had reached the square before the Winter Palace. One member delivered an emotional speech demanding that the City Council march in a body to the Winter Palace, "to die together with Russia's chosen representatives."

The members of the Petrograd City Council and the Soviet of Peasants' Deputies went out into the street and marched toward the Winter Palace, singing the "Marseillaise." At the

Kazan Cathedral they were halted by a Bolshevik patrol and marched no farther.

Inside the Winter Palace the isolated, outnumbered defenders were preparing for their last stand. Among them were Socialists and conservatives, a unit of the Women's Battalion, veteran workers, and men of wealth. Of the military defenders, young Cadets predominated.

Looking out on the Neva River, the Ministers of the Provisional Government could see the guns of the cruiser *Aurora*, manned by Bolshevik sailors. The guns were expected to open fire at any moment. In the square, the Bolsheviks were bringing up armored cars, fieldpieces, machine guns.

Kishkin arrived from Military Headquarters and announced:

"I have received an ultimatum from the Military Revolutionary Committee. I propose that we discuss it."

The ultimatum demanded surrender within twenty minutes, warning that fire would be opened from the *Aurora* and the Fortress of St. Peter and St. Paul.

It was resolved to ignore this ultimatum.

The hand of the clock passed eight. The Ministers turned out the overhead lights. Suddenly a loud report was heard, then another. The hands of the clock crawled on till it was past nine. Some of the besieged sat, some reclined, others paced soundlessly over the soft rug that covered the entire floor.

A new sound was heard, muted, but distinct from all others.

"What is that?" asked someone.

"It is from the *Aurora*," replied the Minister of the Navy Verderevsky.

The earlier noise had been blank shots from the guns of St. Peter and St. Paul and the *Aurora*. These signaled an intensified exchange of small arms fire which lasted an hour. Then the *Aurora* aimed a six-inch shell which exploded in the palace corridor and spread confusion among the defenders.

Thirty or forty Bolsheviks, armed with guns and revolvers, broke into the palace. But they were instantly disarmed and arrested. . . . They surrendered their arms without resistance.

Immediately after this, several sailors made their way into the palace, climbed to the upper gallery in the lobby, and dropped two grenades. They were small and poorly made. The sailors were seized and disarmed.

Maliantovich relates:

Suddenly a noise arose somewhere and began to grow, spread, and roll ever nearer. And in its multitude of sounds, fused into a single powerful wave, we immediately sensed something special, unlike the previous noises—something final and decisive. It suddenly became clear that the end was coming. . . . The noise rose, swelled, and rapidly swept toward us in a broad wave. . . . And poured into our hearts unbearable anxiety, like a gust of poisoned air. . . . It was clear; this is the onslaught, we are being taken by storm. . . . Defense is useless—sacrifices will be in vain. . . .

There was a noise behind the door and it burst open. Like a splinter of wood thrown out by a wave, a little man flew into the room, pushed in by the onrushing crowd which poured in after him and, like water, at once spilled into every corner and filled the room. The little man wore a lose, open coat, a wide felt hat pushed back off his forehead over his long, reddish hair, glasses. He had a short, trimmed red mustache and a small beard. His short upper lip rose to his nose when he spoke. The eyes were colorless, the face tired. He flew in and cried in a sharp, small, insistent voice:

"Where are the members of the Provisional Government?"

"The Provisional Government is here," said Konovalov, remaining seated. "What do you wish?"

"I inform you, all of you, members of the Provisional Government, that you are under arrest. I am Antonov, chairman of the Military Revolutionary Committee."

"The members of the Provisional Government yield to force and surrender, in order to avoid bloodshed," said Konovalov.

"To avoid bloodshed! And how much blood have you spilled?" shouted a voice from the mob behind the ring of guards. Many approving exclamations echoed from all sides.

Antonov stopped the outcries.

"Enough, comrades! That's all! We'll straighten all that out afterward. . . . Now we must draw up a protocol. I am going to write it now. I shall ask everyone. . . . But first I request you to surrender all arms in your possession."

The military surrendered their arms, the rest declared that they carried none.

The room was jammed with soldiers, sailors, Red Guards, some carrying several weapons—a rifle, two revolvers, a sword, two machine-gun ribbons.

When it was learned that Kerensky had fled, vile oaths were heard from the crowd. Some of the men shouted, inciting the rest to violence:

"These will run off too! . . . Kill them, finish them off, there's no need for protocols! . . ."

"Run them through, the sons of bitches! . . . Why waste time with them! They've drunk enough of our blood!" yelled a short sailor, stamping the floor with his rifle—luckily without a bayonet —and looking around. It was almost a call to action. There were sympathetic replies:

"What the devil, comrades! Stick them all on bayonets, make short work of them! . . ."

Antonov raised his head and shouted sharply:

"Comrades, keep calm! All members of the Provisional Government are arrested. They will be imprisoned in the Fortress of St. Peter and St. Paul. I'll permit no violence. Conduct yourself calmly. Maintain order! Power is now in your hands. You must maintain order! . . ."

The members of the Provisional Government were then led away toward the Fortress of St. Peter and St. Paul. Along the way they were met with jeers and threats from the crowds on the streets.

On the fortress bridge they were met by a small group of soldiers and escorted inside the fortress.

Antonov began to write the protocol. When he finished reading it, he raised his head, placed his right hand, palm down, on the paper, and intoned slowly, almost dreamily: "An historic document! . . ."

When news of the arrest of the Provisional Government was transmitted to Smolny there was a rush to the great hall where the Soviet Congress was in session. Lenin took off the handkerchief covering half his face.

"Remove your wig," whispered Bonch-Bruyevich.

Lenin did so, and his comrades saw the familiar bald head.

"Give it to me; I'll put it away," offered Bonch-Bruyevich. "It may come in useful again someday. . . . Who knows?"

When Lenin appeared on the rostrum he received a thunderous ovation. He stood before the packed assembly, hands in his pockets, his head slightly bowed. When the applause subsided, he raised his head and began to speak.

"Comrades, the workers' and peasants' revolution, whose need the Bolsheviks have emphasized many times, has come to pass.

"What is the significance of this revolution? Its significance is . . . that we shall have a Soviet Government, without the participation of a bourgeoisie of any kind. The oppressed masses will themselves form a government. The old state machinery will be smashed to bits and in its place will be created a new machinery of government by Soviet organizations. From now on there is a new page in the history of Russia, and the present Third Russian Revolution shall in its final result lead to the victory of Socialism.

"We have now learned to work together in a friendly manner, as is evident from this revolution. We have the force of mass organization which conquered all and which will lead the proletariat to world revolution.

"We should now occupy ourselves in Russia in building up a proletarian Socialist state. Long live the world-wide Socialist revolution!"

Late that night Lenin went to the home of Bonch-Bruyevich in a state of complete exhaustion. Bonch-Bruyevich made his own bed in the adjoining room, determined to retire only when Lenin was asleep. He locked all doors and prepared his revolvers for instant use. "Who knows? Someone may come to arrest or murder Lenin," he thought to himself. "This is only the first night of our victory. Our success is not yet assured. Anything may happen."

At last Lenin put out his light. Bonch-Bruyevich was beginning to doze off when he noticed lights go on again. Lenin had risen, tiptoed to the door, and thinking Bonch-Bruyevich asleep, had seated himself at his writing table and began to work. He wrote, made revisions, and finally prepared a clean copy. The autumn dawn was breaking when Lenin finally went to sleep.

When the household was assembled for tea late that morning, Lenin saluted them with: "Greetings on the first day of the Socialist Revolution." Then he took out of his pocket the manuscript he had prepared during the night and read his now-famous decree expropriating the landed estates.

"Now we must see to it that the decree is made public and broadcast throughout the country. Then let them try to take it away," Lenin asserted. "No! No power on earth will be able to take away this decree from the peasants and return the land to the nobles. This is the most important achievement of our revolution! Today the agrarian revolution will occur and will become irrevocable!"

"But they will accuse us of having stolen the program of the Socialist Revolutionaries," someone remarked.

"Let them say what they will," Lenin replied with a grin. "The peasants will understand that we always support their justified demands. . . . We must identify ourselves with the peasants, with their wishes. And if there are fools who laugh at us, let them laugh. We never intended to give a monopoly over the peasants to the Socialist Revolutionaries."

The immediate question was the form of the new government. What should its members be called? "Anything but Ministers—that is a vile, hackneyed word," said Lenin.

"We might call them commissars, but there are too many commissars," suggested Trotsky. "Perhaps supreme commissars? No, 'supreme' does not sound well either. What about People's Commissars?"

"People's Commissars? Well, that might do, I think," replied Lenin. "And the government as a whole?"

"A Soviet, of course—the Soviet of People's Commissars."

"The Soviet of People's Commissars? That's splendid, savors powerfully of revolution!" said Lenin.

Despite the capture of the Winter Palace, more than one hundred delegates at the all-Russian Congress of the Soviets protested against the proceedings and walked out of the Congress, leaving the Bolsheviks and their Allies to pass a formal resolution taking over the government.

The Congress promised that "the authority of the Soviet gives peace, land, the right to soldiers' and workers' control, bread and necessities, the Constituent Assembly and self-development of the nationalities included in Russia." After warning the soldiers against Kerensky and Kornilov, the Congress adjourned, at six o'clock in the morning of November 8.

When Lenin and Zinoviev appeared that afternoon before a joint meeting of the Congress, the Petrograd Soviet and members of the conference of the garrison, they were greeted with "tempestuous and ecstatic applause." That evening the Congress established what was to be the fundamental law of the Russian Socialist Federated Soviet Republics.

The All-Russian Congress of the Workers', Soldiers', and Peasants' Deputies decrees:

To establish for the administration of the country, until the Constituent Assembly provides otherwise, a Provisional Workers' and Peasants' Government, which is to be named "The Soviet of the People's Commissars." The management of the different branches of life of the state is to be entrusted to Commissariats, the personnel of which secures the accomplishment of the program announced by the Congress, in close contact with the mass organization of workingmen, workingwomen, sailors, soldiers, peasants, and employees. The governmental authority rests with the *collegium* of the chairman of these Commissariats; viz., with the Soviet of People's Commissars.

Control of the activity of the People's Commissars and the right to recall them belong to the All-Russian Congress of the Soviets of the Workers', Soldiers', and Peasants' Deputies and its Central Executive Committee.

For the present the personnel of the Soviet of People's Commissars is as follows:

Chairman of the Soviet of People's Commissars, Vladimir Ulianov (Lenin)

People's Commissar of the Interior, A. I. Rykov

People's Commissar of Agriculture, D. P. Milyutin

People's Commissar of Labor, A. R. Shliapnikov

War and Navy Committee, V. Antonov-Ovseenko, N. V. Krylenko, and Dybenko

People's Commissar of Commerce and Industry, V. P. Nogin

People's Commissar of Education, A. V. Lunacharsky

People's Commissar of Finance, I. I. Skvortsov (Stepanov)

People's Commissar of Foreign Affairs, L. D. Bronstein (Trotsky)

People's Commissar of Justice, G. E. Oppokov (A. A. Lomov)

People's Commissar of Supply, I. F. Theodorovich

Post and Telegraph, N. P. Avilov (Glyebov)

People's Commissar of Nationality Affairs, J. V. Djugashvili (Stalin)

(Soviet of People's Commisars was later shortened in the Russian to Sovnarcom.)

Lenin, Stalin, and Krylenko, without awaiting the approval of the Central Committee of the Soviets, issued an order to the soldiers to fraternize with the Germans on the front "by battalions, by companies, and by platoons." Many Bolsheviks maintained that this would destroy Russia's capacity for resistance, should the German Government turn down their peace offer.

Lenin's ambiguous answer was: "We appealed for fraternization not by armies but by regiments. We relied in this case on the military experience of Krylenko, who pointed out that such fraternization was absolutely possible."

Trotsky issued the following order to the Army:

Soldiers! Peace is in your hands. You are not going to allow the counter-revolutionary generals to tear the great cause of peace away from you. You will surround them by a guard in order to avoid the lynchers who are unworthy of the revolutionary army, and in order to prevent those generals from escaping trial. Let the regiments at the front at once elect representatives for an armistice with the enemy. Soldiers! the keys of peace are in your hands. Watchfulness, restraint, and energy, and the cause of peace will prevail.

On the night of November 22 Lenin and Stalin spoke over the direct wire with General Dukhonin, the chief of staff, ordering him to cease military operations and open negotiations with the Germans for an armistice. In his account of this episode Stalin says: "It was a tense moment. Dukhonin and the General Staff categorically refused to obey the orders of the Council of People's Commissars. . . ."

Lenin proposed that they go at once to the radio station and broadcast an order dismissing General Dukhonin, and appeal to the soldiers "to surround the generals, cease military operations, establish contact with the Austrian and German soldiers, and take the cause of peace into their own hands."

Accompanied by a detachment of sailors and Red Guards, Krylenko departed for Moghiliev to take over command. Dukhonin, who refused to yield his authority, was slain by a mob of soldiers. Krylenko then dispatched emissaries to the German command for preliminary armistice negotiations.

On November 27 the German commander in chief replied to the Soviet Government that he was ready to open negotiations at Brest-Litovsk.

The delegation sent by Lenin to Brest-Litovsk had instructions to accept any conditions the Germans laid down. There was little else to do. The Russian Army had virtually ceased to exist after Lenin's peace decree and the order for fraternization. The first peace delegation, headed by Joffe, included a staff of military experts, as well as a worker, sailor, peasant, and a woman, who went along for the propaganda effect.

14 DICTATORSHIP

WHILE THE STREET FIGHTING BETWEEN THE BOLSHEVIKS AND
the adherents of the Provisional Government was still in
progress, the Bolsheviks opened negotiations with the Left
Mensheviks and Socialist Revolutionaries for the formation
of an all-Socialist cabinet. Kamenev and Rykov headed the
Bolsheviks, who seriously favored this coalition, but Lenin
urged these negotiations mainly as a cover for military operations against Kerensky's forces.

An important part in the fall of the Provisional Government was played by monarchist officers stationed in Petrograd
and on the northern front. In remaining aloof during the critical fighting, the monarchists were pursuing their own shortsighted strategy. With Kerensky out of the way, they believed
they would quickly dispose of the Bolsheviks as well.

Many of the old Bolsheviks continued to oppose the coup
d'état even after its success. Men such as A. A. Bogdanov,
Leonid Krassin, Bazarov, Gregory Alexinsky, Professor Rozhkov, Maxim Gorky, and other Bolshevik leaders during the
Revolution of 1905, and intimate friends of Lenin, called the
Bolshevik seizure of power "an absurd adventure," the work
of people "in the grip of madness," and Lenin himself "utterly
irresponsible." They described the Soviet regime as an *"opera
bouffe* government, in throes of an incredible and dangerous
delirium."

On November 21, two weeks after the Bolshevik revolt,
Maxim Gorky wrote in his paper *Novaya Zhizn:*

Blind fanatics and unscrupulous adventurers are rushing head-
long toward "social revolution"—as a matter of fact it is the road
to anarchy, the ruin of the proletariat and the Revolution.

The working class cannot fail to realize that Lenin is experi-
menting with its blood, and trying to strain the revolutionary mood
of the proletariat to the limit, to see what the outcome will be.

The working class must not allow adventurers and madmen to
thrust upon the proletariat the responsibility for the disgraceful,
senseless, and bloody crimes for which not Lenin, but the proletariat will have to account.

On November 17, 1917, a number of Bolshevik Commissars, headed by Rykov, resigned in protest against Lenin's
refusal to form a coalition government with all the Socialist
parties. Simultaneously, Kamenev also resigned as president
of the All-Russian Central Executive Committee of the
Soviets.

Following Kamenev's resignation, Lenin promptly summoned Sverdlov.

"Jacob Mikhailovich," he said, "I want you to become president of the Central Executive of the Soviets. What do you say?"

Sverdlov hesitated, but finally was persuaded to accept.

"Begin at once to create some order," said Lenin. "First of all, convene the Bolshevik section of the Central Executive. Then create an organization of non-partisans selected from workers, and, if possible, from the peasants. After that, select the most trustworthy and responsible among our comrades and plant them among the non-partisans. Bring about frequent recesses, and thus give the members of our faction an opportunity to deliberate all the questions with the non-partisans. Above all, they must be able to discover the attitude of every person. We must know what every comrade there thinks. Report to me concerning everything that transpires there. Act immediately, as if you were already president, and we will call a meeting of the Central Committee to whom I will propose that your appointment be confirmed. I believe that the Central Committee will not refuse to confirm you. After that, we will pass it through our faction in the Central Executive of the Soviets and immediately proclaim you president. Count all votes we have in the committee in advance and see to it that all adherents of our faction are present at the meeting."

Leonid Krassin wrote from Petrograd in a letter to his wife in Sweden:

The Bolsheviks, after smashing Kerensky and occupying Moscow, have failed to reach an agreement with other parties, and they go on issuing new decrees on their own responsibility daily. All work is coming to an end. It means the ruin of production and transport; meanwhile the armies at the front are dying of hunger. All the leading Bolsheviks, Kamenev, Zinoviev, Rykov, et cetera, have come around, *excepting* Lenin and Trotsky, who remain as uncompromising as ever and cannot be persuaded to alter their attitude. I am afraid the outlook is black indeed; paralysis of the whole life of Petrograd, anarchy, and probably pogroms.

Krassin elaborated on this in a conversation with Solomon soon after the latter's return to Petrograd from Stockholm. "My dear man," he said, "this is just a case of staking everything on the immediate introduction of Socialism, that is to say a utopian ideal pushed to the very limit of folly. All of them here, including Lenin, have lost their minds. Everything that the Social Democrats have been preaching has been forgotten. . . . And Lenin? Why, he is altogether irresponsible. The whole thing is just an incredible and dangerous delirium. We are banking everything not only upon the success of Socialism in Russia, but on the outbreak of a world revolution, regarded from the same Socialist angle, of course. Those who surround him are very diffident to Lenin. They do not say a word against him, and that is how we have actually come back to our old absolutism."

Vorovsky, later one of the leading Soviet diplomats, was of the same opinion.

Solomon writes:

. . . Vorovsky, according to his own statement, did not believe in the permanence of the Bolshevik Government, nor in the ability of the Bolsheviks to do anything sensible, and regarded the whole matter as an absurd adventure, a "hard nut" on which the Bolsheviks would break their teeth! . . .

Solomon brought these feelings to an interview with Lenin. "Tell me, Vladimir Ilich, as an old comrade of yours, what is going on here? What is this? Is this really a gamble on Socialism on the island of Utopia, only on a more extensive scale? I cannot understand it. . . ."

"There is no island of Utopia," Lenin replied. "It is a question of creating a Socialist state. From now on Russia will be the first state in which a Socialist order has been established. I see you are shrugging your shoulders. Well, you have another surprise coming. . . . It isn't a question of Russia at all, gentlemen. I spit on Russia. . . . This is merely one phase through which we must pass on the way to a world revolution."

Solomon smiled. Lenin squinted his small, narrow eyes and said:

"You are smiling? You mean to say that it is all a fantasy, a dream? I know what you are going to say. I know the whole stock of those stereotyped, threadbare Marxist phrases which in reality are petit-bourgeois futilities which you cannot for a moment discard. By the way," he suddenly interrupted himself, "I remember Vorovsky wrote to me about your conversation with him and that you had called it all a dream and all that. Let me tell you, we are past all that. All that has been left behind. All that is nothing but Marxist hairsplitting. We discarded that as one of those inevitable children's diseases which every society and every class must go through and with which they part when they see a new dawn gleaming on the horizon. . . . Don't even attempt to contradict me!" he exclaimed, waving his hands. "It's no use. You and your Krassin with his theory of natural evolution are not going to convince me. We are turning more and more toward the Left.

"Yes, we will destroy everything and on the ruins we will build our temple! It will be a temple for the happiness of all. But we will destroy the entire bourgeoisie, grind it to a powder." He laughed. "Remember this—you and your friend Nikitich [Krassin]—we will stand on ceremony with no one. Remember that the Lenin whom you knew ten years ago no longer exists. He is dead."

When Solomon protested, Lenin sharply interrupted:

"I will be merciless with all counter-revolutionists, and I shall employ Comrade Uritsky [chief of the Petrograd Secret Police] against all counter-revolutionists, no matter who they are. I do not advise you to make his acquaintance."

Meanwhile, the job of creating some sort of order out of chaos was proceeding. Requisitions and confiscations were in full swing. But it was necessary to get control of the banks. A decree to that effect was issued. To carry out the seizure, Lenin appointed Menzhinsky Commissar of Finance. "You are not much of a financier," Lenin told him, "but you are a man of action."

"The appointment was made late in the evening," writes Bonch-Bruyevich. "Menzhinsky was extremely tired from overwork. In order to put the government's order into immediate execution, he personally, with the aid of one of the comrades, brought a large sofa into the room, placed it by the wall, wrote in big letters on a sheet of paper: 'Commissariat of Finance,' tacked it over the sofa, and lay down to sleep. . . ."

"Comrade Menzhinsky," relates Petskovsky, an old Bolshevik, "half-reclined on a sofa, looking tired. The wall over the sofa was graced by a sign: 'People's Commissariat of Finance.' I sat down near Menzhinsky and began to talk to him. With the most innocent air, Comrade Menzhinsky questioned me about my past and wanted to know what I had studied. I replied, among other things that I had studied at the University of London, where I took up several subjects, among them finance. Menzhinsky suddenly sat up, pierced me with his eyes, and declared categorically: 'In that case we shall appoint you director of the State Bank.' . . . In a short time he returned with a paper which certified, over the signature of Ilich, that I was director of the State Bank."

He begged Menzhinsky to cancel the appointment. But the latter explained: "We need money desperately—at least a few millions. The State Bank and the State Treasury are on strike. We cannot get any money by legal means. The only way is to change the head of the bank and take money."

Two days later Menzhinsky released him. Petskovsky's career as director of the Russian State Bank was ended.

Incredibly enough, most of the early business of the new Soviet regime was transacted in this manner. While the Council of People's Commissars was enacting decrees which changed Russia's economic and social structure and gave a new course to world history, the main actors were wandering through the corridors of Smolny looking for space, desks, chairs, stationery.

A description of the nationlization of banks is furnished by Bonch-Bruyevich, who prepared the whole undertaking, wrote the orders, organized the transportation, the twenty-eight detachments of sharpshooters, et cetera. It was necessary to occupy twenty-eight banks, arrest twenty-eight bank directors.

"I requested the commandant of Smolny, Comrade Malkov, to set aside a comfortable room," writes Bonch-Bruyevich, "completely private from the public and prepare twenty-eight cots, tables, and chairs. He was also to be ready to feed twenty-eight persons, and to begin with, serve them tea and breakfast by 8 A.M." The occupation of the twenty-eight banks proceeded without difficulty. It took place on December 27, 1917. "In the shortest time, the Commissar of Finance appointed new workers to the banks. Many of the directors who had been arrested expressed a desire to continue their work under the Soviet Government, and were immediately released. Commissars were appointed for each bank, and the work continued in so far as it was necessary for the concentration of all funds and operations in the State Bank."

Lenin's counsel, on the eve of the coup d'état, had been: "Let us seize power, try to nationalize the banks, and then see what to do next. We shall learn from experience."

It was on this theory that he now proceeded. The first day after their victory the Bolsheviks published two decrees. One of them disposed of the big landed estates, which were handed over to local agrarian committees, "pending the decision of the Constituent Assembly." Another decree ordered the nationalization of banking institutions.

Private property, however, was not abolished. Small land holdings were left untouched and the withdrawal of sums from current bank accounts up to fifteen hundred rubles monthly permitted.

Lenin was still hesitant about the immediate nationalization of the factories. "Socialism cannot be introduced before the working class learns to lead and assert its authority," he said, explaining why his measures appeared to be "incomplete and contradictory." On January 24, 1918, he declared in a speech at Petrograd:

"Very often delegations of workers and peasants come to the Soviet Government and ask what to do with such and such a piece of land, for example. And frequently I myself have felt embarrassment when I saw that they had no very definite views. And I said to them: you are the government, do as you please, take all you want, we will support you, but take care of production, see that production is useful. Take up useful work; you will make mistakes, but you will learn. . . ."

Human nature being what it is, he wrote in *State and Revolution,* it craves submission. Until Socialism was established the proletariat needed the state not to establish freedom, but solely to "crush the antagonists."

In the meantime, the course was quite clear. "As the state is only a transitional institution which we are obliged to use in the revolutionary struggle in order to crush our opponents forcibly, it is a pure absurdity to speak of a Free People's State. During the period when the proletariat still needs the state, it does not require it in the interests of freedom, but in the interests of crushing its antagonists." To crush the antagonists was the principal aim of the "proletarian dictatorship," "an aim to be attained at any cost."

On November 10, 1917, the Soviet Government published a decree curtailing freedom of the press, accompanied by the assurance that the repressive measures were only temporary and would become inoperative "as soon as the new regime takes firm root."

The Liberal press was promptly silenced.

But it was just as important for Lenin to gag Socialist opinion. From the first days of Soviet power he insisted on shutting down the Socialist Revolutionary and Menshevik papers. According to Trotsky, at every opportunity Lenin would say: "Can't we bridle those scoundrels? Tell me, what kind of a dictatorship do you call this?"

Step by step the opposition papers were suspended and shut down.

At a session of the All-Russian Central Executive Committee of the Soviets on November 17, 1917, Lenin defended the suppression of these publications. "To tolerate those papers," he declared, "is to cease to be a Socialist. . . . The state is an institution built up for the sake of exercising violence. Previously this violence was exercised by a handful of moneybags over the entire people; now we want . . . to organize violence in the interests of the people. . . ."

And three months later, at the Fourth Congress of the Soviets, to the outcries of the Socialists, *"Our papers have been closed,"* Lenin replied: "Of course, unfortunately not all of them! Soon all of them will be closed. . . . The dictatorship of the proletariat will wipe out the shameful purveying of the bourgeois opium."

After the Brest-Litovsk Treaty, when the German Army occupied large Russian territories and Lenin had reason to fear the worst, the censorship was relaxed somewhat, and a few newpapers were allowed to reappear, with the proviso that they were to print on their front page all Soviet decrees and statements by Bolshevik Commissars. In addition, the press was subjected to huge fines for every bit of news that did not please the eye of the censor. Thus Gorky's *Novaya*

Zhizn was fined 35,000 rubles for an "unfavorable" news item.

But even this slight concession did not last long. Early in May 1918 the regime clamped down the lid, closing *Dyelo Naroda, Dyen,* and *Novy Looch,* and, somewhat later, all the remaining opposition papers, including Gorky's newspaper. Nor was Gorky permitted to resume publication when he made his peace with Lenin.

The freedom of speech and press for which generations of Russian revolutionaries had fought since the days of the Decembrists was completely destroyed within a matter of months.

15   LENIN SILENCES THE CONSTITUENT ASSEMBLY

THE IMMEDIATE CALLING OF THE CONSTITUENT ASSEMBLY HAD been one of Lenin's main slogans from April to November 1917. Time and again Lenin had promised that when the Bolsheviks took power the Assembly would be speedily convened.

The Bolshevik pledge was plain enough. But the Bolshevik leaders were well aware that the elections, scheduled by the Provisional Government for November 25, would not give them control of the Constituent Assembly.

"On the very first day, if not the first hour of the Revolution," relates Trotsky, "Lenin brought up the question of the Constituent Assembly. 'We must postpone the elections. We must extend the right of suffrage to those who have reached their maturity (eighteen years). We must outlaw the adherents of Kornilov and the Cadets,' said Lenin."

Despite considerable Bolshevik coercion, when the election returns came in, the result was even worse than Lenin had expected.

Of the thirty-six million Russians who went to the polls, only nine million voted for Bolshevik candidates, while nearly twenty-one million, or about 58 per cent, voted for the Socialist Revolutionary Party. Of 707 deputies, the Socialist Revolutionaries elected 370—a clear majority; the Bolsheviks only 175; the pro-Lenin Left Socialist Revolutionaries, 40, the Mensheviks, 16; the Populist-Socialists, 2; the Cadets, 17; 86 were representatives of national minority groups; and 11 unaffiliated candidates. The Russian people, in the freest election in their history, voted for moderate Socialism against Lenin and against the bourgeoisie.

From the standpoint of Soviet public relations, no more disastrous result was possible. But Lenin was prepared, even for this.

The arrangements for this opening had been well thought out. Who should address the Assembly, and on what topics they should speak, who should guide the respective factions—these and kindred problems had already been debated. "Everything was provided for except—the bands of drunken sailors who filled the galleries of the Tauride Palace and the non-parliamentary cynicism of the Bolsheviks," comments Boris Sokolov, a Socialist Revolutionary delegate. These were not on the agenda, but were quite observable in the proceedings.

After repeated postponements, the date for the opening of the Constituent Assembly was fixed for January 18, 1918.

Meanwhile the Bolsheviks were conducting a skillful campaign to foster a feeling against the Socialist Revolutionaries in the minds of the working people. The astuteness and thoroughness exhibited by the Bolsheviks in their preparation for the November coup d'état were exhibited now in their plans for the dissolution of the Constituent Assembly. They left nothing to chance. As they had previously prepared the Army, so now, by assiduous cultivation of a number of regiments of the Petrograd garrison, they secured military support for a fresh attack upon public institutions. The Bolsheviks started with the great advantage of position. Theirs was the only party organization among the soldiers which had survived the November coup.

The laboring masses had been subjected to a greater amount of propaganda by the Bolsheviks. Though friendly to the Constituent Assembly, the workers' attitude rather inclined to an indifferent skepticism. The large majority of the Petrograd workingmen were neutral, not more than 15 per cent having voted for Bolshevik candidates in factory elections.

The Izmailovsky regiment hesitated for a long time before deciding its course of action. The Bolsheviks conducted a vigorous campaign among the soldiers. A large meeting was held in January in the theater of the regiment. Krylenko and Piatakov spoke for the Bolsheviks, Fortunatov and Sokolov for the Socialist Revolutionaries. Krylenko and Piatakov delivered the customary onslaught upon the "imperialistic war," and attacked the Entente, Clemenceau, the "bourgeois" Provisional Government, et cetera. Then they spoke of the Constituent Assembly. Immediately the soldiers shouted, "Don't dare to touch it! Let there be Soviets and a Constituent Assembly! Do you think we elected our deputies for nothing?"

On January 16 Krylenko went to the Semionovsky regiment in order to prepare the ground for the dissolution of the Constituent Assembly by "clearing away," as he said, "the heavy atmosphere of counter-revolution which filled the barracks." He was not favorably received, and was advised to be very careful in what he said; otherwise the soldiers might not listen to him.

Krylenko's words were lost in the clamor that arose from every part of the room.

After Krylenko had left, a soldier spoke, amid cheers, of the necessity to defend the Constituent Assembly.

The Socialist Revolutionary Military Committee became aware that the Bolsheviks intended to utilize the sailors of the First and Second Baltic squadrons in the demonstration against the Constituent Assembly. The Socialist Revolutionaries had a small organization among the sailors of the Second Squadron, the chairman of the squadron committee, an intelligent sailor called Safranov, being on the side of the Socialist Revolutionaries. A meeting was held on January 16, and, after speeches by Safranov and others, an enthusiastic sailor leaped on to the platform and shouted:

"Brothers, comrades, let us swear that we will not go against the People's Assembly."

The sailors swore not to go against it—as for defending it, that was another question.

The Assembly was scheduled to open on the morning of January 18. In anticipation of the long-awaited event, Lenin ordered a detachment of Lettish sharpshooters to Petrograd. Lenin knew that the Lettish troops had no particular sentimental ties with the Russian people and would carry out their orders with the loyalty of a pretorian guard.

In the meantime the League for the Defense of the Constituent Assembly—organized by the Socialist Revolutionaries and Mensheviks—decided to greet the opening of the Constituent Assembly by a peaceful procession to the Tauride Palace. This was at once labeled as an attempt at counter-revolution.

In addition to the Letts, marines were summoned from Kronstadt, and cruisers, supplemented by several submarines, the *Aurora,* and the battleship *Republic,* were brought up along the Neva. Sailors and Red Guards were stationed at the entrance to the Tauride Palace. All passes for the visitors' gallery were issued by Uritsky, chief of the Petrograd political police.

At about eleven o'clock on the morning of January 18 from all sections of the city came large crowds of unarmed workers and students, waving red banners and placards, with the inscriptions: "Proletarians of All Countries Unite!" "Land and Freedom!" "Long Live the Constituent Assembly!" They marched to Mars Field, where they were joined by members of the Executive Committee of the Peasants' Soviet.

As the procession was turning into a street leading to the Tauride Palace, it was suddenly met by fire from Bolshevik rifles and machine guns. All the streets leading to the Constituent Assembly were barred by picked Bolshevik units whose orders were: "Spare no shells!" One hundred men and women were killed and wounded in Petrograd that day.

The Tauride Palace presented a strange spectacle. The halls and assembly room were jammed with heavily armed soldiers and sailors. At each door marines and Red Guards armed with rifles and hand grenades gruffly demanded admission cards. The public galleries were occupied mainly by Uritsky's Bolshevik claque.

Instead of opening in the morning, the Assembly did not begin its session until four in the afternoon. The Bolsheviks and Left Socialist Revolutionaries occupied the extreme left of the house; next to them sat the crowded Socialist Revolutionary majority, then the Mensheviks. The benches on the right were empty. A number of Cadet deputies had already been arrested; the rest stayed away. The entire Assembly was Socialist—but the Bolsheviks were only a minority.

Lenin, accompanied by his wife, sister, and Bonch-Bruyevich, entered through a side door when the Assembly was already filled. They checked their coats in the anteroom and went into a small chamber where they sat, talked, and ate a buffet dinner.

"Since we have really been guilty of such foolhardiness as to promise to call this assembly, we must open it today," said Lenin with a wry grin, "but as to the time of its closing, history is still silent."

Sverdlov entered the chamber and conferred with Lenin on the order of business. A few minutes later Lenin said: "Well, it is time to begin," and arising, proceeded through the long corridor to the great hall. When he entered, the session had begun—and it was not proceeding according to Lenin's plans.

In accordance with custom, the parliament was opened by the oldest deputy. From the Socialist Revolutionary benches rose aged Deputy Shvetzov, a veteran of the People's Will. As he mounted the platform, Bolshevik deputies began slamming their desks while soldiers and sailors pounded the floor with their rifles. Some of the Left Socialist Revolutionaries joined in the clamor. From the gallery one soldier aimed his rifle at Shvetzov.

Shvetzov finally found a lull in the noise to say: "The meeting of the Constituent Assembly is opened." An outburst of catcalls greeted his words.

Sverdlov then mounted the platform, pushed the old man aside, and declared in his loud, rich voice that the Central Executive Committee of the Soviet of Workers', Soldiers', and Peasants' Deputies had empowered him to open the meeting of the Constituent Assembly. Then on behalf of the committee he read the "Declaration of Rights of the Laboring and Exploited Masses," written by Lenin, Stalin, and Bukharin. The declaration demanded that all state power be vested in the Soviets, thereby destroying the very meaning of the Constituent Assembly. It had been adopted by the Bolshevik-controlled Soviet Central Executive Committee, which had also passed a resolution that "all attempts on the part of any person or institution to assume any of the functions of government will be regarded as a counter-revolutionary act. Every such attempt will be suppressed by all means at the command of the Soviet Government, including the use of armed force."

Sverdlov asked the Assembly to decide immediately whether it would accept the program of the Sovnarcom. Instead, despite the continuing tumult, the majority succeeded in moving for the election of a chairman. Victor Chernov, leader of the Socialist Revolutionary Party, won by a large margin.

In his opening address, Chernov expressed hope that the convocation of the Constituent Assembly meant the end of Russia's nebulous transitional period. The land question was already resolved, he said; the soil would become the common property of all peasants who were willing and able to till it. The Constituent Assembly would pursue an active foreign policy, striving for a democratic general peace without victors or vanquished but would not sign a separate peace with Imperial Germany.

The Constituent Assembly, as the freely elected parliament of the Russian people, was entitled to full legislative power, said Chernov, but it was willing to submit all fundamental decisions to popular referendum. If the Soviets joined hands with the Assembly and respected the will of the people, there would be peace and freedom in Russia; if not, civil war was inevitable.

Under the fire of constant interruptions, Chernov succeeded in finishing his speech. He was followed by Bolshevik orators Bukharin and Skvortsov. Bukharin proposed that the Soviet declaration be passed at the head of the agenda—in order to decide whether the Constituent Assembly sided with the "factory owners, merchants, and bank directors, or with the gray coats, the workers, soldiers, and sailors." The reference to factory owners, merchants, and bank directors brought ironic laughter from the Socialist majority.

Skvortsov, turning to the Socialist Revolutionaries, said: "Everything is finished between us. We are carrying the October Revolution against the bourgeoisie to the end. We are on opposite sides of the barricades."

The Bolshevik speakers were heard in silence by the Socialist deputies. Nor were they interrupted when they used abusive language.

When Tseretelli rose to reply, rifles were pointed at his head and sailors brandished pistols in front of his face. The chairman's appeals for order brought more hooting, catcalls, obscene oaths, and fierce howls. Tseretelli finally managed, nevertheless, to capture general attention with his eloquent plea for civil liberty and his warning of civil war. He was followed by a Socialist Revolutionary deputy who spoke on the peace program of the Constituent Assembly.

Lenin did not speak. He sat on the stairs leading to the platform, smiled derisively, jested, wrote something on a slip of paper, then stretched himself out on a bench and pretended to fall asleep. The sailors continued to point their rifles at the Socialist Revolutionaries. The galleries were in an uproar, shouting, whistling, stamping their feet.

The Bolshevik spokesmen again pressed for the acceptance of their declaration. After much debate the Constituent Assembly majority rejected the Bolshevik platform and voted to record their stand on the war, the agrarian problem, and Russia's form a government. Thereupon the Bolshevik deputies rose in a body and marched out.

Dawn was already breaking when the remaining deputies, representing the elected majority, started to read their decrees. The galleries emptied out and they remained alone with Lenin's sailors and soldiers. The Socialist revolutionaries and Mensheviks knew their time was short. Chernov was reading the decree on land when a sailor seized him by the arm and said, "It's time to finish. We have an order from the People's Commissar."

"Which People's Commissar?" asked Chernov.

"An order—you can't remain here any longer—the guards are tired and we'll turn off the lights," replied the sailor.

"The members of the Constituent Assembly are also tired," said Chernov, "but they cannot rest until they fulfill the mandate given to them by the people to decide the questions of peace, land, and government."

Not allowing the sailor an opportunity to continue, Chernov went on reading the decrees. Russia was proclaimed a federated republic with national autonomy for all its constituent peoples. The guards continued to shout: "Come on, time to finish. We'll turn off the lights." But the deputies went on with their work, voting for the transfer of land to the peasantry and a democratic peace program in line with Chernov's speech. When the chair finally recessed the meeting, it was morning.

Before noon, when the Assembly was slated to reconvene, the deputies found the entrance to the Tauride Palace barred by a detachment of troops with rifles, machine guns, and two fieldpieces. On the same day—Januray 19, 1918, a decree of the Sovnarcom abolished the Constituent Assembly. Newspapers that printed accounts of the January 18 session were seized from the stands and from newsboys by soldiers and burned.

A the meeting of the All-Russian Central Executive Committee of the Soviet on January 19, 1918, Lenin declared:

"The people wanted the Constituent Assembly summoned, and we summoned it. But they sensed immediately what this famous Constituent Assembly really represented. And now we have carried out the will of the people, which is All Power to the Soviets. We shall break the backs of the saboteurs. . . .

"To hand over power to the Constituent Assembly would again be compromising with the malignant bourgeoisie. The Russian Soviets place the interests of the toiling masses far above the interests of treacherous compromise disguised in a new garb. . . . And when the Constituent Assembly again revealed its readiness to postpone all the painfully urgent problems and tasks that were placed before it by the Soviets, we told the Constituent Assembly that they must not be postponed for one single moment. And by the will of the Soviet power the Constituent Assembly, which has refused to recognize the power of the people, is being dissolved.

"The Constituent Assembly is dissolved. The Soviet Revolutionary Republic will triumph no matter what the cost."

That speech was for the record. Privately, after the dissolution decree, Lenin bluntly told Trotsky:

"We made a mistake in not postponing the calling of the Constituent Assembly. We acted very incautiously. But it came out all to the better. The dissolution of the Constituent Assembly by the Soviet Government means a complete and frank liquidation of the idea of democracy by the idea of dictatorship. It will serve as a good lesson."

16 BREST-LITOVSK

PEACE AT ANY PRICE WAS NECESSARY FOR LENIN IN ORDER TO consolidate the power of dictatorship. But he also was so convinced of the immediacy of revolution in Germany that the result of a German-dictated peace was without terror for him. He therefore stubbornly persisted all through the period of negotiations in pressing his colleagues to do anything and everything to achieve peace.

The Soviet peace delegation, headed by Joffe and Trotsky, had been dispatched to Brest-Litovsk at the end of November. On December 27 the Petrograd press published a statement by the Soviet peace delegation claiming that "the principles of a general democratic peace without annexations are accepted by the nations of the Central Powers," that "Germany and its allies have no plans whatsoever of territorial aggrandizement, and similarly have no desire to destroy or limit the political independence of any nation."

* * *

When the Soviet delegation heard the German terms, General Skalon, one of the Soviet experts, committed suicide on the spot. Another Soviet delegate, Professor Pokrovsky, said with tears in his eyes: "How can one speak of peace without annexations if Russia is being deprived of territories equal in size to approximately eighteen provinces?"

The majority of the Bolshevik delegation, now headed by Trotsky and Bukharin, were flatly opposed to the German peace terms. This division became so sharp that it nearly precipitated a major split in the Soviet Government.

On January 21, 1918, the Bolshevik Central Committee met with the Bolshevik deputies to the Third Congress of Soviets to discuss the German terms. Lenin spoke in favor of signing peace even at the cost of ceding considerable territory. Trotsky, on the other hand, recommended that war be declared at an end without signing the peace terms. By this device of "no peace, no war," he hoped that the German and Austrian armies, demoralized by inactivity and revolutionary propaganda, would revolt. The third suggestion was to wage a "revolutionary war" against Germany and her allies. Fifteen voted for Lenin's recommendation, sixteen for Trotsky's, and thirty-two for "revolutionary war."

Three days later the Central Committee again took up the question of peace. Lenin again insisted on immediate acceptance of the German terms.

* * *

Bukharin, as well at Trotsky, Uritsky, Lomov, and Dzerzhinsky, declared that to accept Germany's peace terms would be to surrender the entire Bolshevik program. Finally, by a vote of nine to seven, Trotsky's formula, "the war is to be discontinued; peace is not to be signed, and the Army is to be demobilized," was accepted.

But they reckoned without Germany. On February 16 General Hoffmann sent an ultimatum to the Soviet Government, and the German Army prepared to resume the offensive. On the receipt of the German ultimatum, the Central Committee called a meeting for February 17. A group of five, consisting of Lenin, Stalin, Sverdlov, Sokolnikov, and Smilga, favored immediate acceptance of Germany's terms. Six members, Bukharin, Lomov, Trotsky, Uritsky, Joffe, and Krestinsky, voted against it. When the question of signing immediate peace or awaiting a German offensive was put to a final vote, it was decided to wait for the results of the German offensive. Perhaps the German soldiers would refuse to fight.

The answer came fast enough. On February 18 the German Army attacked once more. The Central Committee was reconvened and Lenin again demanded immediate signing. Again he had the support of only a minority. Toward evening, as news of fresh German advances came in, the general attitude changed. Lenin, with greater determination than ever, pressed for prompt acceptance. He could not understand the concern of his comrades over ceding "some Russian territory." To Lenin the sole important issue was whether or not the German peace terms imperiled the Soviet power.

"If the Germans should demand the overturn of the Bolshevik Government, then, of course, we would have to fight," he said. "All other demands can and should be granted."

On a final vote Lenin won seven votes of a total of thirteen. A wire was sent to the German Government announcing that the Soviet Government was willing to accept the peace terms offered at Brest-Litovsk and would reply immediately to any new conditions.

Germany's reply, on February 22, contained more drastic terms, involving not only surrender of the entire Baltic area, including Finland, but Soviet recognition of a German-sponsored "independent" Ukraine. When these conditions became known, they created renewed opposition.

The Left Socialist Revolutionaries who were then participating in the government proposed acceptance of Allied aid in order to resist the Germans. Trotsky and Sokolnikov favored the acquisition of arms. Lenin was absent from the meeting but sent the following message to the Central Committee: "Please add my vote in favor of taking potatoes and arms from the Anglo-French imperialist bandits." However, at the next meeting of the Central Committee Lenin stated that the policy of "playing with revolutionary phrases" must end.

"If it is to be continued," he threatened, "I will resign from the government as well as the Central Committee, and will begin an open agitation against the two. In order to wage a revolutionary war, an army is needed, and we haven't got it. Consequently, we must accept the peace terms."

A heated discussion ensued. But Lenin's opponents were reluctant to accept his challenge. On March 3, 1918, the Soviet delegates signed the Treaty of Brest-Litovsk.

*   *   *

Lenin had no illusions as to the terms he had accepted. "I happened to be in Lenin's room," related Stasova, his secretary, "when Karakhan brought the draft of the Brest-Litovsk peace treaty. He wanted to unfold it and show it to his chief. Lenin protested vigorously. 'What, not only do you want me to sign this impudent peace treaty, but also to read it? No, no, never! I shall neither read it nor carry out its terms whenever there is a chance not to do so.' "

Brest-Litovsk gave Germany control over the resources of the Ukraine and released many German divisions for the Western Front. But within six or seven months American, French, and British troops were on the offensive which cracked the Hindenburg Line and forced Germany to sue for an armistice. The allied victory compelled the Germans to disgorge the territories they had acquired under the peace treaty which Lenin signed.

17 THE BEGINNING OF TERROR

IMMEDIATELY AFTER THE BOLSHEVIK COUP, CAPITAL PUNISHment for desertion at the front was abolished.

"That is a mistake," Lenin protested, "an unpardonable weakness and pacifist illusion," and recommended that the order be rescinded immediately. Convinced that this move would make an unfavorable impression, he accepted a compromise: to disregard the new law and shoot deserters.

"That was the period," says Trotsky, "when Lenin at every opportunity kept hammering into our heads that terror was unavoidable.

" 'Where is your dictatorship? Show it to me. What we have is a mess, not a dictatorship. If we cannot shoot a man who sabotages . . . then what kind of revolution is this?' "

Once, when Lenin heard a report about a series of counterrevolutionary attempts, he grew angry and exclaimed:

"Is it impossible to find among us a Fouquier-Tinville to tame our wild counter-revolutionists?"

Lenin found his Fouquier-Tinville in Felix Dzerzhinsky. He was fair, slightly round-shouldered, with a short pointed beard and transparent eyes with dilated pupils. There were moments when his friendly smile gave way to icy sternness. At such times his eyes and ascetic bloodless lips revealed a demoniac fanaticism. Rigorous self-denial, incorrigible honesty, and a frigid indifference to the opinions of others completed his make-up. His natural modesty, unassuming air, and quiet manners set him apart. He was the great puritan, the "saint" of the upheaval.

Dzerzhinsky was the son of a rich Polish landowner of the Vilno province. As a student he became a member of the Lithuanian Social Democratic Party, was exiled at an early age, later joined the Polish Social Democratic Party, and spent most of his life in jails and in Siberia. The Revolution released him from a cell in the Taganka prison in Moscow.

Upstairs, in the Smolny Institute, Lenin and his lieutenants were drafting the blueprint for a new society. Lenin had supplied the word, but the sword was needed to consolidate Soviet power. Downstairs, in a small dark corner room at the end of the long corridor, sat Dzerzhinsky. He had just been appointed commandant of Smolony. At his disposal were several detachments of Lettish sharpshooters, whose job was to

keep the machine guns placed in the windows properly oiled.
A modest task. The spotlight on the huge yellowish building
did not reach the dark corner where Dzerzhinsky sat.

For some days everybody came and went freely in Smolny.
All were feverishly busy, with important-looking portfolios
under their arms, rushing from one floor to another, giving
and taking orders, exchanging greetings.

Dzerzhinsky knew that Lenin's power was not secure until
the enemies of the Bolshevik Revolution were crushed, their
forces scattered and destroyed. No quarter could be given in
the fight.

While the Sovnarcom was in session, a polite but firm order
came from the commandant's little room, ordering everybody
in Smolny to appear for examination. Those who failed to
appear were rounded up as they entered or left the building.
The guards had been stationed at every entrance and stairway.

"Ah, good day, comrade!" was Dzerzhinsky's quiet greeting
to all callers.

There followed a businesslike interrogation.

Those who aroused no suspicion were supplied with passes
permitting them to enter the building. Some were ordered out
with the warning not to return. Others found themselves prisoners pending further investigation. Soon a network of
espionage enveloped the building which had once been a
fashionable school for girls.

On December 20, 1917, Lenin instructed Dzerzhinsky to
organize an Extraordinary Commission for Combating Coun-
ter Revolution and Speculation. Under the name Cheka, this
Soviet secret police soon became the symbol for a system of
terror such as the world had never seen. In later years its name
was changed to OGPU, NKVD, MVD, but its purpose remained the same. Dzerzhinsky became the first head of the
Cheka.

Then followed a series of uncovered plots, some true, others
fantastic, against the Bolsheviks and conspiracies against the
lives of the leaders. In his little room Dzerzhinsky was constantly sharpening the weapon of the Soviet dictatorship. To
Dzerzhinsky was brought the mass of undigested rumors from
all parts of Petrograd. With the aid of picked squads of Chekists, Dzerzhinsky undertook to purge the city.

Little time was wasted sifting evidence and classifying
people rounded up in these night raids. Woe to him who did
not disarm all suspicion at once. The prisoners were generally
hustled to the old police station not far from the Winter
Palace. Here, with or without perfunctory interrogation, they
were stood up against the courtyard wall and shot. The stac-
cato sounds of death were muffled by the roar of truck motors
kept going for the purpose.

Dzerzhinsky furnished the instrument for tearing a new

society out of the womb of the old—the instrument of organized, systematic mass terror. For Dzerzhinsky the class struggle meant exterminating "the enemies of the working class." The "enemies of the working class" were all who opposed the Bolshevik dictatorship.

At meetings of the Sovnarcom, Lenin often exchanged notes with his colleagues. On one occasion he sent a note to Dzerzhinsky: "How many vicious counter-revolutionaries are there in our prisons?" Dzerzhinsky's reply was: "About fifteen hundred." Lenin read it, snorted something to himself, made a cross beside the figure, and returned the note to Dzerzhinsky.

Dzerzhinsky rose and left the room without a word. No one paid any attention either to Lenin's note or to Dzerzhinsky's departure. The meeting continued. But the next day there was excited whispering. Dzerzhinsky had ordered the execution of all the fifteen hundred "vicious counter-revolutionaries" the previous night. He had taken Lenin's cross as a collective death sentence.

There would have been little comment had Lenin's gesture been meant as an order for wholesale liquidation. But, as Fotieva, Lenin's secretary, explained: "There was a misunderstanding. Vladimir Ilich never wanted the executions. Dzerzhinsky did not understand him. Vladimir Ilich usually puts a cross on memoranda to indicate that he had read them and noted their contents."

Early in 1918 the Soviet leaders transferred the seat of government to Moscow.

On his arrival in the ancient capital with his staff, Dzerzhinsky set out to find suitable quarters for his organization. He chose the Rossiya Insurance Company building at 22 Lubianka Street. It was a comfortable structure with plenty of rooms, many side entrances, spacious cellars, and a broad courtyard. As the main office of the Cheka, 22 Lubianka Street was to become the most notorious address in Russia.

18 IN THE KREMLIN

ON THE FIRST OF MAY LENIN STOOD ON THE KREMLIN WALL, where Napoleon once had watched Moscow burning, and gazed down at the May Day demonstration in Red Square.

Settled under the same ancient bulb-shaped cupolas and church walls where centuries of Russian autocrats had been crowned, the new master lived a very frugal existence. The rooms adjoining his apartment smelled of cats and carbolic acid. Sharing the apartment were Krupskaya, his sister Maria, and their maid. They ate out of the Czar's silver and china, but their food was rather tasteless and often insufficient. Despite their red caviar, occasional butter, cheese, and jelly, it was poor fare compared to the table of an ordinary citizen before the Revolution. There was never enough firewood to heat the rooms properly, nor sufficient teaspoons for their guests.

"We are good revolutionists," said Lenin, "but I don't know why we feel obligated to prove that we also stand on the heights of foreign culture. As for myself, I don't hesitate to declare myself a barbarian."

* * *

Not having industrial and consumer goods in sufficient quantity to exchange with the peasants for grain, the Soviet Government on May 10, 1918, issued an order for the requisitioning of grain from "rich" peasants. A month later, on June 11, the so-called "Committees of the Poor" were created to enforce the decree in every village. An ugly atmosphere of suspicion, espionage, and betrayal was created among the peasants. Neighbor spied upon neighbor. Peasants slaughtered their cattle and refused to sow their land, rather than turn over their food supplies to the government. And the countryside seethed with local uprisings, which were crushed by punitive expeditions of Cheka troops.

The complete suppression of civil liberty, the dissolution of the Constituent Assembly, the Cheka terror, and the Carthaginian peace of Brest-Litovsk—which deprived Russia of its richest regions—brought increasing revolt from every stratum of the Russian people.

The Petrograd regiments which had overthrown Kerensky were on the verge of a new revolt and had to be disarmed as were other military and naval units. The Lettish sharpshooters became the only regular armed force on which Lenin could rely with complete certainty.

After the dissolution of the Constituent Assembly, all political parties except the Left Socialist Revolutionaries raised the standard of revolt against Lenin's dictatorship.

In the spring of 1918 the Right Center, whose members were always more or less pro-German, entered into secret negotiations with German representatives, hoping with German aid to overthrow Lenin and re-establish the dynasty.

The League for the Regeneration of Russia, on the other hand, looked to the aid of England, France, and the United States, and made an official request to these countries to restore an Allied front in Russia.

Until Brest-Litovsk, the Allies still expected that the Soviet regime would be forced to resume the war against Germany. After the Brest-Litovsk peace was signed, the Allies became interested in the proposal of the "League for the Regeneration

of Russia" for the revival of an Eastern Front. At this time a
new group, the "National Center," was formed. In June 1918
the Allies agreed to send military forces to help these anti-
Bolshevik forces carry on the struggle against Germany and
the Soviet regime.

Earlier, the Japanese had landed several detachments in
Vladivostok and other strategic points in Siberia, where tremendous supplies of Allied ammunition and raw material
were stored. In Siberia there were also large numbers of
German and Austrian war prisoners. Ostensibly the Japanese
acted to prevent the Germans from gaining access to these
stores and utilizing the prisoners. Actually there was reason to
believe that the Japanese intended to remain. British, French,
and American troops were landed in Vladivostok in July 1918
to counteract the Japanese. Most of these troops remained in
the vicinity of the port city. About the same time British and
American detachments landed at Murmansk and Archangel.
After Brest-Litovsk the Czechoslovak Legion of war prisoners,
who had fought as volunteers in the Russian Army, were
ordered by the Allied Command to proceed to France via
Siberia and the Pacific. Thereupon Berlin informed the Soviet
Government that Germany would consider the passage of the
Czechs as a breach of the Treaty.

Trotsky, the Commissar of War, ordered the legion disarmed. On May 26, when an attempt was made to carry out
this order, the Czechs, then in the Volga region, rebelled and
arrested the local Soviet officials.

When Lenin was handed a telegraphic report of the Czech
uprising he became extremely agitated. The cabinet meeting
suspended and Rosengoltz, a strong-armed Bolshevik, was dispatched to the Volga, armed with blanket authority.

On June 8, workers and soldiers allied with the Socialist
Revolutionary Party joined the Czechs. And a Committee of
"Members of the All-Russian Constituent Assembly" was
formed which began to organize a volunteer People's Army.
Cossacks from the Urals joined forces with the Czechs and
the People's Army. Within a short time a vast territory from
Samara on the Volga to Vladivostok on the Pacific was in the
hands of anti-Bolshevik armies. At the same time the Ukraine
and other parts of South Russia were held by German and
Austrian troops.

In the Don Region, Generals Alexeiev and Kornilov, former
commanders in chief of the Russian Army, organized a White
Army. In January 1918 their forces numbered 3,000 men. To
crush this force, the Bolsheviks sent an army of 10,000. Since
the peasant population of the region was not in sympathy with
the program of the generals, their troops were forced to retreat to the steppes. General Kornilov himself was killed in
action.

Two months later the remnants of the volunteer army, numbering only about one thousand men, organized a new offensive and this time found recruits among the Cossacks. In June their number increased to 12,000; in July to 30,000. By October 1918 this army swelled to 100,000 and occupied a front of two hundred miles, under the command of General Denikin.

In the summer of 1918 the Left Socialist Revolutionaries—the only non-Bolshevik political group that had supported Lenin and which had participated in the Soviet Government—also staged a revolt. They submitted a five-point program to the Congress of the Soviets demanding (1) the abolition of the grain-requisitioning squads; (2) the dissolution of the standing Red Army; (3) the abolition of Dzerzhinsky's secret police, the Cheka; (4) peace with the Czechoslovak Legion, and (5) a declaration of guerrilla warfare against Germany.

Lenin flatly rejected these demands and ordered the arrest of some leading Left Socialist Revolutionaries. With the connivance of several anti-German Chekists, the Left Socialist Revolutionaries then devised a plan for an armed uprising coupled with terrorist acts against German diplomatic representatives in Russia. On July 6, 1918, Blumkin, a Left Socialist Revolutionary, who was armed with credentials of the Cheka, assassinated Count Mirbach, the German Ambassador in Moscow.

With the support of several squads of soldiers and a rebel Cheka detachment, the Left Socialist Revolutionaries arrested Dzerzhinsky and seized a number of public buildings, including the Moscow Telegraph Office. Telegrams were at once dispatched throughout the country, summoning the people to revolt.

With the telephone system still at his command, Lenin acted swiftly. He mobilized the Communist workers of Moscow, under the command of his loyal Lettish guards, and with their aid order was quickly restored in Moscow. Dzerzhinsky was released unharmed.

In the provinces there was still danger because of the peasant following of the Left Socialist Revolutionaries. To Stalin in Tsaritsyn (now Stalingrad) Lenin sent this message:

"We shall liquidate the revolt this very night, ruthlessly, and tell the people the truth, 'We are at a hairbreadth from war. . . . It is necessary everywhere ruthlessly to crush these wretched and hysterical adventurers who have become tools of the counter-revolutionaries.' "

To this Stalin replied: "As regards the hysterical ones, you may rest assured that our hand will not falter. We shall treat the enemies as enemies should be treated."

The assassination of Count Mirbach brought stern protests from Berlin. The Soviet Government promised an investigation and swift punishment for the assassin, but Blumkin was not caught. In order to appease German wrath, Lenin ordered the execution of about twenty Left Socialist Revolutionary hostages.

"We will make an internal loan from our 'comrades,' the Socialist Revolutionaries," Lenin told Krassin, "and thus both preserve our 'innocence' and promote our interests."

Meanwhile, in the Urals, Left Socialist Revolutionary Muraviev, who was still nominal Commander-in-Chief of the Red Army, "declared war" on Germany in a telegram to Berlin on July 11, 1918, and ordered his troops to advance on Moscow. Before his orders could be implemented, however, Muraviev was killed by a Bolshevik commissar. With his death, this revolt also collapsed. But Moscow and Petrograd were still cut off from most of Central Russia, Siberia, the Ukraine, Crimea, and the Caucasus.

While the Czechs and Bolsheviks were fighting in the Urals, ex-Czar Nicholas and his family were executed in Ekaterinburg on July 16, 1918. They had been placed under arrest immediately after the March Revolution and confined to Tsarskoye Selo. In July 1917, when the Bolshevik trend developed in Petrograd, the Provisional Government had sent them to Tobolsk, Siberia. In March 1918 the Bolshevik organization of the Urals demanded that they be removed to Ekaterinburg, where they would be in "safe hands."

Soon after the arrival of Nicholas, his wife, and children in Ekaterinburg, the leaders of the local Soviet began to discuss their execution. The majority, however, refused to assume responsibility without Moscow's approval. The local Bolshevik leader Goloschokin was sent to settle the fate of the Romanovs.

At first the Central Committee debated the advisability of holding a public trial in Ekaterinburg, but the precarious military situation forced this plan to be abandoned. The Czechoslovak Legion was approaching Ekaterinburg. The verdict was death for Nicholas and his family and the destruction of the bodies "in order not to give the counter-revolutionaries an opportunity of using the 'bones' of the Czar to play on the ignorance and superstition of the masses." A special commission was appointed to carry out this order.

"On July 16," relates Bykov, one of the Ural commissars, "the persons named to execute the sentence of the Romanovs congregated in the chamber of the Commandant of Ipatyev's house, where the Czar's family resided. It was decided to bring the entire family into the cellar and there carry out the sentence. Until the very last moment the Romanovs were unaware that they were to be executed. At midnight they were awakened, ordered to dress, and go down to the cellar. In order not to arouse their suspicions, they were told that a

'White' attack upon the house was expected that night. All the other inmates of the house were ordered to assemble in the cellar as well. When they had all congregated, the verdict was read to them and all eleven members of the Romanov family, Nicholas, his wife, his son Alexei, his four daughters, and the members of his suite were shot on the spot."

The bodies were wrapped in blankets, loaded on a truck, and driven to a deserted mine shaft several miles beyond the city. There they were temporarily deposited. The next morning the work of destroying them was begun. It was not until the afternoon of July 18 that this task was completed.

The mission was carried out by a detachment of Lettish Chekists, under the command of Yurovsky, a member of the Ural Soviet. The bodies were hacked to pieces with axes, soaked in benzine and sulphuric acid, and burned. The charred remains were dumped into a swamp some distance from the mine, and the soggy ground was raked up and covered with moss and leaves to hide all traces.

"The Soviet power," Bykov later wrote, "liquidated the Romanovs in an extraordinary fashion. The Soviet power in this incident displayed its extremely democratic nature. It made no exception for the All-Russian murderer and shot him as one shoots an ordinary bandit."

Official announcement of the execution was made on July 18.

The Sovnarcom was in the midst of discussing the draft of a new public health decree. Commissioner of Health Semashko was speaking, when Sverdlov walked into the room and seated himself near Lenin. When Semashko had concluded, Sverdlov whispered something to Lenin.

"Comrade Sverdlov asks the floor to make an announcement," Lenin said.

"I wish to announce," said Sverdlov, "that we have received a report that in Ekaterinburg, in accordance with the decision of the regional Soviet, Nicholas has been shot. Nicholas wanted to escape. The Czechoslovaks were approaching the city. The presidium of the Central Executive Committee has decided to approve this act."

There was no comment.

"Now let us proceed to read the draft point by point," Lenin resumed. The Council of People's Commissars returned to Semashko's health decree.

On July 19, 1918, *Izvestia* stated that "the wife and son of Nicholas Romanov were sent to a safe place." Apparently the extermination of the former Czarina, the Czarevich, and his four sisters, was too unsavory for the public. Moreover, no code of laws, even summary revolutionary justice, could admit the "execution" of the former Czar's physician, cook, chambermaid, and waiter.

The night following the death of the former Czar seven other members of the Romanov family were executed in a town in the Urals. Earlier, Grand Duke Mikhail had been shot in Perm.

Ruthless and violent action against all potential enemies was now the order of the day.

In his orders to his subordinates Lenin minced no words. The following order of August 9, 1918, is a typical example:

It is necessary to organize an extra guard of well-chosen, trustworthy men. They must carry out a ruthless mass terror against the kulaks, priests, and White Guards. All suspicious persons should be detained in a concentration camp outside the city. The punitive expedition should be sent out at once. Wire about the execution of this order.

Chairman of the Sovnarcom, LENIN.

Almost from the beginning of Soviet rule there were rumors of plots on Lenin's life, and as his regime adopted increasingly repressive measures, the fears for his safety increased. In January 1918 an unidentified assailant had fired at Lenin's car but missed his mark.

On Friday, August 30, 1918, Lenin was to speak at a labor rally in Moscow. Among the latecomers in the hall was a woman who sat close to the platform, resting her elbows on the table, listening carefully to every word that was spoken, while nervously puffing one cigarette after another.

Lenin arrived on schedule and spoke for only a few minutes. Then he descended the platform, put on his hat and coat, and left the hall, preceded by several workers and followed by a large crowd. The chain-smoking woman left at the same time.

Lenin emerged into the open court of the building, where an automobile was waiting for him. At the door he was accosted by the same woman who asked him some questions. As he walked toward his waiting car Lenin tried to answer her. He had one foot on the running board when she fired three shots at him, point-blank, from a distance of only a few feet. Lenin dropped to the ground. "They've killed Lenin! They've killed Lenin!" someone shouted. The excited crowd surged forward, then scattered in confusion. But Lenin got back on his feet and asked to be driven home. With the help of his chauffeur and bystanders, he staggered into his car and took his usual seat. The car sped at breakneck speed to the Kremlin.

His condition was not so grave at it seemed at first, despite the fact that one bullet pierced his neck and another his collarbone.

The woman who had tried to assassinate Lenin was cap-

tured a few blocks from the scene. She was brought to the
Lubianka late that night. At the Cheka hearing she wrote:

My name is Fanya Kaplan. . . . Today I shot at Lenin. I did
it on my own. I will not say from whom I obtained the revolver.
I will give no details. . . . I had resolved to kill Lenin long ago.
I consider him a traitor to the Revolution. . . . I was exiled to
Akatoi for participating in an assassination attempt against a
Czarist official in Kiev. I spent eleven years at hard labor. . . .
After the Revolution I was freed. . . . I favored the Constituent
Assembly and am still for it. . . . My parents are in the United
States. They emigrated in 1911. I have four brothers and two
sisters. They are all workers. I was educated at home. I shot at
Lenin.

In Petrograd, on the same day Fanya Kaplan attempted to
kill Lenin, a young Jewish student named Leonid Kanegiesser
assassinated the chief of the Petrograd Cheka, Uritsky.

The murder of Uritsky and the attempt on Lenin were followed by a period of unbridled terror in Petrograd, as Red
Army bands combed the streets in search of bourgeois and
intellectuals. Only Communists and important service men
felt safe. Arrests were spontaneous; no questions were asked,
no quarter given.

Zinoviev could tell the masses of soldiers: "The bourgeoisie
kills separate individuals; but we kill whole classes." Inflamed
by slogans of this sort, the soldiers went about their bloody
work with redoubled vigor. Kanegiesser was killed without a
trial, and Kronstadt's sailors added fuel to the rising flame of
civil war by shooting nearly five hundred of the bourgeois
hostages held in the prison of the Baltic bastion.

The Commissar of Internal Affairs, G. Petrovsky, broadcast the following order to all the local Soviets:

All the right-wing Socialist Revolutionaries known to the local
Soviet authorities should immediately be placed under arrest. A
considerable number of hostages should be taken from bourgeois
and officer ranks. The slightest show of resistance or the slightest
move made by the White Guardist circles should be met unre-
servedly by mass executions. . . .

Even before the attempt on Lenin's life, in the "Catechism
of a Class-conscious Proletarian," *Pravda,* on August 4, 1918,
had preached mass terror against the enemies of the Soviet
regime:

Workers and paupers, grab the rifle, learn how to shoot, be
prepared for the uprising of the kulaks and White Guards. Stand
up against the wall those who agitate against the Soviet power.
Ten bullets to everyone who raises a hand against it! . . .
The bourgeoisie is our eternal enemy, forever boring from within. The rule of capital will die with the last breath of the last
capitalist, nobleman, priest, and army officer.

In the space of a few days the Petrograd Cheka shot 512 hostages.

Izvestia of October 19 contained a report of a meeting of the Conference of the Extraordinary Commission: "Comrade Bokiy gave details of the work of the Petrograd District Commission since the evacuation of the All-Russian Extraordinary Commission to Moscow. The total number of persons arrested was 6,220. *Eight hundred were shot.*" These were official figures only for the district of Petrograd and for a limited period.

The professed aim of the Red Terror was "to exterminate the bourgeoisie as a class." But the term "bourgeoisie" as interpreted by the Cheka was so elastic as to include, potentially at least, virtually every non-Bolshevik. M. Latsis, one of the chiefs of the Cheka wrote: "We are exterminating the bourgeoisie as a class. Don't look for evidence of proof showing that this or that person either by word or deed acted against the interests of the Soviet power. The first questions you should put to the arrested person is: To what class does he belong, what is his origin, what was his education, and what is his profession? These should determine the fate of the accused. This is the essence of the Red Terror."

When Angelica Balabanoff protested against the reign of terror she had witnessed in the Ukraine, Lenin intimated with a sardonic smile that her usefulness to the Bolshevik cause was about over.

In an address delivered during this period before the Cheka, Lenin expressed his surprise at the outcries against the shooting of innocent people. We learn from mistakes, he asserted. The important thing was that the Cheka was putting teeth into the dictatorship.

"When I study the activities of the Cheka," said Lenin in 1918, "and at the same time hear the numerous criticisms that are made against it, I say that all that is idle talk of the petit bourgeois. . . . We shall drive them out through self-criticism. The important thing to us, however, is the fact that the Cheka is putting into effect the dictatorship of the proletariat, and in this sense it is of inestimable value. . . . This is the business of the Cheka and in this lies its service to the proletariat."

In October 1918 Lenin had blandly denied the charges of terrorism directed at the Bolsheviks. He had declared that Kautsky and "all the heroes of the Yellow International lie about Soviet Russia on the question of terrorism and democracy." And at the Seventh Congress of the Soviets he said: "Terror was imposed upon us. . . . People forget that terrorism was brought forth by the invasion of the world power of the Allies." The factual record of this period is a refutation of this apology.

In November 1918 Roman Malinovsky, whom Lenin had
reported dead in 1915, suddenly appeared in Moscow.

Now he was brought before a Bolshevik Revolutionary
Tribunal to face the very charges Lenin had labeled as slander
years before. Malinovsky's trial was held behind closed doors
with Lenin present throughout. Malinovsky made no attempt
to deny the documented charges brought against him. He
told the court that at the time he left the Duma he made a
full confession to Lenin.

Lenin sat facing Malinovsky, his head bent over a desk
while he wrote on a pad. It was obvious, according to Olga
Anikst, a Bolshevik witness, that Lenin was undergoing an
emotional conflict. He remained in the same position for
hours. When the defense counsel said that if Malinovsky had
had friends to guide him he would never have become a spy,
Lenin stirred, looked up at Malinovsky, and nodded his head
many times.

When the verdict of death by shooting was read, Malinovsky began to tremble and his face was distorted by fear. He
had obviously expected Lenin's intercession. It is possible that
before appearing he had been promised clemency. Lenin himself was undecided. A delegation of Petrograd Bolshevik workers attending the trial demanded to be allowed to witness the
execution, apparently fearing that Lenin might commute the
sentence of the agent provocateur who once enjoyed his full
confidence. The next day *Izvestia* reported that Malinovsky
had been shot.

19   COMINTERN

THE BOLSHEVIKS BEGAN TO PREPARE FOR WORLD REVOLUTION
soon after they seized power. On December 24, 1917, the Sovnarcom had allocated two million rubles to "the foreign representatives of the Commissariat of Foreign Affairs for the
needs of the international revolutionary movement." In an
order signed by Lenin, Trotsky, Bonch-Bruyevich, and Gor-
bunov, and published in *Izvestia* two days later, the Sovnarcom declared that it considered it necessary "to come to the
aid of the Left Internationalist wing of the working-class
movements of all countries with all possible resources, including money, quite irrespective of whether these countries are at
war or in alliance with Russia, or whether they occupy a neutral position."

Despite the fact that Russia was in the midst of civil war,
Lenin did not for a moment lose sight of his goal of tri-
umphant Marxian revolutions all over the world. Conditions
in central and eastern Europe following the armistice were

chaotic; soldiers returning from the front were weary, disillusioned, and embittered. In Germany and Austria-Hungary the monarchies were overthrown, the Austro-Hungarian Empire collapsed; Poland and the Balkans were in a state of ferment. Workers in Allied countries were also restless. The soil seemed fertile for Communism.

Germany was the first country outside Russia in which the Bolsheviks began to further their aims of world revolution. Revolutionary propaganda, leaflets, and other such material were brought in by the Soviet diplomatic representatives. The Bolsheviks sent a delegation consisting of Joffe, Rakovsky, Radek, Bukharin, and Ignatov. The delegation was barred by the German military, however, and only Radek, in disguise, succeeded in getting to Berlin.

Radek's first appeal was to the powerful Independent Socialist Party. In the name of Soviet Russia he denounced the Social Democratic government headed by Ebert and Scheidemann and called for a real revolutionary government. This government, said Radek, would unite with Russia at the Rhine to declare a new war on the imperialist Allies.

Soon afterward Radek was instructed to conclude a secret pact with Karl Liebknecht, the Spartacist leader. Under the agreement Lenin promised to furnish funds for Spartacist propaganda and weapons, and to recognize Liebknecht as the president of the German Soviet Republic. In January 1919 the Spartacists staged a revolt in Berlin, which was quickly suppressed, and Liebknecht and Rosa Luxemburg were killed.

After the Communist Revolution in Hungary, Lenin concluded a similar agreement with Béla Kun, the Communist dictator, in March 1919. This agreement provided that Russia and Hungary would extend economic and military aid to each other.

When Radek was arrested at the Bolshevik Propaganda Bureau in Berlin on February 12, 1919, the police found in his possession the draft of a plan for a general Communist offensive in central Europe, scheduled for that spring. A German Communist revolt was to be synchronized with a Red Army march through Poland to Germany.

In January 1919 Lenin addressed an open letter to the workers of Europe and America urging them to found the Third International. On January 24 Soviet Foreign Minister Chicherin sent out invitations for an international congress to meet in Moscow early in March. The conference proposed by the British Labor Party was denounced as a "gathering of the enemies of the working class"; all "friends of the Third Revolutionary International" were instructed to stay away. The manifesto, which had been written by Trotsky, ended with: "Under the banner of Workers' Soviets, of the revolutionary fight for power and the dictatorship of the proletariat, under the banner of the Third International, workers of all countries unite!"

The First Congress of the Communist International (Comintern) was opened in the Kremlin on March 2, 1919.

According to Angelica Balabanoff, former secretary of the Zimmerwald Union, most of the thirty-five delegates and fifteen guests had been hand-picked by the Bolshevik Central Committee from the so-called Communist parties in the small nations which had belonged to the Russian Empire, such as Estonia, Latvia, Lithuania, and Finland. Others were war prisoners or foreign radicals who happened to be in Russia at the time. Holland, the Socialist Propaganda League of America (made up mainly of Slavic immigrants), and the Japanese Communists, were all represented by a Dutch-American engineer named Rutgers, who had once spent a few months in Japan; England by a Russian émigré named Feinberg who had served in the Soviet Foreign Office; Hungary by a war prisoner who later escaped with a large sum of money. Jacques Sadoul, who had come to Russia during the war with the French military mission and remained to throw in his lot with Lenin, had been suggested as a French representative, but another delegate was produced. When word was received that Guilbeaux, the anti-war French editor, was on his way to Russia, a special train was sent to the border to pick him up and rush him to Moscow in time to vote for France. As the so-called representative of the French left wing he was given five votes.

The Swiss delegate was Platten, who had helped arrange Lenin's return to Petrograd, had accompanied him through Germany, and had been in Russia ever since. Boris Reinstein, of the American Socialist Labor Party, who had also come to Russia in 1917, declined to act as an American delegate, except in a fraternal capacity, on the ground that he had no credentials from his Party. In fact, the only duly-elected delegate from beyond the Russian orbit was a young German named Eberline, who represented the Spartacist Union. And it was Eberline who protested most vigorously when the Russians proposed that the gathering constitute itself as the First Congress of the Third International.

"I heard," relates Balabanoff, "that Radek was organizing foreign sections of the Communist Party with headquarters in the Commissariat of Foreign Affairs. When I went there to investigate, I found that this widely heralded achievement was a fraud. The members of these sections were practically all war prisoners in Russia. Most of them had joined the Party recently because of the privileges which membership conferred. Practically none of them had any contact with the revolutionary or labor movement in their countries, and knew nothing of Socialist principles. Radek was grooming them to return to their native countries, where they were to work for the Soviet Union. Two of these prisoners—Italians from Trieste—were about to return to Italy with special credentials from Lenin and a large sum of money. I understood that they knew nothing of the Italian movement, or even of the elementary terminology of Socialism. I decided to take my protest directly to Lenin.

"Vladimir Ilich," said the first secretary of the Comintern, "I advise you to get back your money and credentials. These men are merely profiteers of the Revolution. They will damage us seriously in Italy."

"For the destruction of Turati's [Socialist] Party," Lenin replied coldly, "they are quite good enough."

A few weeks after this conversation, word came from Italy that Lenin's two emissaries had squandered the money furnished to them by the Soviet Government in the cafés and brothels of Milan.

By 1920 the Comintern was able to check effectively a movement for democratic government in Italy. The Fascists were not yet a strong factor in Italy but former Premier Francesco Nitti recognized the serious danger posed by royal and military influences, and he proposed the overthrow of Victor Emmanuel and the proclamation of a democratic republic.

To Vladimir Diogot, Lenin's personal emissary to Italy, came Bombacci, secretary of the Central Committee of the Socialist Party, with two Communist comrades:

"Nitti has proposed the deposition of the King and the proclamation of a republic," Bombacci explained. "Seratti almost agrees. Tomorrow the question must be decided at the Central Committee. I would like your opinion to convey to the committee."

"In the name of the Comintern," Diogot replied, "you can tell the Central Committee of the Party that participation in such a coup d'état represents the betrayal of the working class. . . . It matters little who is on the throne—Nitti or the King. We must rather stir up the revolution from below more energetically, so as to destroy both the King and Nitti. . . . Then *we shall proclaim the dictatorship of the proletariat.*" Diogot, speaking for Lenin, thus killed the Nitti proposal. The Socialist Party, then Italy's largest single party, consistently refused to enter coalition and attacked all coalitions formed by other democratic groups. After the Party had split in January 1921 at Livorno, the Communists concentrated all their attacks on the other Socialist factions. In May they completely dismissed the Fascist menace, asserting that a temporary white reaction was necessary to destroy the influence of the Social Democrats. The elections held that month they called "a trial of the Socialists." In October 1922 Benito Mussolini provided the

Communists with their "temporary white reaction," which lasted a generation.

The Comintern was organized to fulfill the historic role of carrying into effect the dictatorship of the proletariat, wrote Lenin. If such success could be achieved in backward Russia the coming revolution in other more advanced countries would accomplish even more.

"The First International (1864-72) laid the foundation for the international organization of the workers for the preparation of a revolutionary attack upon capital," Lenin explained. "The Second International (1889-1914) was the international organization of the proletarian movement whose growth was extensive rather than intensive, and therefore resulted in a temporary drop in the revolutionary level and in a temporary increase of opportunistic tendencies, which finally led to the shameful downfall of this International. . . .

"The Third International took over the work of the Second International, but cut off its opportunistic, social-chauvinist, bourgeois and petit-bourgeois rubbish, and began to carry into effect the dictatorship of the proletariat.

"The international union of parties heading the greatest revolution in the world, the movement of the proletariat for the overthrow of capital, now rests upon the firmest ground; namely, the existence of several Soviet republics, which are putting into practice, on an international scale, the dictatorship of the proletariat, its victory over capitalism."

Lenin was convinced that the Soviet regime could not survive unless it provided the spark to ignite the fires of revolution in other parts of Europe.

Despite reverses and civil war, Lenin continued his intimate contact with the work of the Comintern.

In June 1920 the Second Congress of the Comintern opened in Petrograd. Later it moved to Moscow, where its sessions continued until August. This time there were delegations of Communist and left-wing Socialist groups from thirty-seven countries.

Acting on the program submitted by Lenin, the Second Congress laid down the methods to be employed for spreading Communist propaganda throughout the world. It evolved the plan of organizing secret Communist centers in every country, for the purpose of fomenting revolutions, while at the same time Communist parties, wherever possible, were to engage in legal political action.

The parliamentary tactics of the Communists were succinctly defined by the International: *"No Parliament can under any circumstance be an arena of struggle for reforms, for betterment of the conditions of the working class. . . . The only question can be that of utilizing bourgeois state institutions for their own destruction."*

One of the keystones of Communist policy throughout the world, this declaration can only be regarded as, in effect, a complete admission that the Communists are basically opposed to democracy.

The only organizations admitted to Comintern membership were those which subscribed without reservation to the complete program of the Third International and were ready to follow the tactics laid down for International Communism by Lenin.

To strike at the colonial sinews of imperialism was essential for victory over world capitalism.

"European capitalism draws its chief strength not from industrial countries of Europe, but from its colonial possessions," declared the Second Congress. "The surplus income received from colonies is the chief source of wealth of modern capitalism. The European working class will therefore be able to overthrow the capitalistic system only when this source has finally dried up."

In July 1921 the Comintern Executive Committee issued an order that national congresses of member parties were to be held after the Comintern congresses, as assurance that the decisions of the local parties would be in line with the edicts of the Comintern.

The Fourth Congress ruled that in the future all delegates to the Comintern should come to Moscow uninstructed, without any definite mandate from their party as to how to vote on issues that were expected to arise. This assured that control would remain on top.

Lenin, as the author of these Comintern provisions and instructions, was forging all over the world rigidly centralized and disciplined Bolshevik parties, modeled after his Bolshevik Party and led by small groups of professional revolutionists, who were subject to the supreme authority of the Central Executive Committee of the Comintern.

*   *   *

Lenin was not only the author of the basic Comintern plans and programs, but also the frank advocate of a system of "revolutionary morality" which justified the use of subterfuge and lies in the political struggle. He wrote:

The Communists must be prepared to make every sacrifice, and, if necessary, even resort to all sorts of cunning, schemes, and stratagems to employ illegal methods, to evade and conceal the truth, in order to penetrate into the trade unions, to remain in them, and conduct the Communist work in them at all costs.

The struggle against the Gomperses [Samuel Gompers was then president of the A.F. of L.], the Jouhaux, the Hendersons . . . who represent an absolutely similar [Lenin's underlining] social and political type as our Mensheviks . . . must be waged without mercy to the end, in the same manner as we have done it in

Russia until all the incorrigible leaders of opportunism and of social chauvinism have been completely discredited and expelled from the trade unions.

The Comintern, after Lenin's death, expanded its operations and vastly increased its international network of agents. But the long-range strategy and tactics remained largely those which Lenin had laid down.

20 KRONSTADT

KRONSTADT WAS THE PROUDEST BASTION OF THE BOLSHEVIK revolution.

On March 1, 1921, the sailors of Kronstadt revolted. Mass meetings of 15,000 men from various ships and garrisons passed resolutions demanding immediate new elections to the Soviet by secret ballot, freedom of speech and the press for all left-wing Socialist parties; freedom of assembly for trade unions and peasant organizations; abolition of Communist political agencies in the Army and Navy; immediate withdrawal of all grain-requisitioning squads, and re-establishment of a free market for the peasants.

The Kronstadt revolt came after a series of peasant revolts in central Russia and strikes in Petrograd and other cities. In the former capital, hungry workers were looting the warehouses.

Russia, in March 1921, was on the verge of economic collapse and new civil war in which foreign intervention played no part. Nationalized industry was at a virtual standstill; labor discipline was rapidly vanishing; workers were deserting the town for the village.

The prices of manufactured goods skyrocketed, while, in Janunary 1921, a gold ruble was worth 26,529 paper rubles.

The requisitioning of grain continued with increasing demands on the peasants.

The Soviet regime now faced rebellion by the very masses of workers, soldiers, and sailors who had been won by Lenin's slogans of "peace, bread, and land."

On March 5, 1921, the Kronstadt sailors formed a revolutionary committee of fifteen men. On the sixth, General Tukhachevsky was already speeding by special train from Moscow to suppress the rebellion. He massed 60,000 picked men consisting of Cheka troops, Communist military cadets, and other dependable forces. To prevent rebellion in neighboring Petrograd, he ordered the entire garrison disarmed.

* * *

But the flag of revolt flew over Kronstadt. Power was in the hands of the Revolutionary Committee, which consisted of nine sailors, four workers, a male nurse, and a school director. The chairman of the committee was Petrechenko.

Kronstadt hoped that the workers and soldiers of Petrograd would join the revolt. But Zinoviev was not asleep. He organized a state of siege in Petrograd, ordered Communist regiments to disperse all crowds and to crush any demonstrations with machine-gun fire. At Kronstadt the officers advised the sailors to begin an offensive against Petrograd at once, otherwise they would be lost. But the sailors said they would not "shed needless blood." They would only defend themselves if Trotsky dared to spill the people's blood.

Trotsky did not wait. He issued an order to the effect that if the rebels did not surrender they would be shot singly, "like ducks in a pond." The sailors refused to yield. On the evening of March 6 Tukhachevsky's airplanes flew over the Gulf of Finland to bomb the houses and forts of Kronstadt.

Tukhachevsky then ordered an assault against the fortress. In the early morning, when the ice was still blue, the advance of the Cheka and Communist troops began. The Communist military cadets were out front, clad in white robes to blend with the snow. They were followed by picked Red Army troops, behind whom were Cheka machine gunners to prevent any desertions. The sailors returned Tukhachevsky's artillery fire with the guns of the fort and the ice-locked warships.

In the nearby city of Oranienbaum several Red Army regiments mutinied and refused to fight the sailors. Cheka units rushed to the scene and shot every fifth soldier.

The Kronstadt sailors resisted so fiercely that Tukhachevsky demanded that Bolshevik Party leaders come to the front to raise the morale of his forces. From Moscow the Tenth Congress of the Communist Party rushed 300 high-ranking officials to the scene. At the same Party Congress, on March 8, 1921, Lenin said in the course of a speech: "I have not yet received the latest news from Kronstadt, but I have no doubt that this mutiny, which quickly revealed the familiar figures of the White Guard generals, will be liquidated within the next few days, if not within the next few hours. There can be no doubt about this."

On the night of March 16 Tukhachevsky redeployed his forces in squares in preparation for storming the fortress. At the same time, his batteries increased their bombardment. The battleships returned fire. The next evening Tukhaschevsky sent all available planes to bombard the fortress.

Trotsky kept his word. On March 17 Tukhachevsky reported to Moscow that Kronstadt was silent. Thousands of sailors and soldiers lay dead in its streets.

Some of the sailors succeeded in escaping to Finland. But

the majority of those captured alive were shot by Cheka firing squads, and the rest were exiled to remote prison camps.

* * *

With the guns of Kronstadt still resounding, Lenin realized that the time had come for compromise if the Bolsheviks were to retain power. Despite "Left" objections, he introduced a New Economic Policy (NEP) in the spring of 1921.

In 1918 Lenin had regarded private enterprise as anathema. Now he admitted that private trade was indispensable for restoring Russia's economic health. The wage system was restored and peasants' property rights in their produce was recognized. The "civil war in the villages" was brought to an end. On March 15, 1921, at the tenth Congress of the Party, Lenin declared:

"We must try to satisfy the demands of the peasants who are dissatisfied, discontented, and legitimately discontented, and cannot be otherwise. . . . In essence the small farmer can be satisfied with two things. First of all, there must be a certain amount of freedom of turnover, of freedom for the small private proprietor; and, secondly, commodities and products must be provided."

Following the introduction of the New Economic Policy, economic efficiency rather than Communist theory became the chief objective of the Soviet industrial experts and technicians. Workers were paid in accordance with the value of their services.

In his address before a conference of Moscow Communist organizations in October of 1921 Lenin frankly admitted that the attempt to introduce Communism at this stage had been a mistake.

He placed the onus for his compromise with pure Communist principles on the failure of the peasants to supply the workers with enough bread.

Lenin recommended that the return to private enterprise be applied first to agriculture and then to small industry. Basic industries and transportation as well as foreign trade would remain under government control. He therefore foresaw no danger of a capitalist revival as the result of the New Economic Policy. The new system Lenin gave the name of "State Capitalism."

A year later Lenin was confident that Russia, under the NEP, was advancing on the road to Socialism.

"Socialism is no longer a question of the remote future. We have brought Socialism into everyday life," he wrote. "No matter how difficult the problem may be, no matter what the obstacles that must be overcome or how many difficulties it may involve, we shall achieve it, not tomorrow, it is true, but surely in the course of the next few years, in such a way that the

Russia of the NEP will be transformed into Socialist Russia."

A short time afterward, however, he was not nearly so confident.

"We have not even completed the foundation for a Socialist economic order," he declared. "The hostile forces of dying capitalism may yet take everything away from us. This must be clearly understood and frankly admitted, for nothing is so dangerous as illusions. On the other hand, there is nothing alarming, nothing to give the slightest reason for falling into despair because we recognize this truth. We have always taught and have always preached that to assure the victory of Socialism it is necessary to have the united forces of the workers of several highly developed countries."

Early in the summer of 1921 Lenin appeared before the Third Congress of the Comintern to define the platform to be adopted in relation to the NEP. He assured the foreign delegates that the NEP was necessary for the advancement of world revolution.

"The development of international revolution which we predicted is progressing," he explained. "But this advancing movement is not as direct as we had expected. . . . The fact must be taken into account that now, unquestionably, there has been reached a certain balance of forces. Consequently we must take advantage of this brief breathing space in order to adapt our tactics to this sort of zig-zag of historical development."

By the end of 1921 Lenin could point to a general economic revival, particularly in the transportation system, mining, and small trade, as the result of the new policy.

The NEP did not, however, come in time to avert the famine resulting from crop failure and the lack of reserve supplies, caused by Communist policy toward the peasants since 1918. According to official Soviet figures, starvation took the lives of no less than 5,000,000 people in 1921 and 1922.

Moreover, although peasant revolts, industrial strikes, and the Kronstadt uprising had forced Lenin to revise Russia's economic structure, he made no political concessions. On the contrary, the last vestiges of political opposition were ruthlessly stamped out. "The place for Mensheviks and Socialist Revolutionaries, open or disguised, is in prison," Lenin wrote. ". . . Terror cannot be dispensed with, notwithstanding the hypocrites and phrasemongers."

Lenin's political police perfected a system of internal espionage that blanketed Russia with a network of agents far more efficient than the Czarist Okhrana. Ironclad censorship imposed complete silence on all criticism of Lenin's policies. The press, radio, cinema, and theater became, for the first time in history, an exclusive instrument of state propaganda. Trade unions lost all power to bargain for higher wages or better working conditions. And the prisons and concentration camps were filled with far more political prisoners than under any of the Czars. Kronstadt had marked the last real revolt of the Russian people. Henceforth Lenin's dictatorship was secure. The totalitarian state was coming into being.

21 DICTATOR WITHOUT VANITY

LENIN MIGHT WELL HAVE SAID: "I CREATED THE BOLSHEVIK Party. I was the brain of the November Revolution. Several times, when our power seemed about to crumble, I saved it by bold improvisation, by signing an unpopular peace in 1918, by introducing the NEP in 1921. I created the Comintern and gave it the revolutionary theory and strategy through which Russian Bolshevism became a world force." Lenin could rightfully have said all this, but never did, for no dictator in history was less vain. In fact he was repelled by all attempts on the part of the men around him to set him on a pedestal.

In reply to a Comintern question whether he spoke any foreign language fluently, Lenin wrote "none," although he spoke at the Comintern's Third Congress in very good German, only occasionally being at a loss for the precise word he wanted. "What are your specialties?" asked the questionnaire of the Tenth Party Congress in 1921. "None," replied Lenin.

When the sculptor Nathan Altman was working on his bust, Lenin refused to assume a pose because he thought it would look unnatural.

Maxim Gorky vainly tried to resolve the riddle posed by the vast contradiction between the man and the political leader. "A passion for gambling was part of Lenin's character," says Gorky. "But this was not gambling of a self-centered fortune seeker. In Lenin it expressed that extraordinary power of faith which is found in a man firmly believing in his calling, one who is deeply and fully conscious of his bond with the world outside and has thoroughly understood his role in the chaos of the world, the role of an enemy of chaos.

"Squat and solid, with a skull like Socrates and the all-seeing eyes of a great deceiver, he often liked to assume a strange and somewhat ludicrous posture: throw his head backward, then incline it to the shoulder, put his hands under his armpits, behind the vest. There was in this posture something delightfully comical, something triumphantly cocky. At such moments his whole being radiated happiness.

"His movements were lithe and supple and his sparing but forceful gestures harmonized well with his words, also sparing but abounding in significance. From his face of Mongolian cast gleamed and flashed the eyes of a tireless hunter of falsehood and of the woes of life—eyes that squinted, blinked, sparkled sardonically, or glowered with rage. The glare of those eyes rendered his words more burning and more poignantly clear."

Yet the same Lenin capitalized on ignorance to weave fantastic charges against his political opponents. Thus when a few days after the Bolshevik Revolution unruly soldiers and sailors of Petrograd broke into the wine cellars of the city, Lenin did not hesitate to charge that the raid had been organized by the Central Committee of the Constitutional Democratic Party.

To discredit his enemies in the eyes of the Russian people everything was permissible. Martov was branded by Lenin as a "traitor" and "renegade," and yet shortly before his death Lenin complained to Gorky: "What a pity Martov is not with us. What a wonderful comrade he is! He is without peer!"

He burst into laughter when he heard of Martov's remark that there were only two real Communists in Russia—Lenin and Madame Kollontai (the latter for her advocacy of sexual freedom). His laughter ended with a sigh, "What a wise man Martov is!"

For Martov, the "traitor" and "renegade," the lifelong foe of Bolshevism, Lenin retained more personal affection than for his most devoted lieutenants. But he did not allow personal feeling to influence his actions. According to Gorgy, he reduced everything to the following formula:

"Whoever is not with us is against us. People who are independent of history are only imaginary. Even if we grant that at some period in the past they did exist, they certainly do not exist now and cannot. They would be useless. Everybody, down to the most unimportant man, is drawn into the vortex of reality tangled as it has never been before."

Lenin constantly preached that all notions of morality had to be harnessed to class interests.

"We repudiate all morality which proceeds from supernatural ideas or ideas which are outside class conceptions," he told a gathering of Young Communists. "In our opinion, morality is entirely subordinate to the interests of class war. Everything is moral which is necessary for the annihilation of the old exploiting social order and for uniting the proletariat. Our morality, then, consists solely in close discipline and in conscious war against the exploiters. We do not believe in external principles of morality and we will expose this deception. Communist morality is identical with the fight for strengthening the dictatorship of the proletariat."

The problem of religious faith was reduced to the same formula.

Lenin wrote long before the Revolution:

Religion is one of the forms of spiritual oppression which everywhere weigh upon the masses of the people crushed by continuous toil for others, by poverty and loneliness. The weakness of the exploited classes in their struggle against their oppressors inevitably produces a belief in a better life after death, just as the weakness of the savage in his struggle with nature leads to faith in gods, devils, and miracles. Religion teaches those who toil in poverty all their lives to be resigned and patient in this world and consoles them with the hope of reward in heaven. But the exploiters are urged by faith to do good on earth because in this way they hope to win a cheap justification for their existence and a ticket of admission to heavenly bliss. Religion is the opiate of the people, a sort of spiritual liquor, meant to make the slaves of capitalism drown their humanity and their desires for a decent existence.

Throughout his career Lenin was backtracking on slogans he had previously preached as gospel. He favored the Constituent Assembly as long as that made an effective slogan against Kerensky. When that body went against him he dissolved it. When it appeared that even in the Soviet he had no secure majority, he established the dictatorship of the Bolshevik Party which finally became the dictatorship of the Politburo. He readily appropriated the ideas of his opponents and used them to new advantage. Yet in a large sense he remained always true to a single idea and a single aim. From the moment he became a "professional revolutionist" he devoted his entire life to the cause of the proletarian revolution —as he understood it. But like Nechaiev and Tkachev, Lenin never looked for harmony between ends and means. All the means that led toward the goal were justified. The end was far more important than the path to it.

He had tremendous admiration for Tkachev and Nechaiev, the apostle of "terrible, complete, and unsparing destruction." After the Revolution, according to Bonch-Bruyevich, "he attributed very great importance to Tkachev, urging everyone to read and study him."

"People completely forget," Lenin said, "that Nechaiev possessed unique organizational talent, an ability to establish the special techniques of conspiratorial work everywhere, an ability to give his thoughts such startling formulations that they were forever imprinted on one's memory."

He studied Clausewitz carefully, often echoing his maxim that war was a continuation of politics by other means. In the margin of Clausewitz's book he wrote: "A good leader."

He was no social dreamer in the ordinary sense. Russia was his laboratory for testing Communism on a grand scale; the immediate welfare of the Russian people was secondary. The enormous sacrifices which his great experiment required were inescapable and irrelevant. Mercy was a bourgeois virtue. The man who loved children, animals, and nature seldom lifted a finger to save human beings from Cheka firing squads.

But although he had no mercy for his enemies, he tolerated

the worst scoundrels provided he could make use of them. "There are no morals in politics," he often said: "there is only expediency."

As an orator, Lenin had a brilliant grasp of mass psychology and a virility of language that captivated audiences. In his mind, the entire political world revolved on the axis of force. The first step was the seizure of power, the next was to retain it. Suppression of all civil liberties and mass terror were the only reliable means. The ultimate goal—a classless society— would be reached someday.

There is no clue whether Lenin in his last days still expected that this state he had created would someday dispense with its all-powerful instruments of suppression. Reducing world politics to the irreconcilable struggle between Sovietism and capitalism, he regarded society as in a continued state of war pending the victory of the world revolution.

By a vast oversimplification of Marxist theory he finally denied all validity to the rights granted by "bourgeois" democracy. He did so only after the Soviet regime, to consolidate and hold its power, was driven step by step to eradicate all political freedom.

22   THE TESTAMENT

TOWARD THE END OF 1921 LENIN'S HEALTH BECAME SERIOUSLY impaired. Sometimes, during his work, he would clasp his head and remain immobile for several minutes. He complained of increasing insomnia and weariness, and his headaches became more frequent. At the beginning of 1922 he developed spells of vertigo which forced him to catch hold of the nearest object to keep from falling.

In the beginning of December he went to his home in the village of Gorki, leaving a note to the members of the Politburo:

"Despite the fact that I have diminished my work and extended my rest, my insomnia has increased devilishly. I am afraid that I will be unable to report either at the Party Congress or at the Congress of the Soviets." From the village of Gorky he still dictated Soviet policies. When Foreign Commissar Chicherin proposed that the Soviet Government agree to certain changes in its constitution in return for economic "compensations" from Europe and America, Lenin replied angrily: "I think that Chicherin should be immediately sent to a sanitarium, and there should be no negligence about it."

The Eleventh Party Congress in March 1922 was the last Lenin attended. It was after this congress that the Central

Committee elected Stalin general secretary of the Communist Party.

The leading medical specialists of Russia and Germany were summoned to examine Lenin. In March 1922 the doctors still found no organic affliction in his nervous system. But early in May he suffered his first stroke. For a short time he lost his speech and the ability to move his right hand and leg. Within a few weeks he could no longer speak or walk. Then he began to suffer attacks that lasted from half an hour to two hours. After these attacks he felt somewhat better. He asked the doctors to tell him if this was the end. If so, he had to leave special orders. The doctors felt reasonably sure that the end was not yet in sight. But Lenin was now an invalid. While his understanding remained unimpaired, he could no longer express himself clearly, even with signs.

Lenin was nursed by his sister Maria, while Krupskaya taught him to write with his left hand and to articulate words aloud.

Driven by his indomitable will, Lenin's body made a terrific effort to recover its normal state. His brain, which had lost the faculty of associating letters with sound, gradually recovered. In the long winter nights he would lapse into a sort of pensive doze. At such moments he wanted to hear music. Piatakov, who was an excellent pianist, would be summoned and would play various selections by Chopin, Brahms, and Bach. While playing, Piatakov often noticed that Lenin's face would completely change, become calm, simple, and childishly earnest. The usual cunning gleam in his eyes disappeared entirely.

In July, Lenin was once more on his feet. At that time came the trial of the members of the Central Committee of the Socialist Revolutionary Party. They were charged with preparing terroristic acts against members of the government and of organizing an uprising against the Soviet power in 1918. Some of the leaders had been in prison since that time. When the Soviet Tribunal sentenced them to death, Socialists all over the world, and even some Communists and Maxim Gorky, protested and demanded that the verdict be repealed. Among the Bolshevik leaders, some demanded that the leaders of the Socialist Revolutionary Party be immediately "liquidated"; others, headed by the German Communist Clara Zetkin, insisted that the Soviet Government show its generosity by reducing the verdict to imprisonment, since their execution would make a bad impression abroad. Lenin agreed with neither side. Prison was not sufficient and shooting might bring terroristic acts of reprisal. Therefore he decided to hold them as permanent hostages, to be shot in the event of any overt act against the Soviet leaders. This was in fact a death sentence in abeyance. The condemned Socialist Revolutionary leaders thus remained in prison for many years, until they were executed by Stalin.

In connection with the trial of the Socialist Revolutionaries, Lenin addressed a note to D. I. Kursky, Commissar of Justice. It was written in reference to one of the articles of the Soviet Criminal Code under consideration in May 1922:

In my opinion it is necessary to extend the application of execution by shooting to all phases covering activities of Mensheviks, Social Revolutionaries, and the like; a formula must be found that would place these activities in connection with the international bourgeoisie and its struggle against us (bribery of the press and agents, war preparations, and the like).

He could scarcely have foreseen the use to which this note would be put. It was published in the Moscow *Bolshevik* on January 15, 1937, just before the trial of Radek, Sokolnikov, and other old Bolsheviks. It was accompanied by the following comment by the savants of the Marx-Engels-Lenin Institute:

"The note to Comrade Kursky was written by Vladimir Ilich on the reverse side of the first page, presented to him in printed form, of the project for the supplementary law in the Criminal Code. Next to paragraph 5 of the law, which dealt with the application of capital punishment for counter-revolutionary expression against the Soviet Government, Lenin wrote on the first page below: 'Add the right to substitute for execution exile abroad by decision of the All-Russian C.E.C. (for a period of years or without limit).' It was the postscript that Lenin had in mind in reference to the note to Kursky above.

"The note to Kursky emphasized the need for capital punishment for the counter-revolutionary activities of Mensheviks, Socialist Revolutionaries, and 'the like.' Lenin demanded capital punishment for the counter-revolutionary activities of anti-Soviet parties connected with the war preparations of the international bourgeoisie against the Soviet Republic and with other forms of the fight of international capitalism against our country. That demand of Lenin's is likewise entirely applicable to the Trotskyist-Zinovievist agents of the Gestapo who acted by direct orders of Fascism and are a counter-revolutionary gang of bandits, spies, and diversionists—vicious enemies of the land of toilers. These scoundrels, murderers of Comrade Kirov, are precisely such enemies of the Soviet Republic for whom Vladimir Ilich demanded severe revolutionary punishment."

Lenin improved to such an extent that he was brought back to Moscow. The doctors permitted him to work from eleven to two and from six to eight, on the condition that he rest two days a week. He again began to preside over the Politburo

and Sovnarcom, and to talk for hours on the telephone and
with visitors, to dictate letters and articles, and issue secret
instructions to Communist agents in other countries. He even
took the risk of appearing at the Fourth Congress of the Comintern. He came into the hall, accompanied by his usual group,
and went directly to the platform. He summoned the Communists abroad to greater activity and promised them Soviet
support.

"Depend on us. We have broad shoulders. Prepare yourself
solidly. Don't accept the battle too early. Gather strength and
strike the bourgeoisie as is necessary. Strike it only in the chest
when you are sure of victory."

In the middle of the speech Lenin's strength began to give
way. His voice grew weaker, and when he finished he was
covered with perspiration. Clara Zetkin ran up and kissed his
hand. Lenin gallantly returned the gesture.

Fotieva, the nurse who attended him, kept a record of
everything that happened during the period of his illness. On
November 25 she reported: "Today the physicians prescribed
absolute rest."

From that day on Lenin's regular work routine ceased. He
did not come to his office regularly, did not receive so many
people. On the other hand, he read more than ever.

Lenin at this time no longer said, as he had in 1918, that
Socialism was "already being realized in fact." On the contrary, he now wondered: "Is it not clear that in a material,
economic, industrial sense we are not yet at the threshold of
Socialism?"

He now dubbed the policy of prohibiting the development of
private trade as "stupid and suicidal." And he embarrassed
orthodox Communists with the order: "Learn to trade." Lenin
was restoring the monetary system and explained: "If we succeed in stabilizing the ruble, we have won."

Lenin no longer wanted to set up compulsory collective
farms and to establish the communal tillage of soil.

"We have done many stupid things with regard to collective
farms. The question of the collective farms is not on the order
of the day. We must rely on the individual peasant; he is as
he is and will not become different within the near future.
Peasants are not Socialists, and building Socialist plans in the
same way as if they were Socialists means building on sand.
The transformation of the peasant's psychology and habits is
something that requires generations. The use of force will not
help. The task before us is to influence the peasantry morally.
We must give consideration to the middle peasant. The efficient
peasant must be the central figure of our economic recovery."
[Underlined by Lenin.]

In December 1922 a second stroke came, this time more severe. By a mighty effort Lenin again fought off this illness. His physicians insisted on complete rest. A month later he began to work on an article about the role of co-operatives in the Soviet economic system. He defined Socialism as "an order of civilized co-operators in which the means of production are socially owned." Parallel to this, Lenin noted that "the political and social revolution in Russia preceded the cultural revolution." The greatest attention should now be directed toward instilling culture among the masses. "The transition to Socialism requires complete transformation of thinking, a whole period of cultural development." A month later, to the astonishment of many, he added: "We could do for the start with some genuine bourgeois culture."

These were his last articles; on December 12 Lenin sat at his desk for the last time in his life.

On December 16 he abandoned his original intention of speaking before the Congress of Soviets. On that day, too, he decided to remain in the city, as the trip to the country by automobile was too arduous an undertaking.

Soon after Lenin suffered a new relapse. Despite his grave condition, he worked to the very limit of endurance until his illness deprived him of the last means of communication with people.

Two months after Stalin's appointment as General Secretary and as Commissar of the Workers' and Peasants' Inspection, *Pravda* of June 4, 1922, published the first bulletin of Lenin's sickness. As Lenin gradually departed from the political arena, there developed a struggle for power between Zinoviev, Trotsky, and Stalin. Zinoviev was the president of the Communist International and of the Petrograd Soviet; Trotsky the chairman of the Military Revolutionary Council and Commissar of War, and Stalin the General Secretary of the Party.

When Lenin relinquished his work, the leadership of the Party went to the triumvirate of Zinoviev, Kamenev, and Stalin. By April 1923 a silent fight for control had developed between Zinoviev and Stalin. Trotsky, for his part, began to campaign against the triumvirate. His post of chairman of the Revolutionary Council was an honorary one and he was not given any key work in the party machine. At the Bolshevik Congress in 1923 Trotsky hinted that he was being sidetracked, and that his abilities were not being sufficiently utilized.

For a time the dominating figure in the Politburo was Zinoviev. He had a majority in the Central Committee, whose members felt that under Zinoviev each would be able to broaden his sphere of influence. Of the six members of the Politburo apart from Lenin, Trotsky was opposed by all, and Tomsky played only an insignificant role. Thus Zinoviev, Kamenev, and Bukharin constituted a majority against Stalin.

But neither the majority of the Central Committee nor of the Politburo ever thought of elevating Zinoviev to leadership, for the recognition of leadership required control of the party Congress. And here Stalin loomed large. Slowly but surely he gradually planted his men as secretaries all through the party organization, stopping at nothing to gain control of the party machine.

By the end of 1922, when it became clear that Lenin's condition was hopeless, Stalin began to work out a series of changes in the governmental structure. Stalin himself did not deny that he had made extraordinary preparations for the forthcoming Congress. "For the last six years," he said, "the Central Committee never prepared for the Congress as at this moment."

In anticipation of death, in January 1923 Lenin prepared a "Political Testament" in which he undertook to evaluate the various Bolshevik leaders, endeavoring to find the man or men capable of succeeding him. In his "Testament" he advocated that the leadership be shared by Trotsky and Stalin, but questioned its feasibility. He forecast a split in the Party should this combination prove impossible. Fearful of this eventuality, Lenin suggested the removal of Stalin as secretary of the Communist Party.

Lenin wrote in his "Testament":

Comrade Stalin, having become general secretary, has concentrated enormous power in his hands, and I am not sure that he always knows how to use that power with sufficient caution. On the other hand, Comrade Trotsky, as was proved by his struggle against the Central Committee in connection with the question of the People's Commissariat of Ways and Communication, is distinguished not only by his exceptional ability—personally, he is, to be sure, the most able man in the present Central Committee— but also by his too far-reaching self-confidence and a disposition to be far too much attracted by the purely administrative side of affairs.

These two qualities of the two most able leaders of the present Central Committee might, quite innocently, lead to a split. If our Party does not take measures to prevent it, a split may occur unexpectedly.

I will not further characterize the other members of the Central Committee as to their personal qualities. I will only remind you that the October episode of Zinoviev and Kamenev was not, of course, accidental, but that it ought as little to be used against them as the "non-Bolshevism" of Trotsky.

Of the younger members of the Central Committee, I want to say a few words about Piatakov and Bukharin. They are, in my opinion, the most able forces (among the youngest). In regard to them it is necessary to bear in mind the following: Bukharin is not only the most valuable theoretician of the Party, as he is the biggest, but he also may be considered the favorite of the whole Party. But his theoretical views can with only the greatest reservations be regarded as fully Marxist, for there is something scholastic in him. (He never has learned, and I think never fully understood, the dialectic.)

And then Piatakov—a man undoubtedly distinguished in will and ability, but too much given over to the administrative side of affairs to be relied upon in serious political questions.

Of course both these remarks are made by me merely with regard to the present time, or on the supposition that these two able and loyal workers may not find occasion to supplement their knowledge and correct their one-sidedness.

December 25, 1922.

Postscript: Stalin is too rude, and this fault, entirely supportable in relation to us Communists, becomes insupportable in the office of General Secretary. Therefore I propose to the comrades to find a way to remove Stalin from that position and appoint to it another man who in all respects differs from Stalin only in superiority—namely, more patient, more loyal, more polite, and more attentive to comrades, less capricious, et cetera. This circumstance may seem an insignificant trifle, but I think that from the point of view of preventing a split and from the point of view of the relation between Stalin and Trotsky, which I discussed above, it is not a trifle, or it is such a trifle as may acquire a decisive significance.

January 4, 1923.

LENIN

On March 5, 1923, Lenin dictated a note to his secretary announcing the severance of "all personal and comradely relations with Stalin."

Trotsky called this the last surviving Lenin document.

As through a daze Lenin sensed what was going on. Forbidden to see his comrades, he could complain to no one. Not only could he sense his authority slipping away from him, but he also felt that Stalin was treating Krupskaya discourteously. Enraged by Stalin's actions, Lenin dictated the note to Stalin in which he notified the general secretary that he was breaking off all comradely relations with him. The note had no practical significance. In March 1923 Lenin suffered his third stroke.

In the middle of May 1923 Lenin was taken from the Kremlin to Gorki for the last time. There was no hope for recovery. All that could be done was to make him comfortable. Toward the end of July he improved slightly and could be taken out into the garden in a wheel chair. His spirits and appetite improved.

His illness meanwhile progressed according to its own laws, with the brain deteriorating. To cheer the patient, he was taken on auto or sleigh rides in good weather. On December 24 his wife set up a Christmas tree and called in the peasants. Lenin was cheerful. At midnight on January 20, 1924, he went to bed in good spirits. But at 6:50 A.M. he suffered a final stroke.

The attack ran an exceptionally violent course. His breathing became interrupted and he fell into a coma. General convulsions and a very high fever preceded the end. At 7 P.M. on January 21, 1924, Lenin died.

The body was embalmed after a thorough macro- and microscopic pathological examination.

"When we opened him up," writes Professor Rozanov, "we found a massive sclerosis of the cerebral vessels and sclerosis only. The amazing thing was not that the thinking power remained intact in such a sclerotic brain, but that he could live so long with such a brain."

From the snow-blanketed village of Gorki the news of Lenin's death reverberated throughout Russia. A long procession of friends and disciples filed past the coffin. On January 23 the body was carried by his Communist disciples to the railroad station for transportation to Moscow. The entire route from Gorki to Moscow, thirty miles long, was lined with people as the train bearing the body of Lenin passed on its way. In Moscow the body lay in state in the House of the Trade Unions. A procession of hundreds of thousands came to pay their last tribute.

On the day of the funeral a large black flag draped the building. At four o'clock in the morning soldiers of Lenin's military guard silently met in front of the house. From afar came the dull, continuous rumble of cannon in Moscow saluting the memory of Lenin. The soldiers of the guard raised their rifles and fired three volleys in salute.

It was very cold that morning as most of Moscow turned out for the funeral procession. The coffin was carried by the members of the Politburo. The entire day endless delegations of workers and Red Army units, delegations of foreign Communists, passed by the bier and left wreaths. Only at four in the afternoon was Lenin's body placed in a crypt to the accompaniment of all the factory whistles of Moscow.

His body was not buried or cremated like the remains of other revolutionary leaders, but was embalmed and lodged in a rich mausoleum in Red Square, decorated with the five black letters of Lenin's name.

Lenin, who detested hero worship and fought religion as an opiate for the people, was canonized in the interest of Soviet politics and his writings were given the character of Holy Writ.

Five days after Lenin's death, on January 26, 1924, Stalin delivered a speech before the Congress of the Soviets in which he said:

"For twenty-five years Comrade Lenin reared our Party and finally raised it into the strongest and most steeled workers' party in the world. . . .

"In departing from us, Comrade Lenin bequeathed to us the duty of guarding the unity of our Party like the apple of our eye. We vow to you, Comrade Lenin, that we will also fulfill this bequest of yours with honor. . . .

"In departing from us, Comrade Lenin bequeathed to us the duty of guarding and strengthening the dictatorship of the proletariat. We vow to you, Comrade Lenin, that we will spare no effort to fulfill also this bequest of yours with honor. . . .

"Lenin told us more than once that the respite we have gained from the capitalist states may be a short one. More than once Lenin pointed out to us that the strengthening of the Red Army and the improvement of its condition is one of the most important tasks of our Party. . . . Let us vow then, comrades, that we will spare no effort to strengthen our Red Army and our Red Navy.

"Our country stands like a huge rock surrounded by the ocean of bourgeois states. Wave after wave hurls itself against it, threatening to submerge it and sweep it away. But the rock stands unshakeable. Wherein lies its strength? Not only in the fact that our country is based on the alliance between the workers and peasants, that it is the personification of the alliance of free nationalities, that it is protected by the strong arm of the Red Army and the Red Navy. The strength of our country, its firmness, its durability, lies in the fact that it finds profound sympathy and unshakeable support in the hearts of the workers and peasants of the world.

"Lenin never regarded the republic of Soviets as an end in itself. He always regarded it as a necessary link for strengthening the revolutionary movements in the lands of the West and the East, as a necessary link for facilitating the victory of toilers of the whole world over capital. Lenin knew that only such an interpretation is the correct one, not only from the international point of view, but also from the point of view of preserving the republic of Soviets itself. Lenin knew that only in this way is it possible to inflame the hearts of toilers of all countries for the decisive battles for emancipation. That is why this genius among the great leaders of the proletariat, on the very morrow of the establishment of the proletarian dictatorship, laid the foundation of the Workers' International. That is why he never tired of expanding and consolidating the union of the toilers of the whole world, the Communist International. . . .

"In departing from us, Comrade Lenin bequeathed to us the duty or remaining loyal to the principles of the Communist International. We vow to you, Comrade Lenin, that we will not spare our lives to strengthen and expand the union of the toilers of the whole world—the Communist International."

As the Soviet leaders themselves have so often said, Lenin is dead, but Leninism lives on. Tactics change to meet new conditions, but the oath that Stalin took at Lenin's bier still guides the destinies of the Soviet Union.

ESSENTIALS OF LENINISM

THE FOLLOWING EXCERPTS FROM LENIN'S WRITINGS
and speeches furnish a master guide—in Lenin's own
words—to the ideology which remains the driving
force behind Soviet actions in the world today.

DICTATORSHIP AND SOVIET DEMOCRACY

"Capitalism cannot be defeated and eradicated without the ruthless suppression of the resistence of the
exploiters, who cannot at once be deprived of their
wealth, of their superiority of organization and knowledge, and consequently for a fairly long period will inevitably try to overthrow the hateful rule of the poor;
secondly, a great revolution, and a socialist revolution
in particular, even if there were no external war, is in-
conceivable without internal war, *i.e.,* civil war, which
is even more destructive than external war, and implies
thousands and millions of cases of wavering and desertion from one side to another, implies a state of extreme indefiniteness, lack of equilibrium and chaos. . . ."

(Lenin, *Izbrannyie Proizvedeniya,*)
(*Selected Works,* Russian, Vol. 2, pp. 277-78.)

"The Soviet Socialist Democracy is in no way incon-
sistent with the rule and dictatorship of one person:
that the will of a class is at times best realized by a dictator who sometimes will accomplish more by himself
and is frequently more needed . . ."

(*Collected Works,* 1923 Edition, Vol. XVII, p. 89.)

CIVIL LIBERTIES

"We declare that we are fighting capitalism as such,
the free, republican democratic capitalism included,
and we realize, of course, that in this fight the banner
of freedom will be waved defiantly at us. But our an-

swer is . . . 'every freedom is a fraud if it contradicts the interests of the emancipation of labor from the oppression of capital.' "

(*Ibid.*, 1923 Edition, Vol. XVI, pp. 203-4.)

"Propaganda to be carried on among workers and peasants should be only of the following kind: The 'freer,' or more 'democratic,' a bourgeois country is, the more fiercely does the capitalist gang rage against workers' revolution; this is exemplified by the democratic republic of the United States of America."

(*Ibid.*, 1923 Edition, Vol. XVIII, p. 100.)

WORLD REVOLUTION

"Uneven economic and political development is an absolute law of capitalism. Hence, the victory of socialism is possible first in a few or even in one single capitalist country taken separately. The victorious proletariat of that country, having expropriated the capitalist and organized its own socialist production, would rise against the rest of the capitalist world, attract to itself the oppressed classes of other countries, raise revolts among them against the capitalist, and, in the event of necessity, come out even with armed force against the exploiting classes and their states."

(Lenin and Zinoviev.
Against the Stream, Russian, *Leningrad,* 1925, p. 156.)

"As long as capitalism and Socialism remain, we cannot live in peace. In the end one or the other will triumph—a funeral requiem will be sung either over the Soviet Republic or over world capitalism. This is a respite in war."

(*Collected Works,* Vol. XVII, p. 398.)

WAR, NATIONAL DEFENSE AND PEACE

"An imperialist war does not cease to be imperialistic when charlatans or phrasemongers or petty-bourgeois philistines proclaim sentimental 'slogans'; it ceases to be such only when the *class* which is conducting the imperialist war and is bound to it by millions of economic threads (or, rather, ropes), is *overthrown* and is replaced at the helm of state by the really revolutionary class, the proletariat. There is no other way of getting out of an imperialist war, or out of an imperialist predatory peace."

(*Ibid.,* Vol. XXIII, p. 377.)

"What would have saved us still more would have been a war between the imperialist powers. If we are obliged to tolerate such scoundrels as the capitalist thieves, each of whom is preparing to plunge a knife into us, it is our direct duty to make them turn their knives against each other. When thieves fall out, honest men come into their own.

"I have pointed to one imperialist antagonism, one which it is our duty to take advantage, the antagonism between Japan and America. Another one is the antagonism between America and the rest of the capitalist world. Nearly the whole of the capitalist world of 'victors' emerged from the war with tremendous gains. America is strong, everybody is now in debt to her, everything depends on her, she is being more and more hated, she is robbing everybody, and she is robbing them in a very original way. . . . We must take this trend of circumstances into account. America cannot come to terms with Europe—that is a fact proved by history."

(*Ibid.,* Vol. XVII, pp. 391-92.)

"We are living not only in a state, but in a system of states, and the existence of the Soviet Republic side by side with imperialist states for a long time is unthinkable. One or the other must triumph in the end. And before that end comes, a series of frightful clashes between the Soviet Republic and the bourgeois states is inevitable."

(*Ibid.,* Vol. XVI, p. 102.)

COMMUNIST TACTICS AND STRATEGY

"Universal suffrage provides an index of the state of maturity of the various classes in the understanding of their tasks. It shows how the various classes are *inclined* to solve their problems. But the *solution* of the problems is effected not by means of the ballot, but by the class struggle in all its forms including civil war."

(*Ibid.,* Vol. XVI, p. 455.)

"No parliament can in any circumstances be for Communists an arena of struggle for reforms for betterment of the situation of the working class. . . . The only question can be that of utilizing bourgeois state institutions for their destruction."

(*Ibid.,* Vol. XXV, p. 149.)

"A Communist must be prepared to make every sacrifice and, if necessary, even resort to all sorts of schemes and stratagems, employ illegitimate methods, conceal the truth, in order to get into the trade unions, stay there, and conduct the revolutionary work within . . ."

(*Ibid.,* Vol. XVII, pp. 142-45.)

"Is there such a thing as Communist ethics? Is there such a thing as Communist morality? Of course there is. Often it is made to appear that we have no ethics of our own, and very often the bourgeoisie accuse us Communists of repudiating all ethics. This is a method of shuffling concepts, of throwing dust in the eyes of the workers and peasants.

"In what sense do we repudiate ethics and morality?

"In the sense that they were preached by the bourgeoisie who declared that ethics were God's commandments. We, of course, say that we do not believe in God, and that we know perfectly well that the clergy, the landlords, and the bourgeoisie spoke in the name of God in order to pursue their own exploiters' interests. Or instead of deducing these ethics from the commandments of God, they deduced them from idealistic or semi-idealistic phrases, which were always very similar to God's commandments.

"We repudiate all such morality that is taken outside of human class concepts. We say that this is deception, a fraud, which clogs the brains of the workers and peasants in the interest of the landlords and capitalists.

"We say that our morality is entirely subordinated to the interest of the class struggle of the proletariat. Our morality is derived from the interests of the class struggle of the proletariat.

"And what is this class struggle? It is—overthrowing the Czar, overthrowing the capitalists, destroying the capitalist class. . . . We subordinate our Communist morality to this task. We say: 'Morality is that which serves to destroy the old exploiting society and to unite all the toilers around the proletariat, which is creating a new Communist society.' "

(*Ibid.*, Vol. XVII, pp. 321-23.)